TM

Minicomputers in Sensory and Information-Processing Research

MARK S. MAYZNER
Loyola University of Chicago

TERRENCE R. DOLAN
Parmly Hearing Institute,
Loyola University of Chicago

 LAWRENCE ERLBAUM ASSOCIATES, PUBLISHERS
1978   Hillsdale, New Jersey

DISTRIBUTED BY THE HALSTED PRESS DIVISION OF
JOHN WILEY & SONS
New York   Toronto   London   Sydney

Lawrence Erlbaum Associates, Inc., Publishers
62 Maria Drive
Hillsdale, New Jersey 07642

Distributed solely by Halsted Press Division

Library of Congress Cataloging in Publication Data

Main entry under title:

Minicomputers in sensory and information-processing
research.

Includes indexes.
1. Senses and sensation—Data processing.
2. Minicomputers. 3. Human information processing.
I. Mayzner, M. S. II. Dolan, Terrence R.
QP435.M56   152.1'028'54   78-15762
ISBN 0-470-26488-8

Printed in the United States of America

Contents

Preface

The central thrust of the present volume is intended to fill what we believe is a significant vacuum in the literature on sensory and information-processing research. Extraordinarily rapid developments during the past decade or so, both in sensory and information-processing research and in the use of digital-computer technology to implement and facilitate such research, have produced a highly dynamic and rapidly changing research environment. Thus, little effort has *yet* been devoted to characterizing and relating such findings clearly to the new and novel methodological strategies made possible by digital computer science and technology. This volume attempts, for certain selective areas, to remedy this situation by presenting broad overviews of research findings and methodologies that employ minicomputer laboratory configurations, which today are appearing with ever-increasing frequency in psychology departments throughout the world.

To provide a conceptual framework for this enterprise, Chapter 1 is designed to provide a historical perspective in the development of computer science and technology and its direct impact on sensory and information-processing research. Chapters 2 and 3 describe the general structure of minicomputer and microcomputer laboratory configurations, respectively, and clearly demonstrate the enormous power and flexibility of such hardware configurations for research in sensory and information processing. Chapter 4 describes some alternative options to a stand-alone minicomputer laboratory involving time-shared interactive terminals within the context of a larger-scale computer system. Chapter 5 presents a wide-ranging coverage of modern psychophysical techniques and their implementation by means of minicomputer technology. In Chapters 6, 7, and 8, an incisive series of analyses demonstrate very forcefully some of the extraordinary developments that have occurred in visual, auditory, and cognitive (learning and memory) research, respectively, partially made possible by minicomputer technology. Chapter 9 discusses the use of a minicomputer lab to conduct neurophysiological research, a relatively new and very exciting applicaton. Finally, Chapter 10 seeks to look ahead "into the future" to discern new innovative trends; in particular, the chapter examines the problem of increasing duplication of both hardware and software configurations, attendant funding, and support problems, and it offers some tentative solutions.

The present volume is directed toward both upper-level undergraduate and graduate courses in experimental psychology and/or sensory and information processing. As a text for such courses, this volume provides a unique integration of a number of different and highly novel research findings and methodological strategies. Experimental psychologists, of whatever persuasion, will find increasingly often that the basic experimental tool at their disposal will be a minicomputer or microcomputer hardware configuration. We hope that a careful study of this volume will contribute significantly to a better appreciation and understanding of such computer systems and the manner in which they can be exploited in a rich variety of research contexts.

ACKNOWLEDGMENT

The preparation of this book was supported in part by NSF Grant No. 75-09800 A02 to co-editor M. S. Mayzner.

MARK S. MAYZNER
Loyola University of Chicago

TERRENCE R. DOLAN
Parmly Hearing Institute,
Loyola University of Chicago
On leave to NSF,
Washington, D.C. 20550

1 Historical Perspectives

M. S. Mayzner
Loyola University of Chicago

W. R. Goodwin
Denver, Colorado

INTRODUCTORY OVERVIEW

The past decade has witnessed an explosive expansion in the use of minicomputers in the behavioral sciences, in general, and in sensory and information processing, in particular. This growth in the use of minicomputers in sensory and information processing has been so extraordinary that one almost hesitates to predict what the "state of the art" will produce during the remainder of this century. It seems highly appropriate and timely, therefore, to (1) assess our present state of development in some selected areas (Chapters 2 through 9), (2) discuss how we attained our present position (Chapter 1), and (3) examine some future considerations (Chapter 10).

In this chapter, we attempt to delineate (1) what we believe have been the crucial historical developments within digital-computer science and technology, and (2) how these developments have had direct impact on developments within sensory and information processing. In attempting to develop this historical perspective, it is important to recognize that such an enterprise will, of necessity, be colored by the specific experiences and biases of the particular writers concerned, particularly so when the writers themselves were deeply and personally involved in many facets of this research and development effort throughout the latter portion of the period (i.e., from 1955 onward).

It is probably unavoidable that the experiential framework that the authors (Mayzner and Goodwin) found themselves embedded within at Bell Telephone Laboratories and the RAND Corporation in 1955, respectively, will be reflected in the historical perspective and assessment of events examined in this chapter. Further, it is important to recognize that since the historical perspectives that we hope to develop are, in strictly historical terms, almost contemporary perspectives, our objectivity cannot be that of the true historian, but must reflect to a certain degree our own personal experiences. Additional complications, which also should be explicitly recognized, as one reads on in this chapter, include: (1) the very palpable fact that much of the material to which we will allude has, until recently, been classified as national security information; and (2) most importantly, the vast bulk of documentation for this diverse research and development effort being studied is highly scattered among the technical reports and memoranda of numerous governmental and industrial laboratories, as well as the military services themselves. It is also likely that certain conceptual breakthroughs have never been properly documented.

A primary impetus for this volume, and for this chapter, in particular, is to provide an overview and historical perspective for the widespread and daily increasing employment of minicomputers in sensory- and information-processing research. It is becoming increasingly difficult, in fact, to read the current research journals in sensory and information processing and find any research that has *not* been conducted, either directly or indirectly, by means of a minicomputer-based laboratory. Chapters 2 and 3 and Chapters 5 through 9 of this volume are vivid testimonials of this basic reality, while Chapter 4 departs slightly from this basic theme to illustrate how a time-shared interactive terminal or terminals interfaced with larger computer systems can often provide a substitute for the smaller stand-alone minicomputer laboratory.

Given the current research environment of a probable exponential growth of minicomputer laboratories in sensory- and information-processing research, the present chapter traces in some detail the often circuitous route by which this exponential growth has occurred. Obviously, in tracing this route a starting point is required, and as will become clear in the next section, we have selected the year 1940 as our initial "point of departure" or "benchmark." However, the interested reader who desires a brief but broader and more historical account of computing in general, beginning as far back as 3800 B.C., is referred to an excellent account of computer history by Hal Borko (1962, pp. 22–49). It is important, also, to recognize that in this chapter only certain delimited portions of computer-science history, beginning with 1940, will be examined. For example, we do not even attempt to trace the historical developments in computer software or programming languages, as this topic alone could easily require several chapters. Further, because of space limitations, we do not attempt to trace computer hardware developments as they have occurred in numerous corporations and military systems over the past 25 to 35 years, but rather are highly restrictive and selective, choosing what we believe have been only some of the most important developments.

HISTORICAL CONTEXT (1940–1950)

General "State of the Art"

In the year 1940, four separate, but extraordinary events were taking place, each totally independent of the other, but which were to constitute the genesis of all subsequent developments in computer science and technology.

Event I. At the Bell Telephone Laboratories in Holmdel, New Jersey,
An advance took place . . . which would contribute fundamentally to the invention of the transistor. Several researchers noticed that some samples of the semi-conductor silicon were effective detectors of high frequency microwaves. One of the researchers, Russell Ohl, became interested in obtaining pure silicon samples and involved several of Bell's metallurgists in the problem. During the cooling of hot silicon ingots, Jack Scaff and Henry Theurer produced the first silicon *p-n* junction; a substantial photovoltaic effect was produced when the silicon was illuminated (this was in 1940). When Kelly (later to become President of Bell Telephone Laboratories) learned of this he recognized that here might be the key for the solid state amplifier. The beginnings of solid state physics at Bell Labs and the first steps towards the transistor were therefore definitely under way at the advent of World War II [Hoddeson, 1977, pp. 28–29].

Event II.
Early in October, 1940, James R. Killian, Jr., who was sitting in the President's office (at M.I.T.) as Karl T. Compton's assistant, had a telephone call from his boss, then in Washington. Could 15,000 square feet of space be found somewhere at the Institute for a special governmental research project?, asked Dr. Compton. Dr. Killian recalls his cautious answer—that I thought it would not be easy. But within twenty-four hours the space had been found, and by November two men named Isador Rabi and Lee A. DuBridge had moved in (thus, formally establishing M.I.T.'s Radiation Laboratories). They brought with them a 10 cm *cavity* magnetron which a British mission brought to Washington six weeks earlier. It was to be the foundation of all the microwave radar developed at M.I.T. during the next five years— and that, in turn, was the source of at least half of the radar used by the U.S. Armed Forces in World War II. In that extraordinary period M.I.T. was gradually transferred from an Institute of Technology into a security conscious beehive of classified research involving over 6,000 people and 15 acres of the campus. Five years later it suddenly emerged as a great natural resource—a new kind of university polarized around science and technology [Anonymous, 1977, p. A11].

For example, Dr. Lee A. DuBridge, the first Director of the M.I.T. Radiation Laboratory, later went on to become President of the California Institute of

Technology. In addition, the Radiation Lab gave the nation five of its seven science advisors to the President, and since the inception of the Lab, all but two of the presidents of Cal Tech and M.I.T. have come from Radiation Lab alumni. More germane to our account, however, was the kind of scientific atmospherics that the M.I.T. Radiation Laboratory generated. It is quite probable that only in this very special research and development environment could the future seeds of computer science and technology grow and flourish as, in fact, they did. Further, with the development of radar as the focal point around which air defense systems were developed during World War II, there gradually emerged an increasing and compelling need for high-speed, high-capacity data-processing capabilities. This data-processing requirement provided an ever-increasing impetus towards digital-computer technology, well before it had even been clearly perceived that such a technology would be urgently needed for our national defense.

Event III.   In December, 1940, the Servomechanisms Laboratory of the Department of Electrical Engineering at M.I.T. was begun under the leadership of Gordon S. Brown, assisted by Albert G. Hill (later to become Vice-President for Research at M.I.T.) and J. W. Forrester. This laboratory was to contribute in a direct and crucial manner a number of fundamental ingredients into the scientific mixture then beginning to ferment within the M.I.T. community and was ultimately to lead to the construction of WHIRLWIND I (the first truly electronic digital-computing device capable of highly complex man–computer interaction in real-time). More generally, these contributions of the Servomechanism Laboratory during the 1940s can only be characterized as a series of truly profound breakthroughs, both in theoretical insights and engineering developments, in the newly emerging computer-science field, and these insights and developments are explicated in detail subsequently in this chapter.

Event IV.   Before describing Event IV in our scenario, it is probably prudent to note that this event is most likely both the most important, but also possibly the most controversial, of the four events being described. As will be seen shortly, selection of Norbert Wiener as a prime cornerstone for computer-science development might cause some readers to ask "What about Howard H. Aiken's MARK I computer at Harvard, on which work began in 1937, or the fundamental contribution of John von Neuman of the Institute for Advanced Study at Princeton, New Jersey, or the work of Eckert and Mauchly at the Moore School of Engineering of the University of Pennsylvania?" In response, we would point out that (1) Aiken's MARK I was an electro-mechanical, not an electronic computer, and (2) Wiener's views were expressed in 1940, not the mid-40s, when von Neumann and Eckert and Mauchly were most active. Specifically, Wiener (1948) in his classic monograph, *Cybernetics*, says the following:

In the summer of 1940, I turned a large part of my attention to the development of computing machines for the solution of partial differential equations. I had long been interested in these, and had convinced myself that their chief problem as contrasted with the ordinary differential equations so well treated by Dr. Bush on his differential analyzer, was that of the representation of functions of more than one variable. I had also become convinced that the process of scanning as employed in television, gave the answer to that question, and in fact that television was destined to be more useful for engineering by the introduction of such new techniques than as an independent industry.

It was clear that any scanning process must vastly increase the number of data dealt with as compared with the number of data in a problem of ordinary differential equations. To accomplish reasonable results in a reasonable time, it thus became necessary to push the speed of the elementary processes to the maximum, and to avoid interrupting the stream of these processes by steps of an essentially slower nature. It also became necessary to perform the individual processes with so high a degree of accuracy that the enormous repetition of the elementary processes should not bring about a cumulative error so great as to swamp all accuracy. Thus the following requirements were suggested: (1) that the central adding and multiplying apparatus of the computing machine should be numerical as in an ordinary adding machine, rather than on the basis of measurement, as in the Bush differential analyzer; (2) that these mechanisms, which are essentially switching devices, should depend on electronic tubes rather than on gears or mechanical relays, in order to secure quicker action; (3) that, in accordance with the policy adopted in some existing apparatus of the Bell Telephone Laboratories, it would probably be more economical in apparatus to adopt the scale of 2 for addition and multiplication, rather than the scale of 10; (4) that the entire sequence of operations be laid out on the machine itself so that there should be no human intervention from the time the data entered until the final results should be taken off, and that all logical decisions necessary for this should be built into the machine itself; (5) that the machine contain an apparatus for the storage of data which could record them quickly, hold them firmly until erasure, read them quickly, erase them quickly, and then be immediately available for the storage of new material.

These recommendations together with the tentative suggestions for the means of realizing them, were sent in to Dr. Vannevar Bush for their possible use in a war. At the stage of preparation for war (i.e., 1940) they did not seem to have sufficiently high priorities to make immediate work on them worthwhile. Nevertheless, they all represent ideas which have been incorporated into the modern ultra-rapid computing machine. These notions were all made much in the spirit of the thought of the time and I do not for a moment wish to claim anything like the sole responsibility for their introduction. Nevertheless, they have proved useful, and it is my hope that my memorandum had some effect in popularizing them among engineers [pp. 9—11].

Thus, the year 1940 saw the beginnings of: (1) the development of the transistor at Bell Labs; (2) increasing requirements for high-speed, high-capacity data processing, emerging from the M.I.T. Radiation Labs; (3) work at the M.I.T. Servomechanisms Lab leading to the development of WHIRLWIND I; and (4) a highly sophisticated theoretical analysis with regard to the general structure of a digital-computing device by Norbert Wiener. With the entrance of the United States into World War II on December 7, 1941, work relevant to all four of these events of 1940 took on increasing significance and led to a rapid acceleration of research and development efforts in all four areas.

Military Pressures

The impact of military needs, requirements, and pressures on the development of digital-computer science and technology cannot possibly be underestimated. From the very beginning of World War II, and most particularly with our own entrance into the conflict in December of 1941, one may easily discern increasing dependence of our military establishment on science and technology. Initially through agencies such as the National Defense Research Committee and the crucially important Office of Scientific Research and Development (OSRD), under the stewardship of Dr. Vannevar Bush, American engineering and science became "equal and responsible partners of the military" in the conduct of the war.

The pressures generated by our entrance into World War II were to have profound effects on the four critical events of 1940 alluded to previously. First, at Bell Labs three basic research groups were established: One group, headed by the chemist Stanley Morgan and the physicist William Shockley, was to pursue basic research in solid state physics. A second group, headed by James Fisk (later to succeed Kelly as President of Bell Telephone Laboratories), was to pursue fundamental work in electron dynamics, while a third group, headed by Dean Wooldridge (later to form the Ramo-Wooldridge Company and still later merging to form TRW), was to study physical electronics. A subsequent subgroup, under Shockley's leadership, including J. Bardeen and W. Brattain began intensive study on the semiconductors silicon and germanium. And in December 1947, Bardeen and Brattain demonstrated the point-contact transistor, and the following year the first junction transistor was developed by Shockley (later all three men, Shockley, Bardeen, and Brattain were to receive the Nobel prize for this work).

Second, at M.I.T. both the Radiation Lab and Servomechanisms Lab were undergoing *rapid* expansion and were rapidly coming to serve as *the* models for the development of such military-university labs throughout the country, required for meeting the challenge of World War II. In particular, developments within the Servomechanisms Laboratory represent one of the most interesting inter-actions between military needs and pressures and the university–science–en-gineering community to emerge during the 40s, and led to consequences that continued to have reverberations throughout the 50s. As noted, these develop-ments within the Servomechanisms Lab are explicated in considerable detail later in this chapter.

Third, Wiener's five recommendations included in his memorandum to Vannevar Bush, which outlined a conceptual framework for electronic digital computers, clearly had a profound effect on subsequent developments in the mid-40s. For example, the Electronic Numerical Integrator and Calculator (ENIAC) designed by J. P. Eckert and J. W. Mauchly at the University of Penn-sylvania was completed in 1946. ENIAC was unquestionably, for its time, a large machine containing some 18,000 vacuum tubes. However, it required different electrical connections each time a new problem was run. Thus, while calculating speed was high, set-up time was excessively long and generally represented a machine with little flexibility. Working as a consultant for the ENIAC project was John von Neumann who in 1945 (e.g., see Goldstine & von Neumann, 1963; von Neumann, 1945) suggested the concept of a stored program computer, the Electronic Discrete Variable Automatic Calculator (EDVAC); the program of operating instructions was to be internally stored directly in the memory of the machine, not handled by different internal circuitry or different electrical con-nections for each new problem, as the ENIAC. In the above context, in which ENIAC employed vacuum tubes rather than the electro-mechanical devices of Aiken's MARK I and in which EDVAC employed an internally stored program with a large central storage and the use of a binary number system, we can clearly perceive elements of the five points made by Norbert Wiener earlier in the 40s in the memorandum to Vannevar Bush.

Clearly, all during the 40s, military needs and pressures were building towards requirements for a high-speed, high-capacity, flexible computing device. At M.I.T., at Bell Labs, at the Institute for Advanced Study, work progressed at an accelerated pace. Interestingly, with the end of open hostilities in 1945, the pace increased in tempo and urgency as the "cold war" began to emerge as a basic reality of the late 40s and 50s. For example, in 1947, General Hoyt S. Vandenberg, Vice Chief-of-Staff of the United State Air Force, communicated to Vannevar Bush, the Chairman of the Research and Development Board, his acute anxiety over our lack of an adequate national air defense system for the North American continent. Further, the explosion of a nuclear device in August 1949 by the Soviet Union, thus breaking America's monopoly many years earlier than had been anticipated, was to lead ultimately to a crash program involving the development of a truly powerful and flexible high-speed, high-capacity, real-time interactive digital computer technology. But we are anticipat-ing events that can only be fully appreciated within the historical context of developments at M.I.T.'s Servomechanisms Lab, to which we will now direct our full attention.

THE SEMINAL CONCEPTUALIZATIONS (1948–1952)

Much of the material discussed in this section has as its source "Project WHIRL-WIND: A Case History in Contemporary Technology" written in 1967 by Kent Redmond and Tom Smith on a grant from the MITRE Corporation, initiated by MITRE's President, Robert R. Everett.[1]

The history of WHIRLWIND I has its beginnings in the period 1943–1944, when members of M.I.T.'s Servomechanisms Lab were pursuing discussions with United States Naval personnel concerning the development of an Aircraft Stability and Control Analyzer (ASCA). In perhaps one of the most dramatic, unexpected, and surprising sequences of events ever to occur in a military funded project, ASCA was never built. Instead, WIIRLWIND I was to evolve slowly and ultimately was to become the *prototype* electronic real-time interactive digital computer system for the aerial defense of the continental United States. A prime objective of the Servomechanisms Lab in 1944 was to design and build an aircraft simulator for the Navy with J. W. Forrester directing the ASCA project. Although Forrester remained in charge, he soon brought Bob Everett into the project, as his second-in-command, and clearly those two scientists jointly structured the direction the project was to take during the ensuing decade. Initially ASCA was to include a simulated cockpit, complete with controls and instruments, a flight engineer-observer station, and calculating equipment most probably analog in nature. Already by the summer of 1945, Forrester was becoming progressively disenchanted with analog computation and was increasingly focusing his attention on digital-computation techniques, and in November 1945, he visited the University of Pennsylvania to gather additional information on the design and operation of ENIAC and its projected successor, EDVAC.

These developments in digital computation and their enormous potential in a rich variety of contexts were clearly perceived by Forrester and Everett, almost at once. Their combined vision and insight in late 1945 and early 1946 was to revolutionize their approach to ASCA. In fact, it was gradually to transform Project ASCA, until Project WHIRLWIND was to emerge as its successor. Thus, in mid-January 1946, Forrester was already beginning to investigate seriously digital-computer techniques. This seemingly radical shift from analog to digital computation was gradually to transform the entire ASCA project. In February 1946, Forrester outlined four principal tasks.:

1. Research, development, and construction necessary to demonstrate digital techniques of the type required for the final computer.

---

[1]We should like to acknowledge, therefore, a very special debt of thanks to Dr. Everett for providing us with a manuscript edition of this project and for his own personal discussions and reflections with us on the WHIRLWIND project, in which he and J. W. Forrester played the key roles.

2. Design of a computer which is adequate for the aircraft analyzer problem.
3. Construct and assemble the computer and associated equipment for control and stability studies on aircraft.
4. Operation of the complete equipment for the selection of aircraft stability problems and application of the computer to other types of scientific computation.

Point 4 is especially important, because we clearly see Forrester's remarkable foresight in that he is already suggesting "application of the computer to other types of scientific computation." In a revised proposal to the Navy submitted in March 1946, the ASCA project was officially christened with its new identity: "WHIRLWIND."

As the year 1946 progressed, Forrester perceived at least a 5-year research and development effort, funded at approximately $100,000 per month over the next 5 years. As Forrester foresaw this effort, the central design problem would be given to Bob Everett, in charge of the Block Diagrams Group, who was charged with designing a complete computer system, including definitions of all components and their interconnections as well as defining computing routines, programming techniques, and component designs for implementing, computing, switching, storage, and overall system programming.

In autumn of 1947, Forrester and Everett prepared two technical memoranda for the Navy that were to portend the application of WHIRLWIND, not yet even built, to highly complex real-time control of military warfare, involving ships, submarines, interconnecting radar and sonar data, and various weapon systems. A prime focus of these two memoranda was the exposition of a radically new and profoundly important conceptual breakthrough, explicitly, the employment of a digital computer for the real-time control and data processing of a rich mixture of diverse inputs, with outputs designed to provide true combat information and control as a given battle configuration was unfolding. We return again and again to this enormously important insight of Forrester and Everett, as it represents probably the first explicit statement describing the function of a digital computer as the central element in a real-time interactive command-and-control system, and thus constitutes the historical benchmark for all future applications of digital computers as the central element in such systems. Further, these two memoranda were to introduce *permanently* into the computer-science field the distinction between the use of a digital computer as either (1) a highly sophisticated computing device or (2) a real-time interactive command-and-control device.

It is important to note, at this junction, that this conceptual breakthrough was to so redirect the energy of Forrester and Everett and their laboratory associates, that ASCA was to fade slowly into oblivion and Project WHIRLWIND was to become the central focus of work and attention from this point onward. This reorientation of effort from ASCA to WHIRLWIND was not totally satisfactory to Navy funding agencies, and a long and complicated sequence of events were to begin unfolding that ultimately led to the withdrawal of funding support from the Navy.

In any case, research and development efforts on WHIRLWIND I continued at an accelerated pace in the period 1948 to 1950 with two extraordinary achievements occurring, which must be noted: first, Forrester's invention of marginal checking in late 1947. Very briefly, marginal checking is designed to test the reliability of a computer and its components by testing it under conditions that exceed normal loads. By use of this technique weaknesses may be uncovered prior to their causing total system breakdowns. Specially designed check and trouble-location problems are employed and the computer itself is thus exploited to locate its own potential faults. This fundamental insight developed by Forrester in marginal checking has, with time, become the principal technique for all computer preventative-maintenance testing. Second, Forrester's dismay with the reliability of available storage tubes and other storage devices, of whatever kind, led him to continue to ponder about this crucial storage component in all digital-computing devices. Developments in electrostatic storage tubes in 1947, 1948, and 1949 left him anything but sanguine about this critical storage problem. Thus, in the spring of 1949, when Forrester noticed that a magnetic material, "Deltamax," was industrially available, an insight he had in 1947 involving three-dimensional arrays, employing interconnected gas-glow discharge cells, recurred to him, but now employing 3-dimensional arrays of reversibly magnetizable intersections. Now totally committed to this magnetic-core storage concept, Forrester along with Everett's assistance, persevered, ultimately leading in 1952 to the construction of a semicopy of WHIRLWIND, namely, the "Memory Test Computer," to test the magnetic core concept. In May 1953, all the previous work and effort was dramatically vindicated when a 32 x 32 x 16 magnetic ferrite storage unit provided high reliability in the Memory Test Computer. The rest is history, but perhaps a final footnote. The transistor developed at Bell Labs by Shockley, Bardeen, and Brattain and the magnetic ferrite core developed by Forrester at M.I.T. are probably the two most important single hardware components of all present day digital-computer technology.

As noted, increasing Navy funding problems were being felt more and more from about 1947 onward, as Forrester and Everett shifted their research and development efforts from ASCA to WHIRLWIND and by 1950 had reached a crisis stage. At this junction Dr. George Valley, a member of the M.I.T. Physics Department, but more importantly, Chairman of the Air Defense System Engineering Committee (ADSEC), often referred to as the "Valley Committee," enters our narrative. The Soviet Union's nuclear detonation in 1949 and our entrance into the Korean conflict in 1950, coupled with hard intelligence data that Russia possessed sufficient aircraft to penetrate our existing manual air defense system easily and most probably would match our nuclear weapon arsenal in the very near future was deeply disturbing news to Valley, his committee, and our military establishment.

Within the above context, Valley recalls a chance meeting on the M.I.T. campus with Dr. Jerome B. Wiesner, another M.I.T. faculty member, and now President of M.I.T., in which he told Wiesner of his search for an information-gathering and correlating center that could process vast quantities of information in real-time. Wiesner suggested that Valley look at Forrester's WHIRLWIND project. Valley quickly followed up this lead by visiting Forrester and most fortunately had the foresight to recognize immediately the extraordinary possibilities of WHIRLWIND for air defense. Three days later, on Monday, January 30, 1950, Valley returned, and accompanying him were three other members of the "Valley Committee," namely, John Marchetti of the Air Force Cambridge Research Laboratory, H. Guyford Stever (later to become President of Carnegie-Mellon University and still later Director of the National Science Foundation), and Charles S. Draper. By the time of his second visit, Valley had read the two technical memoranda Forrester and Everett had written in 1947, described earlier, and Valley and his three committee members were further convinced that WHIRLWIND held great promise as a central data-processing device for air defense. Valley, and through him ADSEC, became almost immediately committed to continue funding WHIRLWIND, when Navy support was withdrawn. The initial funding was supplied by Watson Laboratories of Red Bank, New Jersey, in the amount of approximately $600,000 (Valley, 1977), as a result of Valley's recommendations. Further, Valley informed Forrester confidentially that the Air Force most probably would soon assume the entire funding of WHIRLWIND, which shortly was to come to pass.

Thus, in December 1950, the Air Force officially requested that M.I.T. establish a laboratory dedicated exclusively to the development of an effective air defense system for the continental United States. The immediate outcome was Project CHARLES, a study conducted between February and August of 1951 to be followed by a prototype air defense system built around WHIRL-WIND, referred to as the Cape Cod System. Valley's foresight and subsequently his own crucial insights into air defense problems were to become inextricably intermingled with those of Forrester and Everett as the Cape Cod System slowly evolved into the SAGE Air Defense System, but again we are getting ahead of the story.

THE EARLY ROOTS (1952–1960)

The Cape Cod System

To appreciate the Cape Cod System fully, so-called because its radar network covered Cape Cod, it is necessary to review briefly the outcome of Project CHARLES, which Valley had been instrumental in funding. On April 20, 1951, employing a single radar at the Hanscom Air Force Base in Bedford, Massachusetts, three computer-control real-time collision-course interceptions were tested successfully (Israel, 1952). These initial successes gained by ADSEC and Project CHARLES achieved the commendation of Air Force Chief-of-Staff Hoyt S. Vandenberg, who noted in a letter to George Valley that the "successfully accomplished digital computation of interception courses with the WHIRLWIND computer gave real hope of being able to eliminate some of the delays and inaccuracies inherent in conventional manual air defense control systems" (Vandenberg, 1951).

With the demonstrated success of real-time computer-controlled interceptions by Project CHARLES, the Cape Cod System was begun. Basically, this system was to consist of a series of radar stations interfaced with WHIRLWIND at M.I.T.'s Barta building in Cambridge, Massachusetts. To manage this rapidly expanding effort effectively, Project LINCOLN was established in 1951, resulting almost immediately in the construction of M.I.T.'s Lincoln Laboratory, adjacent to the Air Force Cambridge Research Center in Bedford, Massachusetts. At this junction, in the autumn of 1951, Project WHIRLWIND was separated from the Servomechanisms Laboratory and reorganized as the Digital Computer Laboratory under Forrester's leadership, and 6 months later those portions of the Digital Computer Lab concerned with WHIRLWIND's applications to air defense were incorporated as "Division VI" of Lincoln Laboratory. Forrester then came to wear two managerial hats, one as Director of M.I.T.'s Digital Computer Lab and the other as Head of Division VI of M.I.T.'s Lincoln Laboratory.

Work progressed from 1952 onward at several levels concurrently. First, the Cape Cod System served multiple purposes: it conceived novel system concepts allowing for high aircraft or track-capacity operations; it allowed for new components and operating computer programs to be tested within an operational air defense system framework; and most importantly, it became a constant source of inputs for a second-generation expanded air defense system to be called "SAGE." Second, and by far its most important achievement, with regard to the impact of this early prototype digital-computing system on sensory- and information-processing studies (detailed in Chapters 2 through 9 in this volume) was the initial development of a cathode-ray tube (CRT) technology interfaced to WHIRLWIND.

Here can be found the true beginnings of the explicit nature by which man could be interfaced or coupled with computer input and output operations. In this sense the Cape Cod System, although primarily concerned with demonstrating the feasibility of a digital-computer system to conduct air defense operations in real-time, was almost incidentally inventing and developing, perhaps, a vastly more important concept. This extraordinarily new and innovative concept placed man as a vital connective link in the total system operation. The implications and consequences of this conceptual breakthrough are still reverberating throughout computer science and technology, as well as sensory- and information-processing research. Basically, as the design of the Cape Cod System evolved, it was recognized that the computer hardware and software (or programs) had definite limitations with regard to several levels of data processing and decision-making. Certain system functions with respect to aircraft identification, tracking, weapons allocation and control, etc., required manual intervention. To achieve such manual intervention capabilities, operator consoles needed to be designed that would allow operator interaction with the total system. Such consoles involved manual intervention switches and a CRT display console readout of system operations. This mode of man–computer interaction represents one of the most important and fundamental contributions of the Cape Cod System, apart from its demonstrated ability to provide air defense. It clearly was to influence all future uses of digital computers and while it is now taken for granted that man and computer should interact in real-time, it was Forrester and Everett and the Cape Cod System that first provided us with this enormously crucial insight and clearly demonstrated its implementation.

Throughout 1952, the main thrust of the Cape Cod System was to develop sufficient understanding of system operations in order that the system could be expanded ultimately to process inputs from a "14-radar overlapping coverage network." By December of 1953, the Cape Cod System was operating with a long-range radar (the FPS-3) located at Truro on Cape Cod and two smaller gap-filler radars, and WHIRLWIND now had the capacity to process the data from these three radars as well "carry the tracks of some 48 aircraft."

As it became increasingly evident that the Cape Cod System was a viable system for conducting air defense, it also became increasingly evident that a second-generation computer would be required. Therefore, on October 27, 1952, M.I.T. issued to IBM a Letter of Intent, which consequently led to the development of WHIRLWIND's successor, the AN/FSQ-7 or Q-7 computer.

The SAGE Air Defense System

In 1953, the United States Air Force, in a decision leading ultimately to the expenditure of several billion dollars, chose M.I.T.'s Lincoln Laboratory as the prime contractor for the development of a continental air defense system to be known as "SAGE" (or Semi-Automatic Ground Environment), and orders were issued for the delivery of the first Q-7 computer to be delivered for installation at Lincoln Lab to develop and test the first system prototype known as the Experimental SAGE Sub-Sector (ESS).

The Q-7, WHIRLWIND's direct descendent, was then, and even by today's standards some 20 years later still is, an advanced and powerful computer, at least in some respects. It was a duplex computer (i.e., all essential hardware was 100% redundant or duplexed), weighing about 115 tons and consuming some 1500 kilowatts of power with its approximately 58,000 vacuum tubes (the use of the transistor was still just over the horizon). Briefly, some of its basic characteristics included a 32-bit word length, a core memory of 8000 registers, later expanded to 69,000 registers, a memory cycle time of 6 μsec, average instruction operating times of about 10 μsec, and included 12 magnetic drums for external storage of about 150,000 32-bit words. For an excellent overview of the SAGE Air Defense System, as initially conceived and viewed in the context of a large-scale man—computer data-processing system, we recommend highly one of the early descriptions of the system that was not restricted by national security regulations (Everett, Zraket, & Benington, 1957). (See Appendix to this chapter.)

Let us now return to a few of the design characteristics of a SAGE CRT display console, which has direct implications for the sensory- and information-processing studies of the 70s, at least with respect to visual information-processing research. Perhaps the most direct connective link between a SAGE or Q-7 computer with its associated CRT display consoles and intervention switches of the 50s, and the minicomputer CRT display lab of the 70s can be found in the fact that most systems involve information displayed on CRTs under digital-computer control. Clearly, the objective of the Q-7 CRT display system, to conduct air defense, was very different from that of our present-day minicomputer CRT display labs, to study visual information-processing. However, the underlying structure of these systems was highly similar. When viewed within this historical context, it is self-evident that the basic concept of real-time interaction between CRT and operators or experimental subjects remains essentially invariant.

It is worth noting that many of the operational features of our present minicomputer CRT labs were initially developed within the military context of the 50s. For example, the present use of a "light pen" (i.e., a hand held photosensitive device that may be positioned directly over displayed information on the CRT) to provide direct interaction between operator or subject and the CRT, was invented in the military environment of the 50s, at which time it was referred to as a "light gun." Further, SAGE CRT displays introduced such features as: (1) intensity controls, i.e., the capability of varying the brightness of the display; (2) display switch options, which allowed for selective presentation of subsets of information; (3) rapid sequential display of selected inputs; (4) spatial expansion and contraction of selective areas of the display; and (5) display of alpha-numerics, symbols, vectors, and points. In brief, all of the CRT display capabilities we today often take for granted were first developed and refined in the SAGE Air Defense System.

The procedures and devices whereby an operator or subject interacted with the information displayed on a CRT also were developed and refined in SAGE. The use of intervention switches and "light guns," which allowed for SAGE operating personnel to enter information into the system and to take actions with respect to the system find their present-day counterparts in teletype or teletype-like terminals. It would not be unfair to conclude that the developments and experiences gained from both the earlier Cape Cod Air Defense System and the later SAGE Air Defense System provided the basic structure for all present-day minicomputer labs, as found in sensory- and information-processing research. Although we have illustrated this point of continuity in man–computer interactions between developments in the 50s involving military computer systems and the minicomputer research laboratories of the 70s, primarily with regard to visual information processing, analogous arguments can be made for other research domains (e.g., auditory information processing, neurophysiological studies, memory and learning studies). Basically, the fundamental conceptual breakthrough, or insights, of Forrester and Everett and their associates was to demonstrate how a digital-computing device could be employed to *control, record,* or *analyze,* with enormous flexibility and very great precision, a remarkable diversity of environmental events with respect to both spatial and temporal parameters, and even today we have hardly yet begun to exploit this truly ingenious insight.

The SAC Command and Control System (SACCS)

The Stratetic Air Command (SAC) had been following the development of large-scale computer applications in SAGE with considerable interest. With the ever-increasing complexity of planning for and controlling a growingly sophisticated mixed-force structure, within frequently changing sets of strategic parameters, SAC perceived a need as might be expected, for a computerized system of their own. Working with the System Development Corporation (SDC) (and what was to become the Air Force Systems Command) in the late 50s, SAC developed a comprehensive set of requirements for Project 465L – the SAC Command and Control System or SACCS.

After approval of the basic system concepts, contracts were awarded to ITT for system development management and hardware, to SDC for operating system design and software, and to IBM for computers. Four large machines (later reduced to three) were envisaged to be installed at the major SAC headquarter locations with sophisticated communications linkages to all remote SAC locations. At a later date, this network was expanded to include an Air Force Command Post as well. Much more detail of 465L is still highly classified, in contrast to SAGE, and, therefore, not subject to general discussion; however, some of the major developments, which are particularly relevant to this book, can be discussed. One major problem facing the designers and builders of System 465L was creation of and evaluation of strategic plans. Suffice it to say that this is an incredibly complicated process, involving many contingent and variable options. Because these must be dynamic plans, which are interactive with a given mission rather than merely a passive blueprint of it, it was necessary to store very large amounts of readily accessible date in the machines. Thus, unlike SAGE, SACCS had both off-line and on-line utilization and, further, both real-time and non-real-time applications to enable the functions of *planning, execution* of a plan, and *monitoring* of that operation all to take place essentially simultaneously.

With only a 65K core, these requirements led to large quantities of peripheral storage to be accessible differentially in accordance with anticipated usage priorities. Thus, SACCS is blessed with Disc, Drum, and Tape storage — lots of it. The necessity of handling all of these data and the recognition that "priorities" develop according to what is actually happening led to a concept, then called *interleaving*, whereby the machine could interrupt any ongoing processing if a higher-priority task came up, remove the lower-priority task from core, save it ("remembering" where it was temporarily stored), carrying out the new processing in core, then returning the prior task and completing it. To handle these transfers, a small routine called the *executive program* was developed, which always resided in CORE and which carried out the priority recognition and data manipulation necessary to effect the "interleaving." This executive program was the precursor of time-sharing. It also demonstrated how efficient and sophisticated a "small" program could be and perhaps was influential in pointing the way to use the smaller machines, soon to be developed, on complicated problems.

Another contribution of SACCS was continuation of the development of ways for men and their machines to work together. Large displays were developed for SAC command posts, and more sophisticated consoles and intercommunication devices were developed and used. Of all equipment innovations, however, perhaps the TCC was the most significant. Developed by ITT, this was a relatively small communication-switching computer, which enabled a pre-sort and prioritization of message traffic within the total SAC system.

All told, with the advent of improved message handling, group displays and sophisticated man—machine interfaces, use of "expectancies" through pre-planning, and dynamic plan-operations interactions, SACCS contributed mightily to management information-system development, and certainly called the attention of the civilian sector to uses for computers other than just bookkeeping or numerical calculation.

THE EMERGENCE OF THE MINICOMPUTER DOMAIN
(THE DIGITAL EQUIPMENT CORPORATION: 1957—PRESENT)

Because this volume is intended to provide a basic understanding of the application of minicomputers to research in sensory and information processing, it seems proper to discuss at least briefly and selectively a little of the history of minicomputers themselves, and how it came about that the early history and development of large-scale digital computers were to evolve, in part, along the dimensions of minicomputers. We shall argue that the rapid developments and progress in digital-computer technology set initially in motion by Forrester and Everett in their work on WHIRLWIND, and rapidly followed-up with the construction of the giant Q-7 computer for the SAGE system, was to produce rather quickly an interesting paradox.

In delineating this paradox, and outlining some of the more important bench-marks in the development of minicomputer technology, our account must include an explicit recognition of Kenneth H. Olsen and his enormous contributions to the minicomputer field.[2]

Ken Olsen, founder of DEC and its President since its inception in 1957, graduated from M.I.T. in 1950 and soon joined Lincoln Labs, where he was to play a key role in the development of Lincoln Labs' TX-0 and TX-2 experimental transistorized computers that were to revolutionize digital-computer technology; for here, finally, in a single machine were the transistors developed by Shockley, Bardeen, and Brattain at Bell Labs and the magnetic ferrite core memory developed by Forrester at M.I.T.

To return to the paradox, mentioned earlier, the WHIRLWIND and Q-7 computers were giant machines and, while introducing the crucial concept of real-time, interactive, command-and-control, were far too large and expensive for laboratory experimentation. While the WHIRLWIND and Q-7 computers allowed for, in fact were designed for, man—computer interaction, experimenta-tion with man—computer interaction was not possible because of size and cost considerations; thus, the paradox: what the machines had been designed to do, their very size and cost made "doing" prohibitive.

Ken Olsen clearly had the insight to perceive this paradox. In a presentation before the New York Society of Security Analysts on February 16, 1973, Olsen (1973) said, in part, concerning the genesis of his company:

> Digital was founded to develop and introduce real-time interactive computing. At that time, i.e., 1957, most computing was done in a batch way. People were pushed away from the computer's console. They were asked to drop their punch cards in a slot in the door and the next day they got the results—usually wrong. It was very commonly believed that one needed at least a whole day to digest the results, and this was good enough. Besides, computers were much too expensive and sensitive to allow users to get near them.
>
> DEC computers were then relatively inexpensive, that is, $120,000 as compared to a few million dollars, and so one could afford to allow the user to work directly on the computer. They were designed to make it easy to tie all types of equipment to the computer so that they could control processes and devices as well as automatically collect data. They

---

[2]We wish to acknowledge a very special debt of gratitude to Kenneth H. Olsen (President, Digital Equipment Corporation), and members of its corporate public relations department, who so graciously supplied us with materials germane to the history of the Digital Equipment Corporation (DEC), which, in our judgment, best characterizes the history of minicomputer technology development in the United States. We do not wish, in any way, to diminish the contributions of other computer and/or minicomputer corporations, but since our account, of necessity, must be brief, we believe that DEC serves as the best single prototype for discussing minicomputer development.

were interactive both for the individual users and for the equipment tied to the computer.

We believe that modern interactive time-sharing as we know it today had its roots in these early computers. At M.I.T. and at Bolt, Beranek and Newman, a Boston-based consulting firm, several terminals were tied to digital PDP-1 computers so that a number of users could simultaneously interact with the computer and share the expense of a large memory. Since those early time-sharing experiments, DEC has been deeply involved in both minicomputers and time-sharing. In fact, our PDP-6, introduced in 1964, was the first commercially-offered, multi-programmed, time-sharing system. We now offer our smallest minicomputer for about $4,000 and a large DEC system-10 time-sharing configuration which can approach $2,000,000.

The demand for interactive computing is mushrooming. The reasons are quite clear. Society is now demanding more services, more supervision, more watching of safety and environment, more economy in use of energy and other resources. In addition, personnel expect to lessen their work load and be less involved in their daily jobs. These things all point toward the need for *interactive* computing [pp. 1–2].

In an address before the American Institute of Industrial Engineering, Ken Olsen (1975), in part, pursued the foregoing theme further:

Small computers are exciting because they make many networks practical. In networks of many terminals, such as an airline reservation system, minicomputers are used for pre-processing or message switching to save on phone line costs. However, networks of computers might be more important. As computers are located in many places within an organization, networks tie them together for communication. The communication link may be a weekly report sent by mail or high-speed transmission lines in continuous use.

Another application of computer networks comes in tieing many small computers together to share resources. For example: a laboratory with many small computers can be tied to one computer which will have large amounts of storage and expensive peripherals. The small computers in the laboratory will have their own terminals and A/D converters and will be able to directly control equipment and experiments. The large computer will hold programs and store amounts of data, and it will unload and load the small laboratory machine quickly and efficiently. In this way people can have small and inexpensive machines to use freely throughout an organization and still have much of the power of a large machine [pp. 3–4].

In light of Olsen's philosophy concerning minicomputer utilization in laboratory and data processing environments, as expressed in the foregoing quotations, it is not difficult to understand how his company, which began in 1957 with only $70,000 in seed money from a Boston venture capital concern (American Research and Development Corporation), and which obtained 70% of DEC for this initial modest investment, has grown today into a corporation with revenues of about $1,000,000,000 per year. It is very likely that Olsen's philosophy, his influence in shaping the minicomputer field, and perhaps being shaped himself, in turn, by the needs and requirements of the field, are in large measure a function of his early experiences at Lincoln Labs, and, of course, the seminal concept of real-time, interactive-computing devices first espoused and continuously and relentlessly pursued by Forrester and Everett over the years. Evidence supporting the foregoing view of Lincoln's and more particularly WHIRLWIND's influence on Olsen's thinking may be found in the following statement by Gordon Bell (1975), Vice-President, Engineering, DEC:

If we look at the ancestry of the minicomputer, it is clearly M.I.T.'s WHIRLWIND. These machines and people had a profound effect on DEC. Ken Olsen, Dick Best, and George Gerelds, and others of DEC are WHIRL-WIND's alumni and I even wrote a program for it once. The PDP-1 was very much like Lincoln Labs' TX-0 (one of the earliest transistorized machines) and the TX-2, like WHIRLWIND. Beginning with WHIRLWIND, we can see four generations of minicomputers. It was operational in 1950 and was packaged in a two-story building. The second, our own PDP-1, was packaged in only four six-foot cabinets. The third generation, PDP-8/I, occupied about eight cubic feet and now, in the fourth generation, we have the single-board LSI (i.e., Large-scale Integrated)-11, which is ½" x 8" x 10", but it also has over ten times the calculating power of WHIRL-WIND. Most important, the price has come down by a factor of nearly 200 these last fifteen years, which amounts to about 41% compounded per year; that is, every two years the price has halved. This permits new uses of the computer that are in the scale of the application.

The size, too, has changed, going from a building to a single board. The input power has decreased by a factor of 3,000 from WHIRLWIND. WHIRLWIND required 150,000 watts and when it ran, lights in Cambridge dimmed. A WHIRLWIND flip-flop, which stores a single binary-digit (bit) occupied a volume of about eight cubic feet. In the LSI-11, the same function takes an area of silicon that is only 100th by 100th of an inch. WHIRLWIND had the five conventional computer elements: input, output, control, arithmetic, and storage. Control was an area of the room that one walked through. The storage tube, invented at Manchester University, was initially used. The arithmetic element gives us the notion of word-length. WHIRLWIND word-length was 32 feet and a bit slice took up about two feet. We could walk along the bits and the various registers were piled on top of one another. The console was also a place one walked around to look at lights and flip switches. Here we've not made similar strides in console design because there haven't been advances in miniaturizing people.

WHIRLWIND made important contributions to computing including the cathode-ray tube and light pen input which most computers still don't have, but eventually will, if they communicate with people. But WHIRL-WIND is probably most remembered for its innovative magnetic core memory, which is still in use over three generations.

REAL-TIME SENSORY AND
INFORMATION-PROCESSING RESEARCH (1955–1970)

Because the principal thrust of this volume is to illustrate the usefulness, if not the explicit necessity, at least, of a minicomputer-based laboratory for research in sensory and information processing, we would be remiss if we did not describe *some* of the early germinal research applications of digital-computer technology to sensory- and information-processing studies. As one might have anticipated, these initial highly innovative, germinal studies developed within the historical context of the real-time, interactive, command-and-control (digital computer) concepts, first advanced by Forrester, Everett, and their associates. It was inevitable, we believe, that the initial application of digital-computer technology to sensory- and information-processing research was to be found among those experimental psychologists working directly with Fred Frick in Lincoln Labs Group 38 and among those few additional psychologists from other labs who were fortunate enough to have interacted with Lincoln Labs Group 38 psychologists.

Our following account of the work initiated by Frick and his associates will be highly selective and restrictive, but hopefully will provide some insight into the early historical foundations of the application of digital-computer technology to sensory- and information-processing research. Very possibly, one of the earliest such applications is to be found in a study by Green, White, and Wolf. This study, which was begun in the mid-50s, was first reported as a Lincoln Laboratory Group 38 report (Green, White, & Wolf, 1956) and presented at the 1956 meeting of the American Psychological Association; subsequently, it was published (Green, Wolf, & White, 1959) in the *American Journal of Psychology*. Very briefly, this study was concerned with the ability of human subjects to detect patterns in "noisy" visual displays. Its uniqueness may be found in the manner in which these "noisy" visual displays were generated. Specifically, the Memory Test Computer, initially developed, you may recall, to provide a semi-copy of WHIRLWIND to test the magnetic core concept, was employed to generate random sequences of dot patterns with horizontal or vertical orientations, on an oscilloscope or CRT. These dot-pattern displays were then photographed at a rate of about ten per minute and served as the stimulus patterns for the study. Several parameters were examined, including exposure duration, average dot probability, display grain, number of bars, location of contours. The results (Green et al., 1956) indicated that, among other things:

For fixed matrix-size and varying dot-probabilities, thresholds of detection were proportional to the standard deviation of the binomial distributions governing the occurrences of the dots. For fixed dot-probability and varying grain (number of rows or columns in the square matrices), the thresholds were inversely related to the grain, but different forms of the relationship were obtained for two different ways of altering grain [p. 520].

A second germinal study by Green (1961), again employing the M.I.T. Lincoln Labs' Memory Test Computer as well as an IBM 704 computer, was directed towards the effects of figure coherence in the kinetic depth effect. As in the preceding study by Green et al. (1956, 1959), the computer was employed to generate displays that were then photographed, and the resultant film strips were used as the stimulus material. In summary, Green (1961) said:

Six experiments examined the extent to which the kinetic depth effect produces perceived coherence and rigidity of random figures. Subjectively rated coherence was greater with (a) more elements in the figure, (b) connections and constraints among the elements, and (c) less complex axes of rotation. The tumbling rotation was shown to be intermediate between simple and complex axes of spinning rotations. Speed of rotation was shown to have almost no effect. A high speed digital computer was essential for producing the stimuli for the experiments [pp. 281–282].

Bela Julesz, at Bell Telephone Laboratories, also employing digital-computer display techniques, combined with photography of the computer-generated displays, began in the late 50s and early 60s (Julesz, 1960) to study problems of binocular depth perception. Julesz's efforts have been highly imaginative in the application of digital-computer techniques to problems of visual information processing and binocular depth perception, and his fairly recent book (Julesz, 1971) summarizes well over a decade of his pioneering work in this regard.

With the application of digital-computer techniques to problem areas within the visual modality, such applications to problem areas within the auditory modality were simultaneously occurring. For example, in the mid-50s, Frick was applying digital-computer techniques to problems of both human and auditory pattern recognition (Forgie, Groves, & Frick, 1958; Frick, 1959). Although Swets, Green, and Winter (1961), in a highly innovative pioneering effort, were developing one of the first truly automated minicomputer labs for the study of auditory discrimination and auditory information processing, and which was to become the *prototype* for almost all computer-automated auditory labs developed thereafter. Here for the first time a digital computer was being employed to generate auditory stimuli, compute their presentation sequence, feed back information to the subject concerning his responses, and analyze results, all in an interactive, real-time mode of operation.

A bit later in time Yntema, Wozencraft, and Klem (1964), in another pioneering computer application to auditory information processing and memory, were to program the Lincoln Lab TX-2 computer (discussed earlier), to speak numbers very rapidly; specifically, at a rate of ten digits per sec. They were concerned with the information-processing capacity of man, when presented with auditory stimuli at these high input rates. As one might have expected, increased rate of presentation sharply degrades recall behavior (i.e., the more rapidly a list is presented, the smaller the number of items recalled). Clearly, the significance of this study was to demonstrate again very early in the history of the use of computers in sensory and information processing, another novel application and way of introducing stimuli or inputs into man's information-processing system, which could not be implemented with conventional devices.

As experimental psychologists slowly began to recognize the enormous potential of digital-computer technology, the early 60s began seeing increasing and diverse applications of this technology. For example, at the System Development Corporation, in Santa Monica, California, Burt Wolin and his associates (Wolin, Weichel, Terebinski, & Hansford, 1965) used a Philco transac S-2000 computer to carry out a multi-subject experiment. Typically, six subjects were run simultaneously, each enclosed in a separate cubicle with his/her own 8 x 12-inch CRT display and response console. The computer presented all stimulus sequences, recorded all subject responses, and provided a printout of analyzed results for all subjects. This study, in many ways, still constitutes the most ambitious attempt to employ digital-computer technology to control, from inception to final output, a complex information-processing research project involving a multi-subject experiment.

Wolin et al. (1965) summarize the findings as follows:

> Prediction behavior was studied in a context of complexly patterned binary sequences. Sequences were generated from non-stationary, event-contingent, partially random sources. A variable of major importance was the presence or absence of a displayed history of the last eight events in the sequence. Evidence was found that people seek and find order to some degree in the environment. The process by which order is sought and found is discussed. Briefly, subjects do not attempt to analyze the sequences formally, but they respond to recurrent patterns. Those sources where relations between events were important were much more difficult to learn than where sheer frequency or location, and not relations, were important [p. 1].

In all of the preceding studies under discussion, while digital-computer technology was the basic ingredient, larger machines were employed, almost without exception, than those now typically associated with a minicomputer lab;

particularly, since the smaller minicomputer market, as exemplified by the DEC product line, was just beginning to emerge. It seems appropriate, therefore, to discuss very briefly, three selective and illustrative research projects (Subsections I, II, and III). Those projects, which began to employ DEC computers, possibly might be considered along with a very few others, as the initial ground swell in the use of minicomputers for sensory- and information-processing research.

I. Bill Harris (Harris, Mitchell, Morfield, Schulman, & Wiesen, 1965) of Lincoln Labs developed in the mid-60s a stereoscopic, dynamic display. Briefly, information for the display was generated through the use of a simulation program (on an IBM 7094) and fed directly to a DEC PDP-1 computer and in turn displayed on the face of a large DEC 340 CRT display console, which was viewed through a special device designed to yield a vivid depth effect. In summary, the system allowed for real-time, dynamic interaction between operator and display, and while its basic function was to display simulated engagements of ballistic missiles, it was a prelude to the application of DEC minicomputers to sensory- and information-processing research.

II. Ray Nickerson (1964), also in the mid-60s, employing a DEC PDP-1 computer interfaced with a DEC 340 large-screen CRT display console, described in some detail further and direct ways in which a minicomputer lab could be employed in an information-processing research context. For example, Nickerson (1964) noted:

1. Presentation of verbal information on the CRT to instruct subject, to provide stimulus materials, and to give periodic feedback to subjects concerning their performance;
2. Recording of responses made by subjects with a light pen, typewriter, or telegraph keys;
3. Measurement of response latencies with millisecond accuracy;
4. Scheduling of temporal order events or spatial arrangements of display elements, according to program rules which may include randomization with or without forcing constraint;
5. Modification of experimental parameters on the basis of performance;
6. Adjustment of the difficulty of a judgmental task to match the capability of the individual subject;
7. Production of a punched tape record of the trial by trial progress of the experiment;
8. Performance of statistical analyses on data as it is collected, thus providing the experimenter with the results of the analyses immediately at the termination of the experimental session.

III. The third research area of the mid-60s results directly from the work of one of us (Mayzner) and constitutes a long-range research program of visual information processing in man.[3] Briefly, as might be expected, considering the personal, historical context of our work at Lincoln and Bell Labs in the mid-50s, it is not surprising to find that in the mid-60s (i.e., specifically, in 1965), we established possibly the first university, experimental computer-based CRT display laboratory dedicated solely to the study of visual information-processing mechanisms, at the Industrial Engineering and Operations Research Department of New York University (Mayzner, Treeselt, & Helfer, 1967). This lab initially involved a DEC PDP-7 digital computer (in fact, the seventh PDP-7 DEC made), a large-screen DEC 340 Master CRT Display, a large-screen DEC 343 Slave CRT Display, and two Fairchild large-screen Slave CRTs. All displays employed in the experimental work (i.e., the DEC 343 Display and the two Fairchild Displays) had an ultra-fast decaying phospher (i.e., a P-24) and represented probably the first computer-based CRT display lab to employ such an ultra-fast phospher explicitly to insure precise display timing.

It is certainly not our intention to describe this research program here, nor would it be appropriate; for those interested, see, for example, two summary articles by Mayzner (1975) and Mayzner and Tresselt (1970). However, we do believe it is important to note one central concept of our approach, which set it apart from most, if not all, of the previous work in sensory or visual information-processing research employing a minicomputer-based CRT display lab. This central concept or motif may best be characterized as an attempt to exploit very directly and explicitly the power of digital-computer technology to employ CRT displays in new ways in the spatio-temporal domain. Very specifically, we did not want merely to use a CRT to generate pictures to photograph later, no matter how complex or tedious it might have been to produce such displays manually or with animation techniques or to employ a CRT merely as a *N*-field tachistoscope, although we have done so. Rather, our major research thrust has been to generate highly complex spatio-temporal display patterns or configurations in real time, that because of their very own complexity, especially with respect to the control of *spatial* and *temporal* parameters, could not be produced by any other technology. In this regard, we have been most fortunate in that, by employing a computer-based CRT, we have over the past decade and more uncovered a variety of new perceptual phenomena, such as sequential blanking, sequential displacement, dynamic visual movement, subjective visual color (Mayzner, 1975; Mayzner & Tresselt, 1970) and have, we hope, helped to develop a methodological strategy that will continue to yield high dividends (e.g., see a recent paper in which Tynan and Sekuler, 1975, described still another

[3]We acknowledge our deep debt to the National Science Foundation for continuing support over the past decade.

new perceptual effect with computer-controlled CRTs, and Sekuler's superb chapter, Chapter 6, in this volume). In brief, it is and has been our firm conviction for well over two decades (i.e., since first being exposed to digital computer and CRT display technology at M.I.T. from 1956 onward), that sensory- and information-processing research, has and will continue to obtain, through the use of computer or minicomputer technology, an ever-expanding harvest of new findings and new theoretical insights.

One final personal observation: Shortly after we established our lab in 1965, Jerry Bruner paid us a visit and within a month had acquired a Fairchild Display for his lab at Harvard, on which Kahneman was later to carry out one of his early studies on masking and apparent movement (Kahneman, 1967). Over the next 2 years or so (i.e., 1965–1967) visitors to our lab included George Sperling, Bela Julesz, Irv Pollack, and Ralph Haber, among others, and shortly thereafter similar labs began being used at the Bell Telephone Laboratories, the University of Michigan, etc. for studies in sensory and visual information processing. A bit later Don Norman, Bill Estes, and Dave Rumelhart, among others, began extensively employing such minicomputer-based CRT display systems for their research programs, and finally as we are approaching the 80s, minicomputer-based CRT display labs have become an almost standard item of hardware, found in almost every experimental psychology department in the country. We would like to feel that historically we played some small role in the beginning development of this new and rapidly emerging technology.

APPENDIX

Perhaps it would not be inappropriate in our review for one of us (Mayzner) to reflect briefly on his own personal recollections and experiences with the Cape Cod and SAGE Air Defense Systems during the period from 1955 through 1960, when I was employed by Bell Telephone Laboratories. Specifically, Bell Labs had accepted a contract with the United States Air Force to provide an evaluation of SAGE operational air defense capability, and I was hired in December, 1955, as an experimental psychologist to assist in this evaluation process and particularly as it impinged on operator performance and its impact on total system performance. My first two years with Bell Labs were spent on assignment to M.I.T.'s Lincoln Labs. At Lincoln it was intended that I should become thoroughly familiar with the Cape Cod and ESS systems in order to be able to assist Bell engineers in their formal evaluation of the first SAGE subsector to become operational (i.e., the New York Air Defense Sector or NYADS) in June of 1958, and which was located geographically at McGuire Air Force Base in New Jersey.

At Lincoln, I soon discovered that there was already in existence a small group of experimental psychologists (known formally as Group 38), headed by Fred Frick (later to become Assistant to the Director of Lincoln Laboratories) and including Bert Green (author of Chapter 2 of this volume), Douwe Yntema, Warren Torgenson, and Bill Harris. Serving at various times as consultants to this group, among others, were Herb Jenkins, J. C. R. Licklider, William J. McGill (later to become President of Columbia University), and George A. Miller, and I recall reading a few of the technical reports of these consultants (e.g., Green, McGill, & Jenkins [1953]; Licklider [1960]; and Miller [1955]). My first assignment, in fact, at Lincoln was to become thoroughly familiar with the work of Group 38 and any implications such work might have for Bell Laboratory's overall assignment.

My most vivid recollections involve, however, being exposed in early 1956 to both the Cape Cod and ESS systems. Both systems were, of course, under very tight security regulations, and my first exposure to the Cape Cod System in the Barta Building on the M.I.T. campus along with the initial tour through ESS at Lincoln Labs was very akin to finding oneself projected into a world of science-fiction. In the Cape Cod System, for example, one found oneself in a large semi-darkened room filled with about 20 CRT display consoles and their associated intervention switch panels, and during live evaluation exercises when aircraft were tracked and live interceptions were carried out by Air Force personnel, it was easy to imagine that one had suddenly been propelled many years into the future.

This feeling was greatly intensified by the ESS system, in which well over 100 highly complex and very sophisticated CRT display consoles were to be found, bathed in an eerie blue light, which was employed to aid readout from the dim CRTs of the mid-50s. However, when the first SAGE subsector (i.e., NYADS) became operational in June of 1958 at McGuire Air Force Base and Bell Labs began its evaluation (ultimately the entire continental United States was partitioned into some 32 subsectors, each with its own Q-7 computer and associated 100+ operator display console positions, all interconnected to the North American Air Defense Command Headquarters—NORAD—located in Colorado Springs, Colorado), the impression most quickly generated was that one was in the middle of a "space war in the twenty-first century."

During 1958 and 1959 approximately monthly evaluations were conducted by the United States Air Force, in which anywhere from 20 to 40 Strategic Air Command (SAC) aircraft would fly live missions against NYADS in which live interceptors under SAGE Direction Center control would carry out live interceptions over the course of a 2- to 3-hour exercise period. As the psychologist in the Bell Labs' evaluation effort, it was my assignment, hopefully, to provide some insight as to the contributions of the some 150 United States Air Force officers and airmen who participated in these live exercises. A full account of these experiences, however, could themselves easily fill several chapters, and, therefore, this portion of our narrative must be presented at another time. Suffice it to note here, though, that in the early mid-60s, when all 32 SAGE subsectors eventually became operational, a few country-wide SAC/NORAD Sky Shield exercises were run in which the entire country was involved, employing during the course of a 12- to 24-hour exercise as many as 100,000 Air Force and related civilian personnel, and costing, some estimate, between eight million and twelve million dollars per exercise. Obviously, the evaluation of such exercises poses the most complex type of evaluation performance measurement problems one could envision and continues to remain even in the late 70s a dramatic challenge to anyone engaged in system design and evaluation research.

ACKNOWLEDGMENTS

The preparation of this chapter was supported in part by Grant No. BNS 75-09800 A02 from the National Science Foundation to the first author.
    The authors express their very depest appreciation and most profound thanks to the following scientists who took the time to provide their crucial insights and reflections to us in our preparation of this chapter. May we hasten to add, however, that any factual errors or misinterpretations of the facts presented herein is attributable solely to the authors of this chapter and in no way reflects the views of those who helped us so much, namely: Robert R. Everett, Fred Frick, Bill Harris, Albert G. Hill, Dave Israel, Ray Nickerson, Oliver Selfridge, John Swets, George E. Valley, and Douwe Yntema.

REFERENCES

Anonymous. Under the domes. *Technology Review,* 1977, *79,* p. A11.
Bell, G. Computer generations. *DEC Museum Project,* 1975.
Borko, H. History and development of computers. In H. Borko (Ed.), *Computer applications in the behavioral sciences.* Englewood Cliffs, N.J.: Prentice-Hall, 1962.
Everett, R. R., Zraket, C. A., & Benington, H. D. SAGE — A data-processing system for air defense. *Proceedings of the Eastern Joint Computer Conference,* Washington, D.C., 1957, pp. 148–155.
Forgie, C., Groves, M. C., & Frick, F. *Automatic recognition of spoken digits.* Paper presented at the meeting of the Acoustical Society of America, Washington, D.C., May 1958.
Frick, F. Research in speech recognition at Lincoln Laboratory (AFCRC TR-59-198). *Speech Compression and Processing,* September 1959, *2,* 12–37.
Goldstine, H. H., & von Neumann, J. On the principles of large-scale computing machines. In A. H. Taub, *John von Neumann collected works,* New York: Macmillan, 1963.
Green, B. F., Jr. Figure coherence in the kinetic depth effect. *Journal of Experimental Psychology,* 1961, *62,* 272–282.
Green, B. F., Jr., McGill, W. J., & Jenkins, H. M. The time required to search for numbers on large visual displays. *Lincoln Lab Technical Report,* No. 36, August 1953.
Green, B. F., Jr., White, B. W., & Wolf, A. K. Visual pattern detection: I. The effects of exposure time and matrix size with simple bar patterns. *M.I.T. Lincoln Lab Group Report, 38-25,* September 1956.
Green, B. F., Jr., Wolf, A. K., & White, B. W. The detection of statistically defined patterns in a matrix of dots. *American Journal of Psychology,* 1959, *72,* 503–520.

Harris, W. P., Mitchell, R. T., Morfield, M. A., Schulman, A. L., & Wiesen, R. A. A stereoscopic display for on-line monitoring of simulated terminal engagements. *Lincoln Lab. Technical Note,* 1965-68, M.I.T. Lincoln Lab, Lexington, Mass., 1965.

Hoddeson, L. H. The roots of solid-state research at Bell Labs. *Physics Today,* 1977, *30,* 23–30.

Israel, D. R. Interception experiments with Bedford Mews. *Lincoln Lab Memo M-1515,* June 1952.

Julesz, B. B. Binocular depth perception of computer-generated patterns. *Bell System Technical Journal,* 1960, *39,* 1125–1162.

Julesz, B. *Foundations of Cyclopean perception.* Chicago: University of Chicago Press, 1971.

Kahneman, D. An onset-onset law for one case of apparent motion and metacontrast. *Perception & Psychophysics,* 1967, *2,* 577–584.

Licklider, J. C. R. Man–computer symbiosis. *IRE Transactions on Human Factors in Electronics,* 1960, *1,* 4–11.

Mayzner, M. S. Studies of visual information processing in man. In R. L. Solso (Ed.), *Information processing and cognition: The Loyola Symposium.* Hillsdale, N.J.: Lawrence Erlbaum Associates, 1975.

Mayzner, M. S., & Tresselt, M. E. Visual information processing with sequential inputs: A general model for sequential blanking, displacement, and overprinting phenomena. *The Annals of the New York Academy of Sciences,* 1970, *169,* 599–618.

Mayzner, M. S., Tresselt, M. E., & Helfer, M. S. A research strategy for studying certain effects of very fast sequential input rates on the visual system. *Psychonomic Monograph Supplements,* 1967, *2*(5, Whole No. 21).

Miller, G. A. Human engineering critique of the maintenance console for the XD-1 version of the AN/FSQ-7. *Lincoln Lab, Group 38 Reports,* 38-10, March 1955.

Nickerson, R. S. The computer as a control device for psychological experimentation. *DEC Decuscope,* Maynard, Mass., March 1964.

Olsen, K. H. *The future of minicomputers and time-sharing.* Address presented to the New York Society of Security Analysts, New York, February 1973.

Olsen, K. H. *Why minicomputers?* Address presented to the American Institute of Industrial Engineers, Washington, D.C., November 1975.

Swets, J. A., Green, D. M., & Winter, E. F. Learning to identify nonverbal sounds. *Journal of the Acoustical Society of America,* 1961, *33,* 855 (A).

Tynan, P., & Sekuler, R. Moving visual phantoms: A new contour completion effect. *Science,* 1975, *188,* 951–952.

Valley, G. E. Personal communication to M. S. Mayzner, March 1977.

Vandenberg, H. S. Letter from Hoyt S. Vandenberg, Chief-of-Staff, USAF, to George E. Valley, Chairman, ADSEC, May 28, 1951.

von Neuman, J. First draft of a report on the EDVAC. Report on Contract No. W–670-ORD-492, Moore School of Electrical Engineering, University of Pennsylvania, Philadelphia, June 1945.

Wiener, N. *Cybernetics.* Cambridge, Mass.: M.I.T. Press, 1948.

Wolin, B. R., Wiechel, R., Terebinski, S. J., & Hansford, E. A. Performance on complexly patterned binary event sequences. *Psychological Monographs,* 1965, *79*(No. 7, Whole No. 600).

Yntema, D. W., Wozencraft, F. T., & Klem, L. *Immediate serial recall of digits presented at very high rates.* Paper presented at the meeting of the Psychonomic Society, Niagara Falls, Ontario, October 1964.

2 Minicomputers in the Psychological Laboratory

Bert F. Green, Jr.
The Johns Hopkins University

INTRODUCTION

The small digital computer has become a common laboratory apparatus in experimental psychology. It functions as a versatile control and recording apparatus. Because it can be readily connected with the special devices needed for particular experiments, it can be used effectively in a wide variety of laboratory investigations. The laboratory computer is quite different from most laboratory apparatus and sufficiently intricate that not many people understand it thoroughly. Although an investigator can make good use of it without knowing very much of its internal operations, a general idea of the structure and function of the computer is important in assessing its potential value in any particular investigaton.

The typical laboratory computer is a small general-purpose digital computer operating on its own, that is, not connected to any larger computer system. Although good use can be made of a small computer terminal connected to a large-scale system (Green, 1972), precise timing and close control require a computer in the lab. On the other end of the size scale, there are a few laboratories with a large computer devoted solely to laboratory work and capable of running several different experiments simultaneously. Such machines have most of the power available at a university computing center. The main focus of the present chapter is neither the computer terminal nor the large time-shared system; the machine discussed here is a small digital computer that runs only one experiment at a time. A typical laboratory set-up is shown in Fig. 2.1. The computer usually consists of one or two racks of equipment plus some kind of a console or terminal for experimenter control of the computer. The computer is connected to the experimental set-up where the subject will be engaged in the activities of the experiment.

(a)

(b)

FIG. 2.1. (a) Laboratory computer, in two tall racks. A large
disk system is at the left. A programmer is working at the computer terminal. (b) A subject is
viewing a remote display generated
by the computer. The subject is
holding a box housing two response buttons. An intercom is at
his right.

The computer has many possible functions. It can be used for stimulus control, for response recording, and for stimulus-response contingency management.
Through a variety of peripheral display devices, the computer can control the
presentation of items to the subject. It can randomize presentations separately
for each subject, randomize other elements of the experiment as required, and
provide precise timing of the onset and offset of stimuli. For example, each of
the subjects in learning experiments can be presented with a different random
sequence of the items on the list to be learned, with precise control over the
length of exposure of each item. The ability of the computer to provide precise
timing for a sequence of events permits the study of such perceptual phenomena
as apparent motion and metacontrast. An an example of the latter, Mayzner,
Tresselt, and Cohen (1966) showed that if the letters in the word *somersault*

were displayed sequentially from left to right repeatedly, the subject will see the complete word *somersault*, whereas if the order in which the letters are presented is *s, m, r, a, l, o, e, s, u, t,* that is, first the odd-numbered and then the even-numbered letters, then under certain timing conditions, the subject will only see the even-numbered letters.

Response recording from the experimental apparatus can include a record of which response was made and the precise time at which it was made. The computer cannot deal with oral responses, except through the use of a voice key that produces an electrical impulse. (The computer could manage to record oral information on a specially connected peripheral audio recorder but could not recognize what was said.) The computer itself cannot make any more elaborate response measurements but can record results from measuring devices such as eye movement sensors, muscle potentiometers, and devices for measuring electroretinograms (ERG) and electroencephalograms (EEG). In the animal laboratory, data from implanted electrodes can also be recorded digitally for later analysis.

The computer is helpful in experiments in which the presentation of stimuli depends on the subject's responses to previous stimuli. The presentation of rewards (in animal experiments) or feedback (in both animal and human experiments) can also be managed in this same fashion. For example, in a two-alternative forced-choice experiment in signal detection, the experimenter may wish to identify each response as correct or incorrect. For a human experimenter to provide such feedback would slow down the experiment intolerably, whereas the computer can respond immediately and accurately. The computer can also detect and screen out anticipation errors in reaction-time experiments. Sometimes in such experiments the subject presses the response button before the stimulus is actually presented or so soon after the stimulus (for example, within 100 msec) that the button press cannot have been literally a response to the stimulus.

The computer can also be useful in managing multi-subject experiments. Studies involving competition or cooperation in problem-solving or decision-making can use the computer to pass messages from one subject to another. The function of the computer can be to screen out messages that are for some reason illegal in the experimental design. For example, Kelly and Chapanis (1977) used the computer in our laboratory to force subjects to use a fixed vocabulary in communicating about a problem being solved jointly. At the same time the computer recorded the messages, which were typed on electric typewriters by subjects, for later analysis.

It is important to emphasize that for most experiments special equipment will be required. The computer itself is an electronic information processor. It receives and transmits electrical impulses. Special devices are needed to transform these impulses into stimuli and to transform the subjects' responses into impulses for the computer. Some standard devices, such as teleprinters, keyboards, and cathode-ray tube (CRT) displays, are offered by computer manufacturers and are commonly available as parts of laboratory computers. But the blinking lights and simple pushbuttons usually found in the psychological laboratory are special-purpose devices not highly respected in the computer industry. They must be built in the laboratory or bought separately and then attached electrically to the computer. This electrical attachment is called an interface and is a serious problem in dealing with the computer in the laboratory. Investigators contemplating the use of a computer should pay particular attention to the interface problem concerned with their particular experimental use. Extra equipment is often needed to construct an interface between the computer and the laboratory devices. This point is discussed below in the section on interfaces

The computer has a wide range of possible applications. As described elsewhere in this volume, it has been used effectively in studies of human perception, learning, and memory, in animal learning and behavior and in a variety of studies of physiological mechanisms involving physiological measurements as well as behavioral indicators. Although most of the studies involve a single subject, studies of human interaction have also made good use of computers for both controlling and recording the experiment and recording the data. The computer is also widely used in education for computer-assisted instruction and computer-assisted testing. These fields are highly developed and currently active, but their problems are generally different from those that arise in using the computer in laboratory investigations, so such applicatons will not be emphasized here. (The interested reader is referred to Holtzman, 1970, and the U.S. Civil Service Commission, 1976.)

A digital computer is a novel device, and although its operation is straightforward, its description involves some new concepts. Jargon has naturally developed; learning how to use a computer is partly a matter of learning what the computer specialists mean when they say "soft copy," "hardware," "interface," and "byte." In the computer world a floppy disk is not a spinal ailment, and a 300-baud line is not a connection with a Shakespearian orgy. K is not even 1000; it is 1024. Jargon is annoying and pretentious, but it is rampant and must be mastered.

A curious feature of computer descriptions is that animate verbs seem the natural choice. Pedantic circumlocution is required to avoid saying that the computer takes, sends, tells, remembers, and knows. Indeed, the computer sometimes needs, refuses, insists, and even thinks. Use of such verbal shortcuts should not be taken to indicate any philosophical position on artificial intelligence. But there is no denying that, once set in operation, the computer acts.

COMPUTER HARDWARE

The term *hardware* applies to the physical equipment and is used to distinguish the equipment from the *software*, or computer programs that are used to make the machine operate. Computer hardware is presently undergoing a period of rapid and technological development. This chapter contains little about the actual physical devices but is concerned mainly with the functional hardware or the logical organization of units.

Functionally, all digital computers consist of a processing unit for manipulating the data, a primary memory unit for fast storage and access of information, one or more secondary memory units for storing large amounts of data and some input and output devices for communicating with the user. Laboratory computers also include a real-time clock. The physical size of the processor, the primary memory, and the clock are rapidly being reduced by present technology. The computers of the early 1970s, which required one or two racks of equipment, are being replaced by a very small box housing all the electronic components. The size of the computer today depends mainly on the requirements for secondary storage and the input and output machinery, which must be big enough to be manipulated by people. The only other design factors are heat dissipation in the electronic units and problems of providing power. Fortunately as the size has gone down, power requirements and heat generation have also been reduced.

Processor

The processor executes instructions that have previously been stored in the computer memory. The sequence of instructions, called a program, causes the processor to do some particular activity that either transforms the stored data or effects an exchange between the stored data and input or output mechanisms. Using a computer involves first putting a program into computer memory. Then data or other information comes into the processor from input devices, under program control, and is stored in memory. The data may be processed and analyzed. Eventually, results are reported on one of the output units.

Within the processor and the memory, all information is stored in binary form. The computer processes only binary digits, or "bits," which have only two possible values, 0 and 1. An item of information is stored as a particular sequence of bits. All information can be stored in this way. Numbers become binary numbers; text is stored character by character, with a 6-bit or 7-bit code for each character, as shown in Fig. 2.2. Even pictures can be stored in binary code, as sequences of bright and dark spots.

Data coming in from an input device must be translated from external form into bits and data to be put out must typically be transformed from binary to some more useful format. For example, the programmer usually communicates with the computer by typing on the keyboard of a typewriter-like terminal. Each keypress is coded into a string of six or seven binary digits, forming a binary number that stands for the particular character being designated. When the computer wishes to type a character on the print mechanism of the typewriter, it must send a sequence of six or seven binary digits designating the particular symbol that is to be printed. Standardized codes are used in such inter-

1st 2 octal digits	Last octal digit							
	0	1	2	3	4	5	6	7
00x	NUL	SOH	STX	ETX	EOT	ENQ	ACK	DEL
01x	BS	HT	LF	VT	FF	CR	SO	SI
02x	DLE	DC1	DC2	DC3	DC4	NAK	SYN	ETB
03x	CAN	EM	SUB	ESC	FS	GS	RS	US
04x	b	!	:	#	$	%	&	'
05x	(	)	*	+	,	-	.	/
06x	0	1	2	3	4	5	6	7
07x	8	9	:	;	<	=	>	?
10x	@	A	B	C	D	E	F	G
11x	H	I	J	K	L	M	N	O
12x	P	Q	R	S	T	U	V	W
13x	X	Y	Z	[	\	]	^(↑)	‾(←)
14x		a	b	c	d	e	f	g
15x	h	i	j	k	l	m	n	o
16x	p	q	r	s	t	u	v	w
17x	x	y	z	{	|	}	(ESC)	DEL

64

FIG. 2.2.   Seven-bit American Standard Code for Information Interchange (ASCII)-1968 character codes. Definition is from the X3.4-1968 version of ASCII. Octal digits translate to binary as follows: $0 - 000$; $1 - 001$; $2 - 010$; $3 - 011$; $4 - 100$; $5 - 101$; $6 - 110$; $7 - 111$. A subset of characters coded by six bits is obtained by deleting the first and last 32 characters. Multiletter indications (e.g., NUL) are nonprinting special control characters. Characters inside parentheses are ASCII-1963 Standard.

changes. The codes convenient for such input and output mechanisms are not convenient for the internal processing of information, so the computer uses a different binary code for its internal storage of information and its internal processing. The computer contains programs for translating from one type of encoding to the other.

The processor and storage units process information as strings of bits. Each computer has a specific string length that is its unit of processing, called a *word*. Information is typically passed from one place to another, one word at a time. The number of bits in a word is called the *word length* and is a design characteristic of each computer. Some computers use an 8-bit word length, but a 12-bit or 16-bit word are the most prevalent. The PDP/8 uses a 12-bit word. The PDP/11 and most other minicomputers use a 16-bit word. There are, however, a number of computers that use a 32-bit word. The IBM-360 and 370 series use a 32-bit word, but in some operations the word length is actually variable in 8-bit units; the basic unit in that machine is an 8-bit unit called a *byte*. The word length of the computer is important because the amount of storage is typically measured in words. Thus, a typical minicomputer might have a 16K memory, meaning that it can store $16 \times 1024 = 16,384$ words. (The IBM machines measure memory in bytes.)

There is not a one-to-one correspondence between numbers and computer words. Sometimes one word is used to store one number, but often two or three words are used per number. On the other hand, if the set of numbers has a small range, the numbers can be packed two to a word, with added programming effort. An investigator with 10,000 numbers to store needs to know how they will be stored to determine whether 5000; 10,000; 20,000; or even 30,000 words of memory are needed. Numbers within a computer processor are stored either as integers or as floating-point numbers. A 16-bit computer might use 15 bits to encode the size of an integer and use the 16th bit for the algebraic sign, either + or −. This permits accurate representation of integers from −32767 to +32767(2^{15} − 1). A floating-point number is stored in two parts, a fraction and an exponent, each with a sign. Thus, the number 3.5 might be stored as +.875(2^{+2}), whereas the fraction .4375 would be stored as +.875(2^{-1}). The exponent is adjusted automatically so that the stored fraction is always at least .5 in size. This format permits a very wide range of numbers to be conveniently accommodated in the machine, but complicates arithmetic processing. For reasonable accuracy, a 16-bit computer might use 8 bits for the exponent and 24 bits for the fraction, thus requiring two computer words per number. A 12-bit machine might use one word for the exponent and two words for the fraction, thus needing three words per number.

Speed.   The processing speed of minicomputers is in the μsec range. That is, a single process within the repertoire of the machine will typically take from 1 to 2 μsec. This fact by itself, however, is not especially useful, except for inspiring awe and wonderment at the speed of the electronic age. What matters is not how fast each particular instruction can be done but how fast a given required operation can be performed. That is a function of the entire computing system.

Speed depends on the repertoire of instructions that the processor can follow. A machine with only a few well-chosen instructions can be made to do anything any other machine can do by properly concatenating the basic instructions. But a machine that can perform a greater variety of instructions has less need for concatenation; its programs will be shorter, and thus will be executed more swiftly. Thus, the number of different instructions that can be given to a machine bears a relation to the speed with which complicated processes can be executed. For example, many minicomputers have limited ability for doing arithmetic computation. Typically, most of the minicomputer processing is encoding and recoding of information, simple counting and storing of information, or detecting the presence of some simple pattern. For most of these operations the integer form of number storage is sufficient, and the only necessary arithmetic is adding and subtracting. Thus, the typical minicomputer has hardware circuits for adding and subtracting integers, but not for other arithmetic operations. This does not mean that multiplication cannot be done. Multiplication is a sequence of additions. Indeed, all arithmetic can eventually be reduced to sequences involving nothing more elaborate than adding and subtracting integers. But it does mean that integer multiplication and division, as well as all floating-point arithmetic must be done by special programs or subroutines for effecting the result by a long sequence of simpler steps. As a consequence, minicomputers are typically much slower at numerical calculations than are the large digital computers usually found in computing centers. Many minicomputer manufacturers offer special units at extra cost for performing arithmetic steps faster. Fixed-point multiply and divide instructions may be available at an extra cost (this is frequently called hardware multiply and divide). Extra hardware may also be available for floating-point operations. Depending on the availability of such hardware, the same processor might be able to multiply numbers at the rate of 100,000 per sec or only 1000 per sec. Of course, this is academic to someone who only needs to calculate one percentage every 2 sec, but is of vital concern to someone who would like a fourier transform of a speech wave in 0.1 sec.

Processors could easily go 10 or even 100 times their present speed, but the processing can go no faster than the rate at which information can be obtained from the primary memory. Since both the program and the data are stored in memory, every processor step involves one and possibly two memory references. The first memory reference retrieves the next program instruction; the second memory reference occurs only if execution of the instruction requires it (e.g., STORE requires that a value be stored in the data area, whereas JUMP does not refer to the data). At present it is impossible to provide large amounts of primary memory that can operate much below the μsec level. When that becomes possible, we shall have to measure speeds in nanosec (a nanosec is 0.001 μsec, or 10^{-9} sec). (An indication of how close to the edge of reality we are drifting is that the speed of light, and of electricity, is approximately 1 foot per nanosec.)

Each processor has a number of special memory locations, called *registers*, to keep track of important information relevant for the process being done. Thus, in randomizing a list, it is necessary to keep track of how many of the items have been rearranged and which particular items are being interchanged at any given instant. If these temporary pieces of information can be kept in registers instead of in primary storage, processing speed can be improved, since the processor need not repeatedly store and retrieve those place-keeping items. In general, the more registers, the more efficient the program can be, of course, up to some limit. Many minicomputers have four, eight, or even 16 registers available for program use.

Interrupts.   Minicomputer applications typically involve a great deal of input and output and relatively little internal processing. Controlling a psychological experiment is a prime example. Mostly, the computer is outputting stimuli or feedback signals and inputting responses and timing information.

Input and output are very slow; the computer can do useful work between successive transmissions of output characters. Many terminals, for example, cannot accept data at a rate above 30 characters per sec. Thus, once each 1/30 of a sec, the computer must transmit a character; this leaves thousands of μsec between characters in which to do additional calculations, after getting the next character decoded and ready for transmission. In large computers a separate processor does the input/output computing and transmission, leaving the central processor free for computation. Minicomputer applications typically involve relatively little internal processing, so a single processor is sufficient. The processor, however, must have some way of being shared. For example, when output is required, the main program should be able to start the output routine that sets up the string of characters to be output, sends the first character to the output device, and then returns to the main program. Computation would then progress in the main program (assuming there is anything to be done). When the output device is ready for another character, the main program must be interrupted, so that the next output character can be obtained and transmitted; then the main program resumes. The interruption must entail keeping track of the main program, so that it can be resumed at the place where it was interrupted.

The interrupt handler is hardware circuitry for doing this automatically. Designs differ among computers. Some depend more on software, others more on hardware to keeping track of the interrupted program and for sensing the purpose of the interruption. A special problem arises when two or more input/output mechanisms are operating concurrently. Each mechanism can interrupt the main program, but, more importantly, the interrupts can overlap. One output device can interrupt while the other's interrupt is being processed. In this case some hierarchy must be established. Usually, the faster device should get priority. In any case, the computer must be able to keep track of a hierarchy if several interrupts occur. A typical application might use the special computer-controlled CRT as a display device, a special response button, and the clock in stop-watch action. When the trial begins, the main program is probably quiescent, but three interrupt programs are in action or ready. The display routine is at work generating and refreshing the display; when the button is pushed, an interrupt activates the response program. If the time limit expires before the button is pushed, an interrupt from the clock activates the no-response program. Some programming skill is needed to manage all of these interrupts, but in the main the computer does the work automatically.

In summary, processors differ in the instruction repertoire, the number of registers, the word length, the interrupt mechanism, and the number of words needed to encode integer and floating-point numbers. Other differences certainly exist. None of these differences says much about the utility of the machine for any particular application, except that more is better for a wide variety of possible applicatons.

Memory

There are two kinds of memory in the computer. Primary memory, usually megnetic core, has very fast access rates, and is used for storing the program and data being processed by the computer. Primary memory can be randomly accessed, which means that any word can be obtained in the same short time, independent of what word has just been accessed. Secondary memory, such as tape and disk, has slower rates of retrieval and recording but can be much larger than primary memory. Secondary memory is usually accessed serially. Once information is located on the device, successive words can be found much more easily than other "random" words. Secondary memory is used for storing programs not currently in use, data that have been collected in earlier sessions, and so on.

Primary memory is usually magnetic core storage, but sometimes other physical devices are used to store information for ready retrieval. Primary memory operates at a rate from 1 to 10 MHz, that is from 1 to 1/10th μsec per memory access. As noted above, the speed of primary memory is the governing factor in the speed of any computer today. The size of memory is also critical. Because memory is needed to store both program and data, large amounts of memory are required. Memory comes in units that are multiples of 2, because memory locations are accessed by a hierarchical binary switch. The amount of memory is measured in K = 1024 words; 8K (8192) words are minimal, 32K (32,768) words are common.

Core memory is volatile, that is, its contents are lost when the machine is turned off. By contrast, tapes and disks are nonvolatile. The information is permanent, except for wear and long-term decay, although information can be erased and new information recorded. Recently, primary memory devices have been introduced that are nonvolatile. Such devices are convenient for storing programs that will be used repeatedly (see Chapter 3 of this volume).

Secondary memory comes in a variety of styles. The major concern in secondary memory is the speed with which it can be accessed and copied into primary memory. The computer almost never refers directly to secondary memory. Rather, information is copied from secondary memory to primary memory for processing. Digested information is copied from primary memory into secondary memory. There are two aspects to such a transfer. One is the access time, how long it takes to find the location of the information on the secondary memory, and, second, the speed of transfer once information has been found. Access times are typically much longer than transfer rates.

Secondary memory mechanisms on minicomputers include magnetic tapes, and magnetic disks including both rigid disks and the unit called the "floppy" disk. Both rigid and floppy disks have magnetic surfaces on which information can be recorded in circular concentric bands. Magnetic tape is recorded linearly on several parallel tracks. Both tapes and disks are recorded digitally. A bit of information is either present or absent. No analog information is recorded. Magnetic tapes, floppy disks, and some rigid disks are removable, which is convenient in case the data are to be taken to a different computer for analysis or kept for use at some later time. Also, by using new tapes or disks the effective storage capacity of the computer can be extended indefinitely.

Secondary memory has two functions. It serves as an extension of primary memory, holding programs that will be needed later and data that have been collected. It also provides a permanent record of programs and data. For the first function, speed of interaction with the processor is the main issue, whereas for the second, convenience of handling, removal, and storage is of major importance.

Rigid magnetic disks are best for interaction with the processor. The rigid disks can be spun at very high speed, with recording and reading heads very close to the surface. This translates to fast access and transfer rates and larger storage capacity. But great care is needed in removing rigid disks, so they are not misaligned or warped, and so they remain clean. Each disk is very costly.

The floppy disks are more like records from an office dictating machine. They are thin, flexible plastic, easily handled for removal and storage. They are inexpensive. But their speed is slow, and their capacity much less than a rigid disk.

Magnetic tape is intermediate in speed and cost. Transfer rates are good, but access times can be very long. Tape is linear in character. To get to a program half-way along the tape, all the intervening tape must be traversed.

Information on secondary storage is generally organized by files, and within files by records. A record is like a punched card or a line of text; a file is like a deck of cards or a page of text. In a program, each instruction or program statement is on a different record; the entire program occupies one file. Usually, the size of a file, as well as the size of the individual records, is of little concern to the user, so long as the storage device has enough capacity to store all that is needed. The user refers to files by name (generally a user-supplied acronym). The system keeps track of where on the secondary memory each file is located. When a new file is to be recorded on a disk that already contains other files, the system puts the new file wherever it will fit, usually breaking it up into pieces so it can be put where there are spaces to hold it. Some tape, notably the Digital Equipment Corporation's patented *DEC*tape, works in the same way. Most magnetic tape, however, has a simpler organization. Successive records are recorded one after the next, each marked by an end of record mark; files are also recorded sequentially with an end of file mark after each file. If a file is to be added, it is added at the end of the tape. If a file already on the tape is to be changed, the new file can be recorded over the old file, but the new file will typically not fit in exactly the same space as the old file, so all information past that file on the tape is lost unless it is rerecorded. For that reason, magetic tape is fairly awkward to use for intermediate storage of results. This kind of a tape unit is useful only for long-term storage of data and is not convenient for handling data that must be changed and updated frequently.

Magnetic tape and magnetic disks can be damaged by dirt. The recording heads can also get dirty and not function properly. It is necessary to clean the recording heads periodically. Fixed-head disks revolve very swiftly with recording heads very close to the surface. If a small piece of dirt were caught, it would cause serious physical damage to the recording head as well as to the disk surface. Stringent air filters are used in such disk units in an attempt to keep dirt out of the unit. Still, it is very important to maintain a clean environment when dealing with magnetic disks and tapes. Smoking in the area of the computer is, in general, poor policy.

Punched paper tape can be used for permanent storage, but is much slower than magnetic devices. Punched paper tape can be read either by very slow mechanical devices that put metallic fingers through the holes to detect them, or by the speedier photoelectric devices that sense a light shining through the holes. Punching the paper tape must, of course, be done mechanically. Punched paper tape has the advantage that information is physically present in a much less destructible form than on magnetic tape. Magnetic tapes can be erased or otherwise disturbed. Of course, both kinds of tapes can be torn and burned but that takes more deliberate action.

Magnetic tape cassettes can also be used for storing programs and data. They are also relatively slow, and have relatively less capacity than, for example, a floppy disk. But they are very inexpensive and are especially attractive for storing programs. In principle, cassettes would be the most appropriate device for off-line data acquisition (Sidowski, 1977), because speed is not essential in most psychological applications. Presently, much use is made of punched paper tape both for experimental control and data recording. Tape cassettes are preferable to punched paper tape, but minicomputer manufacturers have not, for some reason, promoted the cassette.

For the record, it should be noted that punched cards can be used as permanent storage. Punched-card equipment is expensive, noisy, unreliable, and generally regarded as outmoded, at least for laboratory applications. For those who can find security only in paper with holes, punched paper tape may provide solace.

Real-Time Clock

Every computer has a processor, primary and secondary memory, and some input and output devices. But a real-time clock is not essential. The computer runs on its own internal "clock" that serves only to synchronize the many detailed steps in the processing of a computer instruction. (The internal "clock" is simply a source of regularly spaced digital pulses. The spacing need not be precise, so that counting pulses does not lead to accurate timing. Still, the device is called a clock by computer designers. Thus, when the need arose for a clock that could actually keep time, the term *real-time clock* was used.) Large general-purpose computers whose main function is calculation need a real-time clock only to bill users for the amount of computer time used. For process control and for laboratory applications, however, a real-time clock is often essential. Further, this clock should have much greater precision than a clock used for billing. The algorithm for calculating computer charges would seldom need accuracy better than 1/60th of a sec. For that, a fairly simple clock can be constructed that counts cycles of alternating current in the basic power supply, just like an ordinary electric wall clock. In the psychological laboratory, events often need to be timed accurately to the nearest msec, and physiological recording needs to be done more precisely than that. Thus, it is frequently necessary to have a clock whose tick rate is 10 kHz or 100 kHz. The real-time clock must provide a source of pulses at a given rate, usually crystal-controlled, so that the rate is accurate and reproducible. Then the computer can either keep time by reading off time, as from a regular clock, or it can have a stopwatch action, measuring an interval of time. These modes of operation are matters of programming convenience.

Input and Output Devices

Computers spend much of their time receiving input and sending output. Input can come from terminal keyboards, analog devices, or special-purpose laboratory equipment, such as response keys. Output can be to printers, displays, other analog devices, and a variety of special-purpose devices. The special devices may need a custom-designed interface. Secondary storage devices can also be viewed as sources of input and receivers of output. Those devices, including magnetic disks, magnetic tapes and cassettes, and punched paper tape were discussed above. Magnetic disks and tapes, punched paper tape, and even punched cards can be used to transfer data from one computer to another. To do so requires that the recording or punching formats be compatible. Otherwise, special programs may be needed to read such files.

Terminals. Programs and other computer commands are usually put into the computer from a terminal that consists of a keyboard and some kind of text display. The display can either be a typewriter-like printer that yields written output on paper ("hard copy") or a T.V.-like display of what was typed. The latter is called "soft copy," because the picture is evanescent, disappearing when new material is to be displayed.

The keyboard and display unit of the terminal are independent units. The keyboard can be connected directly to the display, for "local" operation, to check the terminal's operation. However, when the terminal is connected with the computer, the keyboard is an input unit that sends data into the computer, and the display is an output unit that receives information from the computer. In normal operation the typed information is input, processed, and output to the display device. The display thus shows what went into the computer, and can disclose the possible presence of transmission errors, as well as typing slips.

Since the input and output are independent, the display is not automatic. For example, when a user "signs on" to most terminal computing systems, he must indicate his password so that his identity can be verified for security purposes. When he types his password, the display does not show it. The system does not send those characters to the display, so no one else can see the user's password. The same sort of independence is used in other applications. In computer-assisted instruction, the display may show the question and require some kind of typed input from the user. That typed input may show up as a filling-in of a blank in a sentence, for example. In this case, the computer program controls where on the display typed input is displayed.

Keyboards are all very much alike, since all are variants of a standard electric typewriter keyboard. Since the computer uses binary symbols, the various keyboard characters must be encoded in binary form. Today most terminals use the 7-bit (128 character) American Standard Code for Information Interchange (ASCII). Some terminals use a 6-bit (64 character) subset. The 64-character set is enough for uppercase letters, numbers, special symbols, and a few control characters. The 7-bit code with 128 values permits distinguishing between upper- and lowercase letters and provides for many more special control characters. Both codes are shown in Fig. 2.2. Other codes are sometimes encountered. BCD is an outmoded 6-bit code from the old punched-card days. EBCDIC is an 8-bit code, of which 7-bit ASCII is a subset. Details on those codes can be obtained from the manufacturers.

Hard-copy printers are all variants of electric typewriters with fixed carriage and moving typehead. Some use a print ball, or print disk, and produce typewriter-like quality. Others use a set of pins, usually seven in number, in a vertical column. When a pin is struck, it prints a dot. To print a character in a 7 x 5 dot matrix, the pins are positioned at the left-most column, selected pins are struck, the pins are moved right, selected pins are struck, etc. Dot printers are quiet and simple. The 7 x 5 matrix will accommodate most characters. The main problem is lowercase *g, p, q,* and *y,* which normally extend below the line; these characters have been redesigned so they stay within the 7 x 5 matrix.

Printers either use an inked ribbon to create marks on plain paper, or specially treated paper that displays marks when hit. The special paper does not require the ribbon or the necessary mechanical linkages to move the ribbon, but the special paper is expensive and typically less legible than the plain paper-with-ribbon product.

Line printers and plotters are available for minicomputers but are of little utility in the computer-based laboratory. Line printers are hard-copy devices that print a line at a time, rather than a character at a time, so they are fast, mechanically complicated, and expensive. Programmers like the speed, but experimenters seldom need much printed output. Plotters can draw graphs on paper. They can be used to prepare unusual stimuli, but the computer-controlled CRTs are often more convenient. Plotters are expensive, mechanically complex, and slow.

The typical soft-copy display is a cathode-ray tube that looks and behaves like a standard television. It contains internal digital storage for the characters to be displayed, and internal circuitry for transforming the coded characters to a visual display. The display is refreshed 60 times a second, in a manner similar to ordinary television, though possibly with slight differences. (There may be no interlace, which is mainly useful for improving the smoothness of moving scenes and is of little use for static lines of characters.)

Although these displays look and act like T.V.s, their circuitry limits them to displaying characters, generally in a fixed pattern. Naive experimenters may expect to use these devices for perception experiments involving elaborate forms and are disappointed to discover that these displays are merely character displays, without even any control over the size of the character. These displays typically form a character in a 7 x 5 dot matrix, in a pattern of 24 lines with 80 characters per line. The circuitry must have permanent storage for the 7 x 5 bit patterns for the ASCII characters, plus primary volatile storage for 24 x 80 = 1920 characters, or 1920 x 7 = 13,440 bits. The economy of this design is easy to understand. A completely flexible system would need to store a bit pattern for the entire display, which would need from 100,000 to 400 000 bits, depending on the grain of the resulting display.

More general displays are called *graphical displays* by the trade. The simplest are CRTs on which the computer can plot points. The computer program treats the display surface essentially like a graph with cartesian coordinates, x on the horizontal dimension and y on the vertical. A pair of x, y coordinates is transmitted digitally to the display-control mechanism, which translates the digital coordinates into the analog voltages necessary to deflect the electron beam to the associated point on the display. The beam is briefly activated, brightening the phosphor at that point on the display. Since the phosphor brightness decays as soon as the beam is deactivated or moved, some additional action is needed to maintain a steady image. One way is to refresh the display, as the character displays do. The image must be repainted at least 30 times per sec and preferably more, to exceed the flicker-fusion frequency of human vision.

Since the computer must send the coordinates of each point in succession to the display unit, the display is restricted to computer speeds. Further, the points are allowed to be independent, so time must be allowed for repositioning the electron beam independently for each point. This operation is very much slower than a television scan. It may require as long as 50 μsec to display a point. At that rate a flicker-free display would contain no more than 500 to 1000 points. Some improvement can be achieved by providing circuitry to "paint" straight line segments between any two specific points. Still, the computer is essentially fully occupied plotting points.

Another way to get a steady display is to store the image somehow. In a storage tube, the activated electron beam deposits a tiny electrical charge on a screen mesh placed just behind the surface of the display phosphor. This charge causes the display to hold its brightness, at that point, constantly displaying the figure. Although a picture can be built up gradually, storage tubes usually do not allow selective erasure. They must be erased completely, and the picture recreated, if anything is to be deleted.

Other devices store the image in other ways and may permit selective erasure. CRT terminals are now available that store the complete bit pattern of the display digitally. Others store the display specifications and use a separate microprocessor to refresh the display.

Analog Signals. Some information occurs naturally in analog form, as a continuously varying quantity, and must be changed to digital form for the computer. Speech, for example, is continuously varying sound pressure. The speech wave is readily transformed by a microphone to a continuously varying electrical voltage. The electrical wave form must then be converted to a sequence of digital numbers, specifying the wave amplitude at regularly spaced temporal intervals. The fidelity of the digital version can be made as good as necessary by spacing the successive readings sufficiently close in time. EEG and other physiological recordings can likewise be represented digitally. In each case, the analog voltage is treated as a continuous function of time; the amplitude of this function is measured and encoded digitally by an analog-to-digital convertor. Since the amplitude is changing continuously, the instantaneous amplitude must be seized, and held long enough for the digital-encoding circuit to operate. This cycle, called "sample & hold" is repeated at a fast rate to obtain a digital version of the varying analog waveform. The critical problem here is the rate at which that can be accomplished and the amount of storage required to store the digitally coded amplitudes. Most electrical recording connected with neurophysiology does not require high frequency. *EEG* activity can be adequately represented by frequencies no more than 100 Hz. Frequencies up to 5 kHz may be needed to represent activity from single neurons, which means that the amplitude of the wave must be sampled at least 10,000 times per second. With such high frequencies, of course, only a few sec of input can be stored at one time in the computer. But there is time for some data processing between successive inputs (remember that the computer is working at rates up to 500 kHz.) Preliminary analysis (e.g., averaging) can sometimes be done as the signal is input, so that the entire signal need not be stored. If the required input rate is too fast, the analog signal can be recorded on analog tape and later played into the computer at a slower speed, so the computer *will* have enough processing time between successive inputs.

A different kind of analog voltage input is needed for devices associated with graphic-display units. It is frequently necessary to point to some part of the display. This can be done in many ways. One way is to control a unit on the display, called a *cursor*, by either setting two knobs for the x and y coordinates at which the cursor is to be set or by a similar device such as a joy stick that provides simultaneous control of both the x and y settings. The knobs and joy sticks can turn rheostats, controlling voltage continuously, or their positions can be directly encoded digitally. In either case, upon signal, the computer must register their positions and transform them into x and y coordinates.

A light pen is sometimes used with a computer-refreshed CRT. The light pen is simply a photoelectric cell that can be pointed at a position on the screen. When that position is lit by the electron beam, the photoelectric cell senses the light and signals the computer, which can instantly read off the values of the x, y coordinates of the point being displayed. The display program in the computer has just sent the x, y coordinate of that point to the computer; the signal from the light pen enables the light pen program to interrupt the display program and retrieve the x, y values before the next point is displayed. No reconversion is required, since the computer is controlling the location of the beam digitally.

Another popular device is called a *tablet*. The user, in effect, draws a picture by tracing with a stylus, on a hard surface. This device works just the reverse of the CRT. The location of the stylus is sensed in one of several ways and the coordinates transmitted to the computer. A variety of other devices is available to sense a person's pointing at or touching a display surface directly.

On the output side, the computer can send a succession of digitally coded amplitudes to a digital-to-analog convertor for production of an analog voltage output. That analog voltage can be used as input to a loudspeaker through an amplifier or can control a needle-type dial or the vibration of a vibrator or any other of a number of special purpose devices that require analog voltage.

It should be noted that sound can be created without the digital-to-analog encoding. The output of a flip-flop or bit in the computer can be connected directly to an amplifier and then to a loudspeaker. The frequency with which this bit is changed then corresponds to the frequency of the sound generated by the loudspeaker. This ancient, venerable technique cannot easily create very complex signals, but simple tones can be generated with no trouble.

Interfaces

The wide variety of input and output mechanisms will meet some laboratory needs, but other needs are not met. Slide projectors must be advanced, shutters opened, lights turned on, responses sensed. These activities are all controlled by switch closings and can be automatically effected by electromagnetic relays. Some laboratory computers provide relay controls for the purpose. But often the connecting circuitry will have to be built. The signal from the computer itself has very small voltage and could not itself control any equipment. Special circuits, called *interfaces*, are needed to take the computer signal and transform it to a signal that can drive a relay on some laboratory equipment.

Similarly, responses from the subject must go through an interface. When the subject presses a button, a certain bit in the computer's input register should be set, but the button cannot be connected directly to the register. The amount of current that needs to pass through the switch to detect its being closed would overwhelm the computer.

The careful design of interfaces is a topic of great importance that has been addressed in an excellent book by Uttal (1967). The problem cannot be treated in detail here. Instead, one example will give a clue to the need for interfaces. The problem is "switch bounce." When a button is depressed, closing a switch, the two contacts do not meet cleanly at the μsec level. The contacts usually meet, separate, and meet again within the msec that may be required for contact to be made. To the computer, watching at the μsec level, it may seem that the switch has closed and opened two or three times before settling down. The computer could easily record two or three responses, unless this chatter is suppressed. An electronic circuit known as a *Schmidt trigger*, is one way of smoothing the transition, so that the computer is given only a single clean step function. Of course, in principle, the computer could be programmed to disregard all responses received within a few msec of another response, but this means much more work and care by the programmer. An interface is a much safer solution.

SOFTWARE

The hardware is a versatile collection of instruments. The hardware is orchestrated by computer programs, which are sets of instructions indicating what actions are to be done when and under what conditions. Programs are so complicated that other programs are needed to help in constructing new programs. The hardware by itself is of little use without a variety of programs called *software*.

Programming the Laboratory Computer

When an experiment has been designed and the needed equipment has been attached to the computer, the next step is to program the computer to run the experiment. A program is a recipe for a sequence of actions that, when followed precisely, will produce the required result. The program is written as a sequence of instructions for the computer, including specific directions to be followed for every conceivable alternative. In a reaction-time experiment, for example, the computer must check for anticipatory responses, responses that occur after the "ready" signal for a trial but before the actual presentation of the stimulus. Such responses are not reactions to the stimulus, and the trial must be aborted. The experimenter, and possibly the subject, must be warned. In the same experiment, if no response is made within, for example, 5 sec, a different anomaly has occurred. (The subject fell asleep or the equipment failed.) The program must also provide for this situation.

Programming the laboratory computer is not very different from programming a large-scale computer. Generally, the program is written in one of the standard programming languages such as Basic or Fortran. Less frequently, it is written in a special purpose language as Psychol or Scat. The nature of these languages will be discussed below but the details of computer programming will not be discussed here. Persons who need to learn programming should consult any good text. It is best to learn a standard language first, such as Basic or Fortran. Persons who know programming will have no difficulty learning the particular language of their computer from the manuals provided.

The first step in preparing a program is to plan its major organization. A flow diagram, or outline, is very helpful. Then the actual program statements must be devised and written on paper before approaching the computer. Some experts can sit down at the computer keyboard and compose a program directly, but most mortals need to have the program all worked out, so they can concentrate on getting it into the computer. All except the smallest laboratory computers come with a variety of utility programs to help the user write programs. The utility programs are usually integrated into a system controlled by a program called a *monitor*. The monitor is of special importance because it must reside in primary storage at all times. Thus, its size is an important factor, since it reduces the available size of primary storage for user programs. The utility programs themselves reside in secondary storage until called in by the monitor. Systems using Basic are organized slightly differently from Fortran systems, in that their various parts are more tightly coupled. We shall first describe the more loosely organized Fortran systems.

One of the utility programs that the user can call through the monitor is an editor. The editor permits program files to be written into the computer. It also facilitates changing existing files. The editor is used both to compose new programs and to correct old ones. Editors vary widely in the power and variety of facilities available to the programmer. A simple editor requires program statements to be typed one line at a time, in sequence. Errors can be corrected only by erasing or replacing an entire line. More elaborate editors permit individual characters to be changed or inserted anywhere in a line; they will search through the program for all occurrences of a specified string of characters and do similar helpful things upon command. Power is achieved at a price, of course. The versatile editors are larger programs, needing more storage, and are more difficult to learn.

When the user's program has been put into the computer, it must then be translated from the programming language in which it is written into machine language. There are two kinds of translators: compilers and interpreters. A compiler will translate the instructions written in programming language into instructions in machine language that can be executed directly by the computer. An interpreter, of which Basic is the prime example, translates each program statement as it is executed, so no machine-language version is ever created. Statements within iterative loops are translated every iteration, which is inefficient for any but the smallest programs.

Most translators also note a variety of errors that they are able to detect, such as syntax errors in construction of the program. For example, right parentheses must match left parentheses in an arithmetic expression. If there are more of one kind than the other, the compiler signals an error. Errors must be corrected by editing the program text, then recompiling.

When the program has been successfully compiled, it must be combined with whatever standard system subroutines are needed for input/output and for computation (e.g., floating-point arithmetic, random-number generator). Every program is actually a combination of a main program and many standard subroutines. This complete set of routines must fit together properly in primary storage, with appropriate cross-references made so that the actual addresses will correspond to where the programs are actually put in the computer. This is a simple but extensive housekeeping task for the computer, requiring a special program called a *linking loader*. The final product is a program in absolute machine language that can be very easily loaded into successive cells of primary storage in the machine and executed immediately.

The final programming step is to run the program to see what is wrong. (Something is always wrong, at first. In 20 years of programming, I have only once written a program that worked correctly on its first run.) The error must be tracked down; then the program text must be edited, recompiled, relinked, and retested. After a few correction cycles, the program is ready for business.

Finally, the system must have facilities for manipulating files and keeping track of a set of files for a programmer, or there must be a special utility program to do this. Programmers will typically have more than one program at a time and a given overall program may have several subsections stored in different files. This set of files is commonly called the programmer's directory. At the least, the programmer must be able to erase and copy a file and to cause copies of program files to be typed out.

One more utility program is frequently needed for programming special devices. The standard languages seldom contain statements that permit special-purpose programming for special devices that have been interfaced with the machine. This must be done instead in a language much closer to the machine language of the computer. No one actually programs in the binary language of the machine. That is, no one actually programs a computer by writing down strings of 1s and 0s. The closest thing to it is a program called an *assembler* that accepts a symbolic form of instruction-by-instruction programs and translates them into the binary codes of the machine. A program at this level will almost certainly be needed for each new piece of machinery interfaced with the computer. Generally, the operation of the special equipment is programmed through a general purpose subroutine that can be linked with the main program. This subroutine only needs to be written once; it is kept in a subroutine library for use by experimenters. But it does need to be written, and thus the assembler is a necessary, if rarely used, utility program.

Systems using Basic perform the functions of editing, translating, linking-loading, and file manipulation, in a more constrained way. Basic was designed for novices; simplicity was the paramount consideration. Program statements and system commands can be freely intermixed. Few options are available, so the system can be learned fast. Editing, in most Basic systems, means no more than retyping a complete program statement. The function of compiling and link-loading are replaced by a simple interpreter. The file manipulator likewise has only a few possible actions. Consequently, the Basic system can be smaller and usually occupies primary storage continually. It is not unusual for a Basic system to need 10K to 12K words of storage, limiting the space available for user programs and data.

If the chief virtue of Basic is its simplicity, its chief flaw is inefficiency. Not only does it need a lot of primary storage space, but Basic programs run slowly. The reason is that the Basic translator is an interpreter, not a compiler. The program is never translated into an equivalent machine language program. Rather, the program is stored in a slightly compressed form of its original typed form; each statement is translated every time it is executed. For large programs, this is time-consuming. For many experiments in cognitive psychology, speed is not essential. A few msec of extra processing is of no concern. But Basic is worthless for programming the CRT, for example, where time is critical.

Basic has a minimal ability to use subroutines. Linkage of several programs, or incorporation of separate subroutines, is difficult. Instead, in Basic it is necessary to define special functions (called *external functions*) for controlling the laboratory apparatus. These special functions must then be written in the computer's assembly language. Thus, there is still a need for a symbolic assembler and a means of installing programs assembled in this way as external functions in the Basic system.

Documentation.   None of these programs is of any use unless there is adequate documentation describing how to use it. It is important to get complete and useful documentation of all software provided by the manufacturer. It is especially important to get good documentation of procedures in a Fortran system for connecting machine language routines with Fortran routines. The explicit details of the way in which Fortran expects subroutines to pass parameters back and forth must be spelled out for the programmer who is going to prepare the machine language routine for the special equipment. The problem is even more serious with the Basic systems: A provision in Basic for externally defined functions, functions defined in terms of machine-language routines, is a nonstandardized extra, not a normal part of the system. As a consequence, it is often very difficult to understand thoroughly how programs for such functions should be prepared.

System software is somewhat dynamic. The user must sometimes communicate with the manufacturer, who provides the software, to understand details such as, for example, machine subroutine linkage with other systems. Further, the software may not work as documentation says it does. There may be bugs in it. All programs contain bugs at first, and the larger the program, the more likely it is to have undetected bugs. Hopefully, most of these areas have been found and repaired, but occasionally new bugs are uncovered. For this reason it is usually necessary for the user to maintain a constant dialogue with the manufacturer to get periodic system updates and corrections. Further, the manufacturer frequently offers new versions or completely new systems of software. Usually, an annual cost is involved in obtaining these software updates.

Another problem with translators, particularly with Fortran and sometimes with Basic, has to do with a particular set of features available at the particular computer installation involved. For example, many computers do not have hardware for floating-point arithmetic. Indeed, the standard unadorned minicomputer will seldom have hardware facilities for multiplying and dividing fixed-point numbers. These processes must be done by subroutines (multiplication is successive addition and division is successive subtraction, so addition and subtraction are all that are required for all arithmetic calculations.) Thus, the standard translator will call the appropriate subroutine when translating an arithmetic expression. On the other hand, if this particular installation owns a hardware-multiply-and-divide option, then the translator must be set so that it makes use of this option. It is important to check translators to be sure that they take full advantage of the particular hardware configuration available at the installation.

As mentioned above, there are wide variations in the efficiency of systems. Basic is typically must less efficient than Fortran. The difference can easily be a factor of 50 in speed. Factors of 10 and 20 have been noticed in speeds of different Fortran compilers for the same computer. A simple Fortran compiler can be written that compiles swiftly but produces machine code that is inefficient when it is run. To produce efficient machine code requires an elaborate compiler. If time is of the essence in computer application, as it might well be in on-line signal analysis of neural recordings, for example, then considerable care needs to be taken in choosing the appropriate system. For the typical tachistoscopic presentation in the human perception laboratory, program efficiency is irrelevant.

Programming Psychological Experiments. Fortran and Basic are the languages most used by minicomputers. Programming an experiment in either language requires extensive calls to subroutines (Fortran) or external functions (Basic) for controlling the clock and the special equipment. For example, in our laboratory at Johns Hopkins, a set of special subroutines has been prepared. To display the word *TIGER* at coordinates $x = -100$, $y = 0$ on the CRT display screen for exactly 2.5 sec, there must first be some preliminary calls to preset the buffers (storage areas for the display coordinator). Then the display buffer is filled by

CALL LDBUF(-100, 0, 1, 'T', 'I', 'G', 'E', 'R').

The display is activated by

CALL TRNON.

The 2.5-sec delay is effected by

CALL WATFOR(2,500).

Here the two parameters specify sec, and msec. Then the display is stopped by

CALL TRNOF.

Alternatively, suppose the subjects' task is to push button #1 if the named animal is a bird, and to push button #2 if not. Then the program would load the buffer and turn on the display, as above, but then must either wait for 2 sec (and 0 msec) or until the subject responds. This is effected by

CALL WRESP(2,0, KEY, RT1, RT2).

The subroutine will return the number of the key pressed — either 1 or 2 — as the value of KEY, and the reaction time in sec (value of RT1) and msec (value of RT2). If no response was made in the specified interval, RT1 and RT2 will both be zero.

The system is versatile but slanted toward a certain class of experiments, and the program is not easy to decipher.

Several general-purpose languages have been prepared to simplify programming for psychological experiments. Among these are Pross (Scholz 1973), Psychol (McLean, 1969), Act (Millenson, 1970), Sked (Snapper, 1975), and Scat. Pross and Psychol are both procedure-descriptive algorithmic languages. Act, Sked, and Scat, by contrast, are state-description languages.

Psychol is an extension of a standard algorithmic language, in this case, Algol. Psychol is merely Algol with some extra permissible statements to define particular conditions, mainly timing conditions.

In Psychol, the program waits for 2.5 sec by means of the statement

WAIT 2.5 SECONDS;

similarly, waiting for either the response or 2 sec is effected by

AWAIT KEY FOR 2.0 SECONDS.

Then the reaction time is obtained by

RT = LATENCY OF KEY.

There are several other nice features of Psychol that simplify timing considerations.

Most minicomputers do not have an Algol compiler. It is usually most convenient to use a large-scale computer to compile Psychol programs for the minicomputer.

Act, Sked, and Scat are quite different from Psychol. They are state languages slanted toward operant-conditioning experiments. (Scat was developed by the Grayson-Stadler Company, a major supplier of operant-conditioning apparatus.) The control section of a Scat program for a fixed-interval reinforcement schedule might look like this:

```
C1:  S1; 15 SEC > 2'
C2:  S1; R(1, 1) > 3'
C3:  S2; 3 SEC > 1'
```

This means, "In State 1, activate Stimulus S1; after 15 sec, change to State 2. In State S2, activate Stimulus S1; after the first response of Type 1, change to State 3. In State 3, activate Stimulus 2; after 3 sec, switch to State 1." Stimulus 1 is a lighted key to be pushed; Stimulus 2 is the reinforcement (i.e., the feed tray). Response 1 is a key push. Note that during the first 15 sec, responses to the key are irrelevant, because the system is in State 1. As soon as 15 sec have elapsed, the system changes to State 2, where the first response does make a difference.

Scat, as extended by Polson (1972), can do anything that Psychol can do and vice versa. But both are capable of doing anything that can be done. Each system is awkward for some things and well matched to others. Act is like Scat, but its language is more transparent to the programmer. No one language or procedure has satisfied everyone. A good source of general information about languages and hardware is the annual meeting of the National Conference on the Use of On-Line Computers in Psychology. The proceedings are published annually in the journal *Behavior Research Methods & Instrumentation*.

On Trading Software. Unless an experiment is especially novel, it has probably already been programmed several times for a computer. It may well have been programmed for the computer model that is to be used. The question then arises whether an existing program should be found or whether a new one should be written. It is feasible, but by no means straightforward, to share programs from other installations. Each installation is, to some extent, unique. There are so many options available on minicomputers that installations frequently have slightly different configurations. The most important issue is the amount of primary storage available. Programs that run on machines with 32K of primary storage will not run on machines with only 16K. Almost certainly the program should be obtained in the original programming language. It is much more transportable in that form than in any later stage. Still the program will need modification. The program will usually be for an experiment that is similar to, but not exactly the same as, the experiment that is planned.

Typically, the person who prepared the program will not have made provision for each adaptation to other experiments. Programs that are easily transported must have been written with parameters that can easily be changed. Novice programmers do not know how to do this, and experienced programmers are usually in too much of a hurry or too lazy to do it. For example, suppose the experimental design calls for a trial to end after 5000 msec, if there is no response. The controlling program statement should not include the number 5000; instead it should use a parameter, perhaps named MAXTIM (or T9, in Basic). The value of that parameter should be set at the start of the program (e.g., MAXTIM = 5000, or T9 = 5000). Then, if in another experiment you wish to wait a different number of sec, or if another installation has a clock that ticks at a different rate, the statement at the beginning of the routine is easily labeled, easily seen, and easily changed. All such constants should be defined at the beginning of the program. For another example, input and output units for typing out either records of results or typing the stimuli for the subject, should not be specified by number but, again, by a parameter name such as IO or SUB that can then be defined at the beginning of the program. The definition can then be changed very easily without going into the heart of the program. This kind of problem is frequently seen and understood in the context of iterative programs where the number of iterations or the step size of some computation need to be controlled externally. But, the pervasiveness of the need for defining parameters symbolically is seldom appreciated.

These techniques should be used even if an experimenter decides to program the experiment from scratch and has no plans to export the program. Undoubtedly the program will be used more than once, possibly with changes in the design. It is remarkable how easily the details of one's own program are forgotten.

MANAGEMENT

Costs

Today (1977), a 16-bit processor with 16K core, a floppy-disk system, a hardcopy terminal, and a computer-controlled CRT display costs from $10,000 to $20,000. But costs are changing rapidly and may be quite different in a few years. Whatever the initial cost of the equipment, there are a number of ongoing costs associated with the machine.

The first need is a programmer/technician, at least on a part-time basis. Someone is needed to get all of the system software set up, to write the necessary control programs for the special devices, and to design any interfaces that may be needed. This person can also be responsible for routine maintenance. Air filters have to be replaced, tape-reading heads have to be cleaned, paper and ribbons have to be changed periodically in the hard-copy terminal, etc. Further, if the machine needs repair, the technician can try to repair it or at least can isolate the problem.

Most computer manufacturers offer maintenance contracts. The value of such a contract will depend on circumstances. Some installations will need a contract if immediate service is vital and if no competent technician is available on-site. Others find the contract much too expensive. The machine seldom needs repair, and when it does, it can often be repaired by laboratory personnel. Even if the computer manufacturer must be called for repair, the cost may be less than the contract unless the calls are frequent.

The costs of acquiring and maintaining a laboratory computer are not negligible, but neither are they overwhelming. Most investigators have found them to be a very good investment.

Other Uses

Experiments are not being run continually. The computer has many idle hours that could be used to advantage. Of course, first priority goes to persons programming future experiments. But when they have been accommodated, the computer is, in principle, available for data analysis, report writing, and other more tangential activities.

Data analysis may not be efficiently done on a minicomputer, but if time is available, efficiency may not be important. What really matters is the availability of a program to do the analysis. If the analysis is nonstandard so that a program must be written in any event, it may as well be written for the laboratory computer. Programs for standard analyses will almost certainly be available at the campus computer center; transferring these programs to a minicomputer is not likely to be cost-efficient.

The laboratory computer surely does not run experiments all night. Some computing jobs, such as Monte Carlo studies, require large amounts of rather routine but tedious computing. Such jobs could be given to the laboratory computer for an all-night run, if the computer may be left running unattended. It is usually considered dangerous to leave disks and tapes running unattended. (We came in one morning to a huge mound of randomly punched paper tape.) But there is no problem in letting the central processor run continuously. If a way can be found to disable the input/output devices, the central computer will cheerfully compute all night and print out the results when the input/output devices are reactivated in the morning.

Minicomputers could be very helpful in text processing. Very little of that is now done but the possibilities are begging to be realized. A document can be typed into the computer just as a program can. The author can then examine his product, make editorial changes, get criticism requiring more changes, without any retyping of the document. The editing program can be used to edit the text file. When the document is polished, it can be typed in final form.

The prime need for text processing is a terminal capable of producing type-script quality. The dot matrix printers will not serve nor will the special paper devices. Several satisfactory terminals are available, however. One mechanism, trademarked *Diablo*, provides the option for typing dots as well as characters. In the dot mode, the paper can be moved vertically and horizontally in small steps, so that graphs or special characters (such as summation signs) can be created, albeit slowly. Form letters, as to graduate school applicants, can also be typed on such a device. This may seem a horrid waste of valuable resources, since the computer has very little processing to do, although it is indispensable. On the other hand, if the computer is otherwise idle, why not use it for a worthwhile job?

Actually the computer is idle much of the time, even when an experiment is being done. Thus, data analysis, text processing, or even new program develop-ment could be done at the same time as experiments, under the right conditions. The minicomputer must have some hardware device for memory management so that when two programs are in operation at once, they cannot inadvertantly interfere with each other. Without this hardware, time-sharing the computer is very unwise.

Another job for a minicomputer may be to service the nearby microcompu-ters. As computers become more plentiful, it will be silly for each of them to have a complete system of utility programs and a complete array of input/out-put gear. It seems more sensible to use the minicomputer to develop and compile programs for the laboratory microcomputers. Indeed, we can expect to see much more cross-compiling and other intercommunication among computers than has occurred heretofore. (For example, Psychol was first implemented by modifying an Algol compiler on a large computer. That computer was used to compile pro-grams for the laboratory minicomputer.)

The laboratory minicomputer is a very versatile machine. Given the right program it can do many things in addition to new experiments. What other uses will be made of it in the future will doubtless depend on the prevalence of other laboratory minicomputers and microcomputers, as well as office computers and classroom computers. Some may feel that a laboratory computer should be devoted exclusively to running experiments. Others, particularly at universities, may feel that the students are better served if they get a chance to see the com-puter flex its abilities.

Technology is changing rapidly. In 10 years, microcomputers may be so plentiful that a new way of organizing activities will be established. For the pres-ent, the best move would seem to be to keep open as many options as possible and proceed into the primary task of laboratory control.

REFERENCES

Green, B. F. The use of time-shared terminals in psychology. *Behavior Research Methods & Instrumentation,* 1972, *4,* 51–55.

Holtzman, W. H. (Ed.). *Computer-assisted instruction, testing and guidance.* New York: Harper & Row, 1970.

Kelly, M. J., & Chapanis, A. Limited vocabulary natural language dialogue. *International Journal of Man-Machine Studies,* 1977, *9,* 479–501.

Mayzner, M. S., Tresselt, M. E., & Cohen, A. Preliminary findings on some effects of very fast sequential input rates in perception. *Psychonomic Science,* 1966, *6,* 513–514.

McLean, R. S. PSYCHOL: A computer language for experimentation. *Behavior Research Methods & Instrumentation,* 1969, *1,* 323–328.

Millenson, J. R. Language and list structure of a compiler for experimental control. *The Computer Journal,* 1970, *13,* 340–343.

Polson, P. G. A brief description of EXTENDED SCAT. *Behavior Research Methods & Instrumentation,* 1972, *4,* 104–105.

Scholz, K. W. A process control programming language. *Behavior Research Methods & Instrumentation,* 1973, *5,* 245–247.

Sidowski, J. B. Observational research: some instrumented systems for scoring and storing behavioral data. *Behavior Research Methods & Instrumentation,* 1977, *9,* 403–404.

Snapper, A. G. A new OS/8 SKED. *Behavior Research Methods & Instrumentation,* 1975, *7,* 233–238.

United States Civil Service Commission. *Proceedings of First Conference on Computerized Adaptive Testing.* Washington, D.C.: U. S. Government Printing Office, #006-000-00940-9, 1976.

Uttal, W. R. *Real-time computers.* New York: Harper & Row, 1967.

3

Structure and Use of Microcomputers

William A. Yost
Parmly Hearing Institute
Loyola University

INTRODUCTION

Researchers in the areas of interest covering information and sensory processing have come to rely heavily on computer technology. Computers generate and/or display stimuli, control experiments, analyze data, display complex results, help to test models and hypotheses, and simulate complex interactions. Although the computer and its peripherals are very helpful and most often necessary, they make state-of-the-art research in these areas an expensive enterprise. Recent advances in microelectronics have helped to keep the cost of computer systems from growing at the same rate as many other commodities in our society. Perhaps the most useful of these advances for the purpose of laboratory computing facilities is the advancement of the microcomputer. The microcomputer can perform many of the tasks of a minicomputer at a fraction of the cost, with far less power, in very little space, and with great flexibility.

This chapter attempts to introduce the reader to the basic structure and use of microcomputers. The hope is that both the reader with knowledge of computers, as well as the researcher or student with little exposure to computers, will be able to learn about microcomputers. The chapter deals only in a general way with microcomputers, since there is a great variety in the manufacture and operation of the available systems. The chapter is intended to indicate the potential use of microcomputers and provide enough background so that the reader can more easily understand the description of microcomputing systems and options that might be provided by a manufacturer.

HISTORY OF MICROELECTRONICS

Any investigator of sensory and information processing who has been in the field for more than 10 years probably recalls the time when laboratories were changing from relays and clipleads to solid-state logic and plug boards. In these 10 years, however, the change from logic systems to large computers to mini-computers and now perhaps to the microprocessors, or microcomputers, has been fast paced. This quick rate of conversion, is, of course, directly related to the tremendous growth taking place in the microelectronic industry.

From 1946 when John Bardeen, Walter Brattain, and William Shockley invented the transistor, microelectronics have invaded every aspect of our society, especially our laboratories. Following the diode and transistor the con-cept of the integrated circuit (IC) resulted in a quantal leap of the application of microelectronics to research and to practically all other aspects of society. The IC is a single sheet of semiconductor material that is functionally equivalent to a number of discrete electronic components (resistors, transistors, etc.) and their

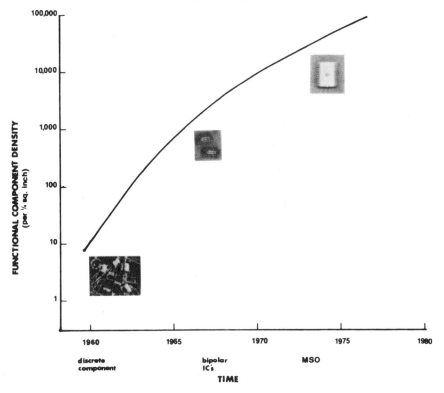

FIG. 3.1.   The approximate functional component density (per ¼ inch) of electronics is shown as a function of time. There has been a many-order-of-magnitude increase in density from single components to MSO technology.

interconnections. Thus, the function of an amplifier, a flip-flop, or now even the central processor of a computer can be performed by a single monolithic (system contained on one chip) IC.

The technology of the IC was enhanced even further by MOS (metal oxide semiconductor) technology. The MOS chip allowed for an increase of several orders of magnitude in the number of circuit elements that could be functionally contained on a small chip of metal oxide. This increase in circuit element density was accompanied by a much lower need for power by the MOS chip than by the previous ICs.

The MOS chip is based on unipolar-field-effect transistor (FET) technology, whereas most ICs are based on bipolar p-n-p or n-p-n junction-type transistor technology (hence most of them are sometimes labeled bipolar ICs). An MOS chip can contain approximately 15,000 FETs that require far less power than junction transistors.

Figure 3.1 diagrams the type of increase in circuit density that has transpired in microelectronics over the past 15 to 20 years. The required power consumption has dropped from watts to fractions of milliwatts in about the same period of time. Thus, today, large-scale integration with MOS integrated circuits allows for massive packing of electronic functions onto small chips of silicon that require very little power to operate.

With the use of film hybrid technology all of the advantages of MOS and IC circuitry can be placed on an enclosed single, sealed unit. The "thin" and "thick" film types of hybrid microelectronic circuits are made by bonding to a system of metallic film conductors and resistors, many ICs, MOS subsystems, and discrete components. This is all assembled on an insulated substrate of metal oxide. At this stage a very reliable LSI circuit is achievable in an extremely small space. This provides a savings in space, in power consumption, and, therefore, in cost of the system. Such hybrids will probably play a large role in the future of microelectronics.

In the late 1960s, a small-scale minicomputer might have cost thousands of dollars and occupied a space of many cubic feet. Today, the same tasks performed by this minicomputer can be carried out using MOS and IC microelectronic technology, which could cost less than one thousand dollars and be no larger than one cubic foot.

WHAT IS A MICROCOMPUTER?

A microcomputer includes a single MOS chip that contains the functional equivalent of the central processing unit (CPU) of a small scale minicomputer called the microprocessing unit (MPU), as well as memory and input/output (I/O) circuits. The microcomputer is usually slower than the minicomputer and has a small instruction set, but the differences are diminishing fairly rapidly with time.

In the 1970s the microcomputer can be thought of as being between a large-scale hardwired logic system and a small scale digital computer (probably closer to the small-scale digital computer). Software is used to program the microcomputer in ways similar to programming minicomputers, but microcomputers are most useful, as are hardware logic systems, to control input/output (I/O) functions and to perform straight-forward arithmetic operations especially when various time-dependent contingencies are involved. In other words, they are ideal for controlling psychological or physiological experiments and providing a fair amount of direct, on-line data analysis. They are not yet suited for real-time

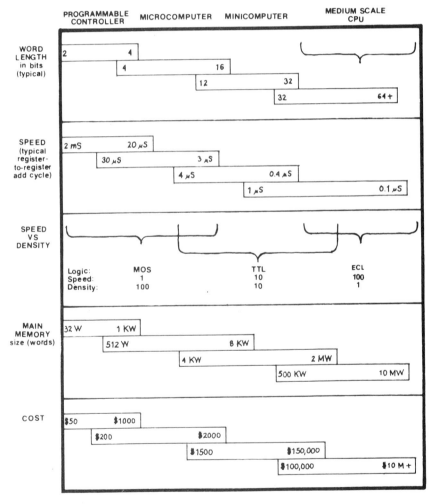

FIG. 3.2. A relative comparison among computing systems is shown (Adapted from Electronic Products Magazine).

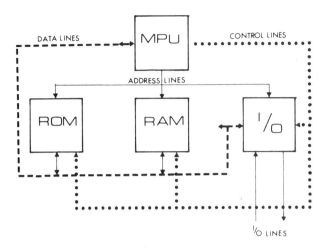

FIG. 3.3. The typical layout of a microprocessor. MPU – microprocessor unit; ROM – read only memory; RAM – random access memory; I/O – input/output device.

signal analysis, complex data analysis, or interactive use of subjects or laboratories.

Figure 3.2 shows a comparison between various sizes and types of computers or computing systems. As can be seen in the dimensions shown, the microcomputer lies between programmable controlled systems such as hardware logic devices and minicomputers such as the PDP 8s and NOVAs. Word length, speed, and memory will be discussed in more detail later in this chapter.

The basic simple microcomputer is diagrammed in Fig. 3.3. The microcomputer usually contains the MPU, a read only memory (ROM), a random access memory (RAM), an input/output unit (I/O), address lines, data lines, control lines, and I/O lines. This basic microcomputer can be extended with additional ROM, RAM, and I/O devices; even additional MPUs can be added for an interactive system. It is this type of versatility that makes the microcomputer so attractive for laboratory use, especially since the additions are usually very inexpensive. A simple microcomputer might be contained on one chip as is shown in Fig. 3.4 or on one PC (printed circuit) board with each MPU, ROM, RAM, etc. being a single chip as is shown in Fig. 3.5. With the addition of power supply, some input and output lines and connectors, and a keyboard for entering programs, the simple microcomputer is ready for use in the laboratory. Of course, the microcomputer system can consists of many other peripherals including discs, video units, analog-to-digital converters (A/Ds), digital-to-analog converters (D/As), etc.

The schematic diagram of Fig. 3.3 shows the very general organization of a microcomputer. Each manufacturer of microprocessors and microcomputers constructs its systems with different methods of operation and options. Thus,

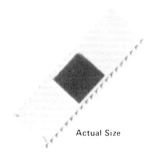

Actual Size

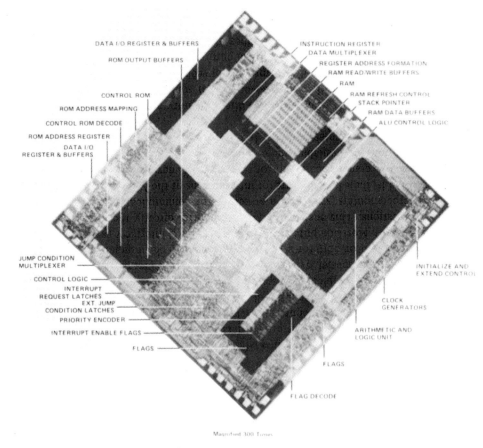

FIG. 3.4.   Layout of a microprocessor on a chip (courtesy of National Semiconductor Corporation – an example of their central processing unit called PACE).

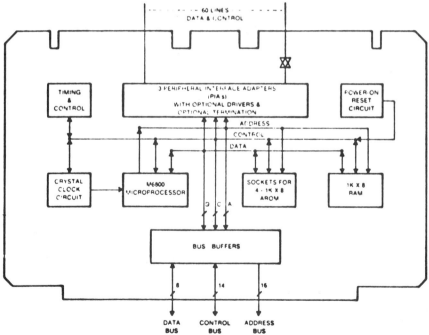

FIG. 3.5.   Layout of a microcomputer on a printed circuit board (courtesy
of Motorola – an example of their M68MM01 Monoboard Microcomputer).

63

since it is difficult to describe in detail the operations of MPUs, ROMs, RAMs, and I/O devices so as to apply to all microcomputers, these devices will be described in a general way so that the reader can become familiar with their overall function and can perhaps more easily understand the more detailed descriptions provided by a particular manufacturer for his microcomputer.

THE CPU OR MPU

The MPU basically contains registers and control logic. The basic binary word of the MPU can range from 4 to 16 bits, with perhaps 8-bit microprocessors being the most common. The MPU is usually organized similarly to the CPU of a minicomputer, with a memory in which a series of instructions is stored. Each location in memory contains one word (between 4 and 16 bits of code). The word stored in some location may be either a particular binary coded instruction that causes a particular task to be executed or a binary coded piece of data. The basic MPU operates on the instructions and data stored in the memory in a serial sequence.

Figure 3.6 shows some of the general elements and organization of a basic MPU. In general, the instructions and data are controlled by the program counter (PC), which keeps track of which instruction was just performed and which instruction should be executed. The PC receives and sends the data and instruc-

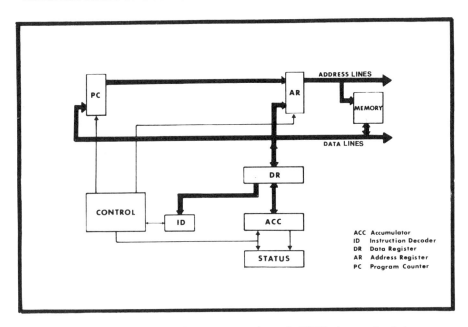

FIG. 3.6.   The layout of a microprocessing unit (MPU). A more detailed description is given in the text.

tions from memory via the address and data registers. The instruction decoder (ID) then interprets the instruction. The arithmetic and logic operations that are to be performed on the data are carried out within the accumulator (ACC) or accumulators. The status registers (STATUS) help determine what is happening in the accumulator. The data register (DR) and the address register (AR) help route data and instructions between the MPU and the memory. The control unit coordinates the activity within the MPU. A clock pulse and its support logic help time the sequence of instructions in the correct order and manner. Thus, data are manipulated in the accumulator, and these manipulations are determined by the instructions that are in a memory and are deciphered by the instruction decoder. The PC, AR, DR, status, and controller help in the bookkeeping and in the timing so that every operation is performed quickly, in the right order, and so that one can interrogate the MPU to determine what is happening at any particular time.

The time it takes to transfer data from register to register is often referred to as the cycle time of the MPU. In addition, the time for one instruction to be executed is also critical in terms of considering how long it will take for the MPU to execute a program. As Fig. 3.2 shows, the timing for microcomputers is usually slower than for minicomputers. The above description gives a very general overview of the hardware aspects of the MPU.

MEMORIES

The device for storing information is the memory. Locations in memory are called addresses, and each address is N bits long (in microcomputers, N is usually between 4 and 16 bits). Figure 3.7 shows the way in which memory is typically organized. The addresses may be accessed randomly by the MPU, in which case the memory is called a random access memory or RAM. Other memories are fixed; that is, the code at each address within the memory cannot be changed. These are called read-only-memories (ROM).

Most RAMs in microcomputers hold data on a "volatile" basis, that is, the stored information is lost when the power supply is removed. RAMs can be dynamic or static. In dynamic RAMs, the information is stored at each address as an electrical charge on capacitors of MOS transistors. The charge will leak if it is not occasionally replenished, which can be accomplished by periodic memory refresh pulses derived from the MPU clock. Static RAMs have the information stored much like setting flip-flops, so that special memory refresh logic is not required. Static and dynamic RAMs differ in the amount of power and support circuitry required to operate them. Static RAMs use more power but have less control circuitry than Dynamic RAMs.

ROMs are also usually semiconductor integrated circuits, in which the data are fixed (therefore, they are not volatile). They are usually used for special purposes and within the MPU. ROMs most often have their data programmed at the

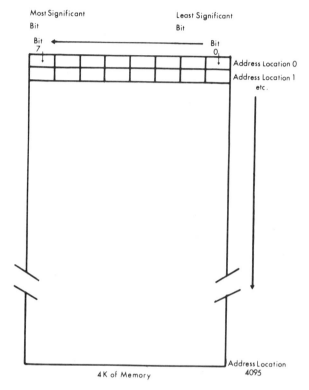

FIG. 3.7.   The way in which memory is typically organized. This example
is for an 8-bit word, 4K memory unit.

time they are fabricated, and they cannot be changed. ROMs whose data can be
altered (that is, whose memories can be programmed *once* by the user) are
called programmable-read-only-memories (PROM). Once a PROM is programmed,
however, its data are fixed. Some ROMs can have their memories altered more
than once, although the processes of rewriting the memory is slow and costly.
Hence these erasable programmable read only memories (EPROMs) are typically
used only for prototyping microcomputer systems.

RAMs and ROMs are often used together in microcomputers. For instance,
a particular statistical program may exist as a set of fixed instructions on a ROM.
The data from an experiment that will be analyzed by the statistical technique is
stored on a RAM, and the MPU reads the data from the RAM and statistical
instructions from a ROM and performs the arithmetic and logical operations
necessary to provide the analysis. One type of analysis, such as a limited slow-
speed FFT (First Fourier Transform), might be programmed in a PROM, and the
low-frequency waveforms to be analyzed are digitized in the RAM. The MPU
uses the stored FFT program on the PROM to determine the spectrum of the
waveform stored in the RAM. Or a particular laboratory procedure could exist

on a PROM as a set of instructions, and the actual stimulus values and the particular subject responses would become addresses in a RAM. Again, there is a great variety of RAMs, ROMs, and PROMs manufactured by the microelectric industry.

INPUT/OUTPUT DEVICES

Obviously, the microcomputer is in a laboratory to help perform some task. The input/output devices (I/O) transfer any data to and from the microprocessor as well as sending or receiving control signals. The device to which or from which the data or signals are coming is usually called a peripheral. The I/O devices that can be interfaced to a microprocessor are varied. Typically, the microcomputer is designed to have special I/O interfaces to handle particular peripherals (e.g., a special connection or port for a keyboard through which programs and/or data can be entered). Most computers treat many of the I/O interfaces as if they were memory locations. This enables the MPU to control directly the peripheral devices. Microcomputers also have a structure for communicating with the I/O devices. That is, there is a structure for interruptions of the MPU activity in order for the MPU to communicate with or service an I/O device. Sometimes priority interrupt options are available whereby the microprocessor user can determine a hierarchy of importance as to which I/O device should be serviced first, second, third, etc.

General purpose I/O devices such as direct memory access (DMA) or peripheral interface adapters (PIA) are also used with some microcomputers. DMAs help to speed the transfer of information between the various elements of the microcomputers. PIAs are usually general purpose devices that lie between some peripheral device and the MPU. The lines of the PIA (usually 8 or 16) can be programmed and considered as either input or output lines. The PIA acts as a register usually with some store (memory) capacity. Thus, the PIA can route data to the MPU under MPU program control, storing some data if the data are not needed at a particular time.

The primary aspect of the microcomputer is to control, read, and write data to and from peripheral devices. Thus, the types of I/O devices used and how they are programmed determine to a large extent how economic and useful a microprocessor is. A very large number of I/O devices are available, and many different types of these devices are manufactured. Thus, one should investigate carefully how a particular I/O device will interface in terms of both hardware and software before a device is purchased.

PERIPHERALS

The peripheral devices are those pieces of apparatus that are connected to the computer to perform certain tasks. Perhaps the most often used peripheral device is a keyboard to enter programs and data into the microprocessor. Many storage devices, most usually floppy disc systems or cassette systems, are also a common peripheral device. There are, in addition, the various laboratory peripherals such as data lines, digital-to-analog (D/A) and analog-to-digital (A/D) converters, clocks, hard copy units such as some sort of teletype or line printer. Many microcomputers have, as part of the PC board to which the MPU, ROM, RAMs, etc. are attached, a receptacle for a keyboard interface. That is, an I/O chip is a programmable communications interface that allows one to connect a keyboard terminal, teletype, or video-keyboard terminal to the microcomputer using either a voltage mode or current mode communication channel.

Before buying I/O devices one should consider:

1. *Word length.* Does the device have the same number of bits as the MPU?
2. *Interconnections.* Is the I/O or peripheral device able to connect directly to the MPU, or are particular connectors, ports, or cables required?
3. *Power.* The MPU will require constant voltage power supplies, usually +5 volts, −5 volts, +12 volts, and/or −12 volts. Many I/O devices and peripherals require different voltage. The more voltages required, the more expensive the system; and problems of power distribution might become serious.
4. *Speed.* It does no good to have a high speed MPU if the I/O or peripheral device is slow and vice versa.
5. *Type of transmission.* Does the I/O device communicate in a serial or parallel fashion, and does the MPU process data in a serial or parallel fashion?

THE OPERATIONAL MICROCOMPUTER

The MPU, ROMs, RAMs, I/O devices, etc., appear as PC boards, chips and combinations of PC boards and chips. To have an operational microcomputer, the devices need to be interconnected and power-supplied; the means of interrogating the MPU must be supplied (i.e., indicator lights), and the peripherals connected. Most of the large microcomputer companies supply all of these items. However, one need not purchase them from a single company, although some care must be exercised in building a system. For instance, the power requirements and power distribution can be rather complex. One must also consider the future expansion of the system before deciding the initial configuration of the microcomputer. Figure 3.8 shows a simple completed microcomputer. The cards contain the various chips for the MPU, ROM, RAM, and I/O devices. There are slots for expansion and connectors for the interface as well as the power supply.

An additional advantage of microcomputer hardware is worth mentioning. Most microcomputer systems contain only a few IC or MOS chips, usually interconnected in a straight-forward manner, and each chip is relatively inexpen-

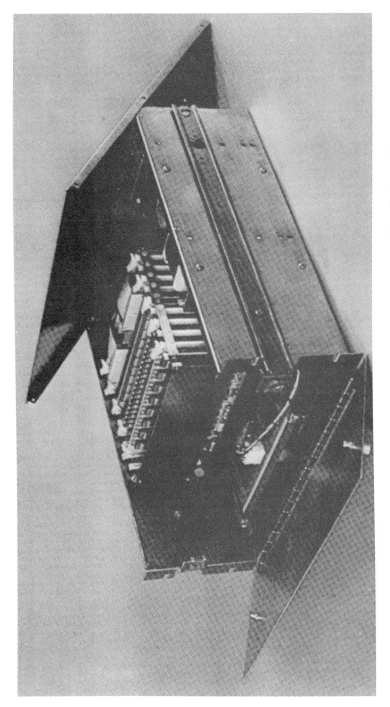

FIG. 3.8. An example of how various options are combined to complete a microcomputer system (courtesy of Motorola – an example of their micro module chassis, card cage, and power supply).

sive. Therefore, if there is a breakdown of the system, it is usually easy to pinpoint the chip and inexpensive to replace the malfunctioning part. Thus, the need for expert computer techicians and/or expensive maintenance contracts is reduced with the use of microcomputers.

SOFTWARE

The variety of hardware options that we have described for microcomputers also applies to software. The basic program instructions for microcomputers are similar to those used by minicomputers, basically because the hardware architecture of microcomputers is modeled after that of the minicomputers.

The basic operation of the microcomputer is, as in any computer, the setting of binary bits. Thus, the basic operations of programming begins with the manipulations of binary numbers. This task is made easier by representing binary numbers as octal numbers (Base 8) or sometimes as hexadecimal numbers (Base 16). Certain combination of bits are interpreted by the microcomputer in a particular manner. These become the instructions of the microcomputer software system. The instructions are symbolic or mnemonic codes. These instructions are translated into the machine language of binary bits by an *assembler* program. There is a large variety of assemblers. The number and type of instruction vary greatly from microcomputer to microcomputer.

TABLE 3.1
Decimal to Octal to Binary to Hexadecimal Counting

Decimal	Octal	Binary	Hexadecimal
0	00	0000	0
1	01	00001	1
2	02	00010	2
3	03	00011	3
4	04	00100	4
5	05	00101	5
6	06	00110	6
7	07	00111	7
8	10	01000	8
9	11	01001	9
10	12	01010	A
11	13	01011	B
12	14	01100	C
13	15	01101	D
14	16	01110	E
15	17	01111	F
16	20	10000	10

TABLE 3.2
Logic and Arithmetic Operations

Logic	
AND	OR
Word 1: 11100101	Word 1: 11100101
Word 2: 01010101	Word 2: 01010101
AND 01000101	OR 11110101
Rule: Two 1's yield a 1. Everything else yields a 0.	*Rule:* A1, 0; 0, 1; or 1, 1: yields a 1. A0, 0 yields a 0.

Arithmetic	
Addition	Subtraction
Word 1: 11100101	Word 1: 11100101
Word 2: 01010101	Word 2: 01010101
100111010	01010101
carry (count)	10101010 one's compliment
	10101011 two's compliment
Rule: 1 + 1 = 0 plus a carry of 1	+11100101
1 + 0 = 1	1 10010000 answer
0 + 1 = 1	carry (do not count)
0 + 0 = 0	*Rule:* *Step 1* — ones compliment of subtrahend is changing each bit (1 to 0, 0 to 1). *Step 2* — two's compliment of subtrahend is adding 1 to one's compliment. *Step 3* — add two's compliment of subtrahend to the minuend.

As was stated previously, the language of the microcomputer is the binary number. However, the language of binary numbers is difficult to program. A string of binary numbers can be divided into groups of three, forming an octal number, or into groups of four bits for a hexadecimal number. Table 3.1 shows these types of conversions. Programming in octal or hexadecimal is easier than in binary, but still inefficient. The symbolic instructions are simply achieved by assigning a particular mnemonic label to a particular unique binary bit pattern. For instance, CLC, which might stand for clearing a register (setting the bits in the register to zero), may be represented by an eight-bit pattern of 00001100.

The primary instructions are simple arithmetic and logic operations that are carried out on data in the accumulator. The crucial instructions are the *AND* and *OR* logic operations and addition and subtraction. Rules for these four operations are given in Table 3.2.

In most assemblers the instructions are stored and operated in a sequential manner. A statement in an assembly language program typically has four fields:

(1) a label field; (2) a mnemonic operator field; (3) a mnemonic operand field; and (4) a comment field. The operator (OP code) and operand fields constitute the instructions, while the label and comment fields are used to aid the programmer in writing the program and in understanding it once it is written. The mnemonic codes in the operation fields define what operation should be performed on the data. The operand field tells the assembler the location of the data that is to be operated on. Thus, the operand field is not always used since every OP code does not require the assembler to go to memory to obtain data. An example of a line or statement in a program is:

| LDA | A   M1 | LOAD ACCA FROM MEM1 |

| label
field | operator
field | operand
field | comment field |

In this line there is no label field, LDA is the mnemonic for the LOAD operation, A is accumulator A, and M1 could stand for memory location 1. Thus, as the comment says, this instruction calls for the MPU to load accumulator A (in some microprocessors there is more than one accumulator) with the data found in memory location M1. The following program would allow for adding two 8-bit numbers (given that one word of the microcomputer contains 8 bits):

```
LDA    A    M1    LOAD ACC A NUM1
ADD    A    M2    ADD TO ACC A NUM2
STO    A    M3    STORE RESULT M3
```

In addition to providing a means to program microcomputers with simple mnemonic labels, the microcomputer assembler also provides an interpreting piece of software that pinpoints errors in the program. Errors of syntax and program logic are identified. There is a wide variety of assemblers available for microcomputing. Some microcomputers have assembly languages that closely parallel those of such well-known minicomputers as the PDP8. There are different types of assemblers, and some large microcomputer systems contain a compiler that allows the user to program in a higher language such as BASIC or, in some cases, FORTRAN.

The programming of the microcomputer often proceeds in the following manner: The MPU first strobs out to the address lines the content of the program counter (PC). The PC allows the first instruction of the program to be obtained from the memory. The operand field of the instruction defines where the data are, and the MPU, after incrementing the PC by one, fetches the data and places it in the appropriate register (perhaps an accumulator). The OP code field of the instructions is then interpreted by the instruction decoder, and the operation is completed. The use of software, especially assembler language, gives the microcomputer a very large range of possibilities. This versatility of the software coupled with the inexpensive hardware makes the microcomputer attractive for laboratory use.

USE OF MICROCOMPUTERS IN STUDIES OF INFORMATION AND SENSORY PROCESSING

As with any piece of laboratory equipment, the type of apparatus used depends on the exact needs of the laboratory. Microcomputers can be used in two general ways: either as a piece of equipment that stands alone or as a complement to an already existing computer. As mentioned previously, the microprocessor can solve arithmetic problems, control experiments, and make decisions, especially those involving knowledge of operations that have already been completed in order to determine which operations should follow.

Although most laboratories probably do not now have a microcomputer to control experiments, they may have pieces of apparatus that contain a microprocessor. Many calculators, recently developed oscilloscopes, digital meters, complex timing devices, wave- or real-time spectrum analyzers, etc., are often based on the operations of a microprocessor.

Microcomputers are particularly useful for tasks that are carried out many times in essentially the same manner. For instance, a microcomputer is ideally suited to control the stimulus presentation and subject data acquisition for psychophysical procedures, especially adaptive or tracking paradigms. The microcomputer can act as a stand-alone device to control the experiment and collect and analyze the data or can act in connection with a minicomputer. The minicomputer might be required for stimulus generation for more complex stimulus control. Or the minicomputer can be used for off-line data analysis, program development, or student use while the microcomputer runs the experiment.

The low cost of the microcomputer often makes it a less expensive option for adding computing capability to a laboratory than adding additional peripherals to another computing system. For instance, experimenters might feel it necessary to add a mass-storage device to a minicomputer because of additional tasks they demand of the system. In some cases a microcomputer that might cost one-half to one-tenth as much as the mass-storage device could perform the same service. In addition, one has the flexibility of another CPU if the microcomputer is purchased.

In laboratories that do not have minicomputers, but have access to a large time-shared computer facility, the microcomputer can make the large computer available in the laboratory. The microcomputer can act as a programmable buffer, multiplexer, and interface between the laboratory and the time-sharing system. For instance, a video-display unit and a microcomputer could be connected to a large-scale computing facility for little more than the cost of the display unit alone in order to control written material presented on the display and to accept subject's responses. The microcomputer acts as the controller, and the large-scale computer deals with the storage and manipulations of the stored words and the analyzer of the responses.

An example of the use of a microcomputer as a stand-alone device is for physiological measurements. Biological signals most often have to be processed on line in order to provide meaningful and useful information to the experimenter. Signal averaging or the computation of histograms can easily be programmed with a microcomputer. The microcomputer, keyboard, display scope (a simple $X-Y$ scope) and an analog-to-digital (A/D) connecter are the primary hardware devices required. The MPU can be programmed to provide the appropriate data analysis. The system, of course, can also be used as a small-scale general purpose computing system when there is not an experiment in progress.

In this chapter, I have attempted to describe in a general way the structure and use of microcomputers. Because of their programming flexibility, low-cost hardware, small space requirements, and ease of expansion, microcomputers will probably soon be an integral part of many laboratories, in which information and sensory processing are studied.

MANUFACTURERS

Although the list of companies that make microcomputers will probably change over time, the following manufacturers have provided a full line of microcomputers and microcomputer support.

Fairchild Semiconductor Company
Intel Company
Microsystems International
Motorola Semiconductor
National Semiconductor
Rockwell Microelectronics

Many other firms offer microprocessors, memories, etc. One should consult a list of electronic manufacturers for a complete description.

ACKNOWLEDGMENTS

I was at the University of Florida with the Institute for the Advanced Study of Communication Processes and the Psychology Department while most of the work on this chapter was completed. I would also like to thank Wayne Harrington for his useful comments on the chapter.

REFERENCES

This chapter has provided only a very general overview of microcomputer structure and use. Most of the manufacturers provide pamphlets on the general use of microcomputers, as well as on the specific use of their own microcomputer. The following pamphlets and books were most helpful in preparing the material for this chapter:

Introduction to Microprocessing, H. Tireford, Motorola Semiconductor Product, Inc., 1973.
Minicomputers in Data Processing and Simulation, R. Souock, Wiley-Interscience, 1972.
Microelectronics in the 1970's, M. S. Parks, Rockwell International, 1974.
Understanding Microprocessors, D. Queyssac (Ed.), Motorola Semiconductor Products, Inc., 1975.

GLOSSARY OF TERMS

The major terms that were used in this chapter concerning microcomputers are defined here. These definitions do not represent any standardized definitions. A complete list of microelectronic definitions can be found in *Microcomputer Dictionary and Guide,* by C. J. Sippl and D. A. Kidd, Matrix Publishers, New York.

Accumulator (ACC) — It is the basic component of the arithmetic unit of the computer. The basic logic and arithmetic operations are carried out in the accumulator.

Assembler — A special program that translates symbolic labels into binary numbers. That is, an assembler allows the programmer to use letter and number symbols as mnemonics for the binary language of the computer.

Bits — A binary digit. Takes the value of 1 or 0.

Bytes — A byte contains 8 bits. That is, a byte is eight binary numbers.

Central Processing Unit (CPU) — In larger computing systems, the central arithmetic and logic control unit.

Compiler — A program that translates a higher language program such as FORTRAN or BASIC into a form closer to the machine code, quite often into a code understandable to an assembler program. Usually for larger computing systems.

Direct Memory Access (DMA) — An input/output device that helps "speed up" movement of data between components of a microcomputer.

Erasable Programmable Read Only Memory (EPROM) — A read-only memory that can have its memory erased and rewritten usually at a slow speed.

Field Effect Transistor (FET) — A means of controlling or gating an electronic field within a semiconductor. The technology used in MOS chips.

Hardware — The electronics and circuitry of a microcomputer.

Hexadecimal — A number system to the base 16. Usually derived by dividing a binary string of numbers into groups of four. The numbers go from 0 to 9 and then from A to F.

Higher Order Language — A language such as FORTRAN or BASIC that allows the programmer to use simple English-like words and symbols to program. A compiler translates these symbols into a machine code.

Hybrids — A single, sealed unit of electronics such that the components are bonded to a substrate of metallic conductor with an insulating surface.

Input/Output (I/O) *Units* — The components of a microcomputer that route data and signals in and out of the microprocessing unit and memories.

Instruction Decoder (ID) — The device in the microprocessing unit that decodes the operation code field of the instructions.

Integrated Circuits (IC) — The placing of many electronic components and their interconnections onto a single chip of silicon.

Interrupt — A processing technique that allows the operation of the basic microcomputer to be temporarily suspended while some signal is transferred to or from the microprocessing unit and then allows for the basic program to begin again at the part at which it was suspended.

Large-Scale Integration (LSI) — The combining of many electronic components onto a single electronic chip of silicon.

Machine Language — The basic language of the microcomputer, which is the operation of binary numbers.

Metal Oxide Semiconductors (MOS) — A transistor fabrication technology using metal deposits and oxide layer to form the device.

Microcomputer — A complete computing system including a memory and input/output devices that is contained on one chip or on one printed circuit board.

Microprocessor — The part of the microcomputer that is equivalent to the central processing unit of a computer and its immediate memory.

Microprocessing Unit (MPU) — The central processing unit of a microcomputer.

Monolithic — Describes any system of electronics that is completely contained on one chip or substrate.

Octal — The number system to the base 8. Usually obtained by dividing a series of binary numbers into groups of three.

Peripherals — Any device that the microprocessor is going to send data to or receive signals from.

Printed Circuit (PC) *Boards* — A board onto which individual MOS and IC chips are placed and interconnected.

Program Fields — The parts of an assembly program that specifies what operation is to be performed (operation field), where the data are (operand field), comments to the programmer (comment field), and an index (label field).

Peripheral Interface Adaptor (PIA) — A built-in register that is an input/output device. The PIA is programmable with a limited memory that aids in the transfer of data within the microcomputer.

Programmable Read Only Memories (PROM) — A read-only memory into which data or instructions can be written once.

Random Access Memory (RAM) — A memory device whose memory is controlled by the program. The memory may be written or accessed in a random rather than in a serial fashion.

Read Only Memory (ROM) — A memory device in which data are programmed at the time of manufacture or in the field and may not be altered once programmed.

Registers — Temporary storage logic, usually a RAM in the microcomputer.

Software — The programs that a user writes to instruct the microcomputer to perform its tasks.

4 Time-Shared Terminals in Research

N. John Castellan, Jr.
Indiana University

INTRODUCTION

During the past 15 years, there have been significant changes in the manner in which psychologists conduct research. In the early 1960s, small computers began to be used in some research laboratories. In the latter part of the 1960s, some laboratories acquired medium-sized computers that, when operated in a time-shared mode, enabled several experimenters to share the resources (e.g., large disk storage, large amounts of core memory) previously available only with larger systems and a greater variety of peripherals than could be supported on smaller systems. Now, in the middle 1970s, the distinction between minicomputers and larger systems is not as clear as before. The reasons for this development are many and include the drastic cost reductions that have occurred for central processors and core memory, the corresponding cost reductions and standardization of interfaces for extended memory (disk, tape, etc.) and peripherals such as printers and teletypes. Moreover, significant developments in hardware and software design have made previously difficult programming tasks much easier and thereby more accessible to the researcher.

While much of the early work in laboratory automation utilized discrete outputs from the computer to control stimulus displays and other experimental contingencies and discrete inputs from subjects such as button and level presses, there were a small number of laboratories dealing with more complex displays and inputs. Such displays included complex visual stimuli presented on a Cathode Ray Tube (CRT), and inputs included verbal responses. (In other applications, particularly psychophysiology, analog inputs and outputs were used; detailed discussion of these are beyond the scope of the present chapter.) This chapter is concerned with the use of a particular device — an input/output (I/O) terminal — in psychological research.

TYPES OF TERMINALS

In the context of this chapter, a terminal may be one of several devices. At the simplest level, a terminal is a teletype by means of which alphanumeric characters can be typed as output from a computer or typed alphanumeric characters can be transmitted to the computer. At the next level of complexity is the video terminal that differs from the teletype in that the text of alphanumeric characters, rather than being typed on paper, is displayed on the face of a CRT. At the next level of complexity is the terminal that has a CRT with some editing capability; such capability lets the display be more complex and versatile than that presented on a simpler CRT. At the next level of complexity is the terminal that permits, in addition to alphanumeric text, the display and control of complex graphic stimuli. Finally, at the highest level of complexity is the terminal that has storage capacity for its own stored programs and that sometimes possesses computing power in excess of some minicomputer systems of 10 years ago.

There are many ways that such terminals may be attached to a computer. While some may be interfaced directly to a small computer, many are interfaced through some communications interface to a large timesharing system. Some may be located in close proximity to a computer center and others may be located miles from the central computer. Regardless of the proximity of the computer, there are distinct advantages and capabilities of terminals attached to a timesharing system. These advantages are not insignificant and include access to large amounts of memory — both primary (core) and secondary (tape, disk, etc.) — large and efficient language compilers, and versatile program libraries for editing and debugging programs and for analyzing data. Also, depending on the number of ports available on the system, several subjects can be run at the same time. In some systems, the users of the terminals may interact with each other through the computer. Finally, and certainly not least for many researchers, the ability to interface through telephone lines makes it possible to bring the experiment out of the laboratory and to the subject. Thus, subjects may be run in the setting most important and relevant to the experimental and theoretical concerns of the project — home, school, hospital, etc.

In the following section different types of terminals will be described and classified. The classification will be in terms of function, and the primary breakdown is in terms of output (displays) and input (responses).

Displays

With I/O terminals, the greatest flexibility and variety of the devices is in terms of output. There are three basic types of displays—printers, video CRTs, and line graphics CRTs. Each of these types is described in turn.

Teletype Display.   This sort of output consists of some sort of printed characters, usually limited to those found on an ordinary typewriter. The output is usually quite legible, and since it is printed, results in a permanent copy for later use and reference. There are two primary limitations to such displays: print speed and the sequential or line-oriented nature of the output. For most printers likely to be used in conjunction with experimental research, the maximum printing speed is between about 10 and 30 characters per sec. For some purposes this data rate is adequate, whereas for experiments requiring relatively fast displays, such speed is too slow.

There are some programming techniques that can overcome the character-by-character printing limitation. Perhaps the simplest is to install a mask over the print mechanism so that a line is not visible as it is printed. Then, when the line is to be displayed, a line feed will bring the entire printed line into view at once. The capability of doing this illustrates the second limitation — that lines of output must be printed in order and usually from left to right. Thus, it is not possible to return to earlier locations and spaces on the page and insert characters or symbols. Further, since the printed copy is available, provision must be made to obscure from view those portions of the printed output that the subject is not supposed to view (such as the stimuli for the previous trial). Another minor limitation is that virtually all print terminals are noisy — some to the point of distraction.

After listing these problems and limitations, for what could a teletype display be used in the psychology laboratory? Although I am not attempting to convince the reader that a printer terminal is the best choice, the following sorts of experiments could be run on them: serial and paired-associates learning, simple decision-making tasks, and concept identification tasks in which the stimuli are simple symbols or short words. Finally, it should be noted that at the present time printer/teletypes are still the lowest cost terminals available, although maintenance costs may be higher.

Video (CRT) Display.   There are many varieties of video display terminals available. Perhaps the simplest type is the display that is a direct teletype substitute. Such a device has the capability of displaying several lines of teletype text. The last line output typically is printed on the bottom of the display. When a carriage return (or "line feed") occurs, the material presented on the bottom line is "scrolled" or "popped up" in order to make room for the next line of text. At that time, the line at the top of the screen disappears, and all others move upward by one line. The size of the display usually consists of 12, 20, or 24 lines of 40, 72, or 80 characters, the most common size now being 24 lines of 80 characters on a 12-inch video screen. The mechanism for generating characters is usually internal to the device, and each character is either drawn as line segments or comprised of a fixed matrix of dot positions that may be filled to form characters or symbols. In practice, it is usually the case that characters formed by a dot-matrix method are more uniform and sharp and result in less eye strain for the viewer. Subsequent references to video CRTs will imply video terminals in which the characters are formed from a dot matrix.

Most of the simple display terminals now available have several basic functions in addition to display. These include the capability to erase all information that may be on the screen and a function that permits a particular line to be referenced (line-addressing). For effective utilization in the laboratory, screen erase and line addressing are essential if the device is to be more than simply a replacement for a teletype.

More sophisticated displays have the following functions that are of use to the researcher: *Tab*, which allows the user to move the cursor (which indicates the location of the next character to be displayed) horizontally by some fixed amount, usually five spaces. *Horizontal line addressing* is also useful and permits movement of the cursor to a specified horizontal position without the necessity of spacing across the screen. Other functions allow the user to *protect* portions of the screen so that displayed information cannot be inadvertently destroyed or obliterated. Another function sometimes available is the capability to make a portion or portions of the screen "blink" so that certain presented information is enhanced. With all of these displays, the information presented remains visible on the screen until it is erased or written over by a new line.

The rate at which information may be displayed on these terminals can be as slow as a hard-copy teletype (10 to 30 characters per second). However, depending upon the type of computer interface, transfer rates up to 1200 characters per sec (9600 baud) are possible. Thus, it is possible to have very rapid display of information.

With basic video displays of the sort described here, there are a large number of different types of experiments that may be run, in addition to those that can be done on teletypes. Instructions can be presented to the subject easily and rapidly on a video display terminal. Experiments in which textual material is used can be run on such a terminal. Examples from the work in linear orderings (cf. Potts, Banks, Kosslyn, Moyer, Riley, & Smith, 1978) and sentence comprehension readily come in mind. Moreover, many other sorts of experiments may be adapted for use with character-oriented terminals, since relatively complex stimuli can be displayed rapidly on the screen. However, because of problems with timing — in the terminal itself, in the interface between the computer and terminal, and the timesharing software — precise timing of a display is not possible. These and other timing problems will be discussed later.

Video Displays With Limited Graphics.   It is reasonable to say that some graphics are possible with a character-oriented display system, since a figure could be drawn using letters and symbols. However, it must be obvious that such a figure would not be especially clear or unambiguous. For example, consider a square made with a pattern of Xs or a triangle made out of Os. A rectangle formed by Is and hyphens will necessarily have spaces between the characters because of the manner in which they are generated. For some applications, such graphics are completely acceptable; in other applications, better quality graphics are required.

Fortunately, there are some video displays that have inexpensive graphics capability, which, while limited, can meet a large number of research needs. Sometimes called "business graphics," these terminals permit clear representation of solid vertical and horizontal lines and rectangular figures. (Bar graphs are especially easy to display in such systems.) One system permits graphics in the following way. Each character location is divided into a 2 x 3 matrix, each position of which may be filled or not filled under program control. The 6 bit ASCII code corresponding to each character is used to determine the position to be filled in the matrix. When the terminal is in the graphics mode, the bit positions containing 1s cause the corresponding part of the grid to be filled. In this manner, solid horizontal and vertical lines may be drawn. They are drawn at the same speed that characters may be presented. This sort of display has been useful for forming many different sorts of stimuli that can be formed from straight lines. Since the graphics characters and alphanumeric characters can be displayed at the same time, this capability is useful for providing neater and clearer displays at modest cost.

Full Graphics CRT.   The most complete and versatile graphics is that provided by a CRT terminal that supports line graphics. In this sort of system (e.g., DECs VR-14), it is possible to display very complex figures. Moreover, with such systems it is also possible to present alphanumeric characters of varying sizes and orientations. Such displays, while versatile, differ from the other sorts of displays described in that effective utilization of them requires more core memory for programs and greater programming skills for the user. Also, for character-oriented displays, the characters are usually less clear than those formed in video systems. Because of their more specialized use and relatively large cost, only passing mention of them is made here.

Input

Most terminals have some sort of input capability. This input is usually accomplished by means of a keyboard similar to a typewriter keyboard with added functions that permit use with a computer. The usual mode of operation is that as a character is typed, it is transmitted to the computer and displayed or typed on the output portion of the terminal.

More complex terminals enable the user to type and display a line, edit it, and transfer the entire line at one time to the computer. Other terminals, especially video terminals, enable the entire display area to be filled, edited, and transmitted to the computer. This sort of procedure is especially useful in preparing programs or editing text, since corrections to the textual material are more easily accomplished than with character-by-character transmission or with line-oriented transmission.

The keyboard on terminals is best suited for experiments in which a verbal response is required – a word, a phrase, or sentence. In such cases, a subject only needs to type the appropriate material on the keyboard. Experiments that require very simple responses – such as a binary response or one of a few number of alternatives – are more difficult with a keyboard. The reason for this is that the large number of alternatives on the keyboard can lead the subject to be confused and errors can result. However, this difficulty is overcome easily by use of a special template placed over the keyboard that leaves only the desired keys exposed. Such a keyboard template is easy to design and fabricate and can significantly reduce subjects' confusion and errors.

One of the most sophisticated inputs for a terminal is a light pen. When the pen is directed at a location on a special CRT screen, the corresponding (X, Y) coordinates are read into the computer. A light pen permits a subject to choose among alternatives merely by "pointing" at them. This capability is an expensive option.

Microprocessor Terminals

Recently, a new type of CRT terminal called a *microprocessor terminal* has become available. These terminals are often described as intelligent or programmable. An intelligent terminal contains a processor, but the user may not have ready access to it. If the terminal is user programmable, the ability to use the processor may require the purchase of special options. These options include hardware – memory, cassettes, floppy disks, paper tape, etc. – and software – monitor, editor, assembler, and perhaps a higher-level language processor like BASIC. By the time the user has obtained the options necessary in order to program effectively, the total cost may exceed that of a larger minicomputer system.

Other programmable terminals may be less flexible: The resident programs may be changed, but the variety of changes permissible is limited. Other systems can be modified, but a Random Access Memory (RAM) and storage device such as a tape cassette or disk is required in order to accomplish the task. Regardless of options, microprocessor terminals are becoming cheaper and more powerful; their capability in the laboratory will be great.

SOME TECHNICAL ASPECTS OF CRT TERMINALS

Most CRT terminals utilize techniques developed by the television industry. The basic display consists of circuitry that allows horizontal and vertical deflection of the beam and a raster-scan control. The horizontal scan rate is approximately 15.75 kHz, and the frame rate is 60 Hz. (The frame rate is the rate at which an entire screen may be filled.) This allows a resolution of 262 lines in a cycle. Many displays use an interlaced scan in which one half of the lines (alternate) are refreshed on each cycle. This allows approximately 520 scans to be used to make up the frame to be viewed. Thus, the resolution possible is approximately 0.002 of the vertical extent of the screen.

Alphanumeric characters are made of a matrix of dots of light. The character sets can be 5 x 7, 7 x 9, and, more recently, 10 x 16 matrices of dots. The presentation of characters is determined by a Read Only Memory (ROM) character generator and a 2K display memory. The ROM contains the basic dot pattern for each character, and the display memory contains coding for which character is to be displayed in a given position on the screen. This permits the display of 24 lines of 80 characters each. If a greater variety of characters is to be utilized, then the ROM character generator needs to be larger. Changes in the number of lines and/or characters per line requires corresponding changes in the size of the display memory. As the cost of memory decreases, larger displays are possible, but in order that the alphanumeric characters be clear and discriminable (a function of the size of the dot matrix), the scan rate has to increase.

As noted earlier, while the simplest terminals have minimal functions (cursor home, carriage return, line feed), many terminals have added functions, including horizontal and vertical line addressing, horizontal tabs, line and character insertion and deletion, field protection, block and page transmission, and blinking fields.

One feature important in the research laboratory is the quality of the video image. Although the size of the dot matrix is important, the spot size on the CRT is also important. It depends on the beam, current, phosphor type, and (unfortunately) the location of the spot on the screen. While contrast, brightness, and focus are easy to deal with and are easily adjusted, most of the former characteristics noted cannot be altered easily. However, the phosphor used in the CRT determines the ease of viewing, color, and decay time, and there is some choice when the unit is originally purchased. The most common phosphor is P4, which is white. It is the standard for alphanumeric displays and is the lowest in cost. One problem with the P4 phosphor for some uses is its 60 μsec decay time (the time for all image to reduce to 10% of its original brightness). Other common phosphors are P21 (green), P39 (yellow), and P42 (yellow). These latter phosphors are better for long-term viewing because eye fatigue is less. Phosphors P21 and P42 have 38- and 8-μsec decay times, respectively. There is a tradeoff in phosphors: the faster the decay time, the worse the quality of the image for long-term viewing and the greater the distortion due to flicker.

Another common problem is glare. Remedies that can be used vary from etched faceplates bonded to the CRT to plastic sheets attached to the mounting frame of the video monitor. The bonded faceplates result in a better image but are more expensive and less versatile than plastic sheeting. Although plastic sheeting is more easily damaged, it is more easily and cheaply replaced.

There is less choice and variety among keyboards – they are typically standard typewriter keyboards in format, with function and control keys located in various positions. Some terminals have a separate numeric pad (such as that found on a calculator) that is useful and convenient in some applications, particularly those requiring numeric responses and other numeric input to the computer.

Timing

One of the greatest problems in the effective use of a time-shared terminal in the laboratory is timing. Although considerable effort has been expended in standardizing the form of timing routines in higher level languages (cf. Castellan, 1976), standards for timing precision have not been forthcoming. Thus, it is difficult to obtain precise control over stimulus duration and accurately measure response time. Although such imprecision makes such terminals inappropriate for some experiments, with careful planning and programming it is possible to make effective use of them in a large variety of situations and tasks in which some timing control is desired.

In a comprehensive study of the factors affecting the precision of latency measures in real-time computing systems, Christian and Polson (1975) identified four sources of errors in the determination of response latency measures. These four factors are: (1) the resolution of the clock; (2) the accuracy of the current clock value: (3) delays in the recording of the time of occurrence of an event; and (4) uncertainty in the time of stimulus presentation if the display is a video display. It should be noted that with the possible exception of (3), these timing errors also are common to experiments that are not done on computers.

If the computer clock is digital, then only discrete values may be recorded, and the initial timing error will be between O and p, where p is the period of the digital clock. If the operation of the digital clock causes an interrupt and updating of an internal counter by the computer, a second error may occur in that there will be a delay in the response to the update interrupt. The lack of perfect synchrony of the digital clock and internal counter can lead to measurement errors in timing as large as approximately $2p$.

In any timesharing system, there are delays in the recording of a response that result from an inability to record a response at the precise moment that it occurs. The magnitude of this error depends upon the priority level at which timing and latency information is processed by the computer, the number and type of instructions necessary to record such information, and other tasks that must be performed by the system at about the same time. The user has greatest control over this type of error, the magnitude of which could be very large. The control is gained by constraining the number of operations performed at critical times and masking out other interrupts and tasks that may require service at the time when a latency interrupt is being serviced. This control is achieved by minimizing the *number* of instructions involved and ensuring minimum *variability* in the number of instructions involved. Christian and Polson (1975) showed that with careful software design, most errors of time measurement may be attributed to the resolution of the digital clock and delays in recording the time of a subject's response.

The final source of error is due to imprecision in the time to presentation of a stimulus. This imprecision is not due solely to the transfer rate of information from computer to terminal, but to the manner in which information is displayed. As noted earlier, for displays that use video interlace scans, information is displayed as the beam scans the screen every 1/60 of a sec. Actually, two scans are necessary to fill the screen — one to display the odd-numbered lines and one to display the even-numbered lines. Thus, it always takes between 17 and 33 msec to display any text; this timing interval is the same whether one displays a single character or fills the entire screen with characters. It should be noted that it is rare that a new stimulus actually could be displayed in 17 msec since that duration only could result when every other raster line would be unchanged from the previous display and only other lines (for example, the even-numbered ones) could be changed. Since most terminals display characters with seven or nine raster lines, it would be very difficult to construct stimuli that would change so rapidly in such a peculiar manner. On some terminals it is possible to control display time — more specifically, reduce its variability — by using options that allow one to turn the CRT beam on and off under program control. However, even with this control, the onset of presentation of stimulus display generally will not be in phase with the raster scans, and thus the display could begin with any random portion of the intended display.

In addition to the timing problems described above, the user has considerable difficulty gaining control over the stimulus and response timing when running in a time-shared environment in which multiple users are competing for computing resources. Potts (1976) described a very simple system that enables an experimenter to obtain precise response times from a CRT terminal. The device provides for all timing to be done externally to the computer. It consists of a constantly running timer that is reset as each character is transmitted to the terminal; then, as soon as a subject types a character, the time on the clock is read and transmitted to the computer as an ASCII number followed by the actual character. The device is placed on the line from the terminal to the computer. It eliminates the sources of error (2) and (3) described earlier. While it is as precise in recording as the phase of the clock, it does not eliminate the problem of display timing on the CRT. Such control boxes may be designed and fabricated fairly easily and also are available commercially.

SOME APPLICATIONS

Time-shared terminals are widely used in research, and it is impossible to give a comprehensive overview of either the current or potential use of them in psychology. Many surveys have been written; especially useful recent ones have been provided by Gregg (1977), who discussed both current and future trends, and Aaronson, Grupsmith, and Aaronson (1976), who discussed the impact of computers on research and theory in cognitive psychology.

Terminals, especially those with graphics capability, have been used in judgment and decision-making studies in which feedback to subjects is dependent upon the sequential characteristics and magnitude of their responses. Such response-contingent studies would be impossible without computers. The role of terminals in complex judgment tasks were described by Hammond (1971). Studies in which complex feedback has been used include experimental studies by the author (Castellan, 1974; Castellan & Swaine, 1977) and clinical studies (e.g., Gillis, Stewart, & Gritz, 1975). Such studies illustrate the crucial role of computers in enhancing our understanding of complex cognitive tasks.

Another important application of terminals is interactive scaling. Chang (1973) described a set of programs that accomplish multidimensional scaling with interactive graphics terminals. The system consists of a program that does the multidimensional scaling proper, and a second program that performs the rotation of points. The latter is the truly interactive aspect of the system. After the initial solution, projections of points onto a three-dimensional subspace are displayed on the video terminal. The user selects the dimensions by entering them on a keyboard. After an initial configuration is displayed, three knobs on a specially designed box may be adjusted to indicate the amount of rotation to be performed for each dimension. Since final solutions (and particularly rotations) are largely a matter of taste in multidimensional scaling, such interactive rotation is especially valuable for improving the understanding of data by the researcher.

Interactive graphics has also been used in nonmetric multidimensional scaling. Schneider and Weisberg (1974) describe an extremely flexible system for interactive scaling. Not only can points be plotted as the Chang program, but the paths of points can be traced from iteration to iteration. Also, the user is able to control not only the rotations, but the actual solution (the number of dimensions, tolerance, stress, etc.) as well. Multidimensional scaling is playing an increasing role in applied measurement and psychological theory. It is to be expected that interactive systems will become increasingly important in future development.

A final example of the use of terminals is the computer enhancement of interaction among scientists. The technique, known as computer conferencing, facilitates the close interaction of scientists at widely physically separated locations. By means of interactive terminals in a network, researchers may communicate with each other by means of shared data, program, and information files (Ruggiero, 1977). Computer conferencing has been shown to be effective in a wide variety of situations: one particularly productive conference that produced a simulation model of transitive behavior in judgment has been described by Thorson and Buss (1977). As the technique becomes more widely known, it is expected that computer-facilitated group interaction will have a significant impact on the manner in which psychologists do research and communicate with colleagues.

The use of time-shared terminals in research is playing an increasing role in empirical research, psychological theory, and scientific communication. As the field develops, psychology is bound to change in many ways, some crucial, some subtle, and some trivial. Prudent contemporary psychologists will invest the relatively small amount of time and effort required to become familiar with the use of terminals and computers. In that way they will be able to share and contribute to the as yet unpredictable developments that will mark the course of research and theory in the coming years.

REFERENCES

Aaronson, D., Grupsmith, E., & Aaronson, M. The impact of computers in cognitive psychology. *Behavior Research Methods & Instrumentation,* 1976, *8,* 129–138.

Castellan, N. J., Jr. The effect of different types of feedback in multiple-cue probability learning. *Organizational Behavior and Human Performance,* 1974, *11,* 44–64.

Castellan, N. J., Jr. Standards: Real-time extensions to programming systems. *Behavior Research Methods & Instrumentation,* 1976, *8,* 207–210.

Castellan, N. J., Jr., & Swaine, M. Long-term feedback and differential feedback effects in nonmetric multiple-cue probability learning. *Behavioral Science,* 1977, *22,* 116–128.

Chang, J. J. On-line multidimensional scaling programs with interactive graphical display. *Behavior Research Methods & Instrumentation,* 1973, *5,* 99–103.

Christian, T. W., & Polson, P. G. The precision of latency measures on real-time computing systems. *Behavior Research Methods & Instrumentation,* 1975, *7,* 175–178.

Gillis, J. S., Stewart, T. R., & Gritz, E. R. New procedures: Use of interactive computer graphics terminals with psychiatric patients. In K. R. Hammond & C. R. B. Joyce (Eds.), *Psychoactive drugs and social judgment.* New York: Wiley-Interscience, 1975.

Gregg, L. W. Maximizing the mini-uses of on-line computers. *Behavior Research Methods & Instrumentation,* 1977, *9,* 67–71.

Hammond, K. R. Computer graphics as an aid to learning. *Science,* 1971, *172,* 903–908.

Potts, G. R. Use of a campus-wide time-sharing computer to run reaction time experiments. *Behavior Research Methods & Instrumentation,* 1976, *8,* 179–181.

Potts, G. R., Banks, W. P., Kosslyn, S. M., Moyer, R. S., Riley, C. A., & Smith, K. H. Distance effects in comparative judgments. In N.J. Castellan, Jr. & F. Restle (Eds.), *Cognitive theory* (Vol. 3). Hillsdale, N.J.: Lawrence Erlbaum Associates, 1978.

Ruggiero, F. An overview of the development of computer modeling for instructional and research purposes. *Behavior Research Methods & Instrumentation,* 1977, *9,* 76–80.

Schneider, E. J., & Weisberg, H. F. An interactive graphics approach to dimensional analysis. *Behavior Research Methods & Instrumentation,* 1974, *6,* 185–194.

Thorson, E., & Buss, T. F. Using computer conferencing to formulate a computer simulation of transitive behavior. *Behavior Research Methods & Instrumentation,* 1977, *9,* 81–86.

Note Added in Proof: There are periodic surveys of terminals published in computer magazines. The most recent survey appeared in the June 1978 issue of *Datamation,* in which specifications of over 170 different alphanumeric display terminals are summarized. Manufacturers names and addresses are also given.   –N.J.C.

5 Psychophysical Methods and the Minicomputer

M. J. Penner
University of Maryland

INTRODUCTION

Sensory psychologists study the remarkable ability of the senses to detect and discriminate changes. For example, increments in loudness can be detected when the intensity of a tone changes by a small amount and this ability to detect holds as the stimulus intensity varies over a range of 10^{12} in magnitude. This magnitude of the dynamic range of the sensory system has triggered excitement and speculation since neural responses to stimuli are known to be restricted to a range of about 10^5 (Katsuki, 1961) so that the abilities of the complete sensory system exceed that of its component parts. By studying conundrums such as this, sensory psychologists aim at understanding how human and animal sensory systems operate.

There are a variety of avenues available for studying the operation of sensory systems. Some researchers choose a molecular approach in which they proceed with a detailed analysis of the physiological response of a single cell or perhaps with the separate response of several cells as well as their interactions. Measurements are of the component parts of the sensory system (as discussed by Rhode in Chapter 9). Other researchers choose a molar approach in which they proceed with a description of stimuli that are detectable or discriminable to a human being (as discussed by Wightman in Chapter 7 or this volume). In carefully designed and well-controlled situations, these researchers test human subjects to arrive at a picture of the functioning of the sensory system.

The issue of whether the physiological or psychophysical approach is preferable is a matter of debate. Some scientists feel that the only way to proceed is to take the system apart and study the parts and their interactions. There is much to recommend this approach, as the cross-referencing seen in physiological and psychophysical journal articles attests. There are, of course, some drawbacks since the sensory systems are large, complicated, and interconnected. In this chapter, I bypass these issues of research strategy and proceed with the experimental situations that are used in the psychophysical attempt to make sense of the senses. An introduction to psychophysical methods in general is provided and, in particular, to two modern methods that can be simply implemented using a minicomputer.

In sensory psychology a variety of questions concerning the stimulus can be addressed. Some experiments are concerned with the problem of detection (whether a stimulus was present), some with the problem of recognition (what the stimulus is), and some with the problem of discrimination (whether two stimuli are the same). In the following discussion, techniques to measure detection thresholds are considered; the techniques may easily be generalized to include tests of discrimination or recognition (although the comparison of the scores derived from the various measures can be a very thorny problem indeed).

AN OVERVIEW

How can we determine whether human beings hear, for example, a 1000 Hz tone? The first and most obvious answer is to ask them. If we present a very weak tone, they are likely to say that they do not hear it; if the tone is intense the subjects are likely to say that they do hear it. Problems begin to arise if these observations are repeated, since human observers do not necessarily always respond in the same way to the same stimulus. Of course some stimuli are so weak that they are never detected and some so intense that they are always detected. In between, however, there is a range of stimulus level in which the subjects' responses are unpredictable, a range in which the experimenter is uncertain of what the subjects' responses will be. For this range of stimulus intensity, responses can only be described probabilistically. Investigators can keep track of the relative frequency, or probability, of a detection response as a function of stimulus level. A typical form of this function, called a *psychometric function*,

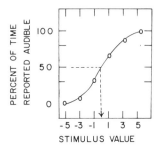

FIG. 5.1.   A hypothetical psychometric function. The value of the absolute threshold, indicated by the arrow, is found graphically to be 0.

is diagrammed in Fig. 5.1. Its shape is a matter of concern to psychologists (Bush, 1963). Smooth curves of this sort can appear when data are averaged over many trials, even though on any one trial there might be a single point at which detection probability changes from zero to one (as long as the position of the single point changes over trials). Thus, a debate has taken place concerning whether detection is a discrete (Larkin & Norman, 1964) or a continuous process (Green & Swets, 1966). Whatever the ultimate outcome of these issues, the absolute threshold is defined as that stimulus value for which the chance of a detect response is p (for example, $p = 0.50$), and it is the determination of this stimulus value that concerns us here. All psychophysical methods employed to measure threshold assume that there is a psychometric function and are fundamentally concerned with finding the threshold that can be determined from it. While attacking the problem of explaining the variety of methods employed, it is important to keep in mind that the methods are prescriptions for tracking threshold. In the slower methods, the signal values are preselected and testing levels are independent of the subject's responses. In the faster methods, the signal values are contingent upon the subject's responses and, in modern psychoacoustics laboratories, they are typically controlled by a minicomputer.

I begin with a description of two commonly used paradigms, yes—no and forced-choice tasks, and then discuss methods of threshold determination. The events of a single trial are defined as specifying a *paradigm* and the technique that tracks threshold is called a *method.*

PARADIGMS

The Yes—No Paradigm

The paradigm described in the last section, in which the investigator presents a tone to subjects and asks them if they hear it, is an example of a yes—no paradigm (yes it is heard or no it is not). In this procedure subjects sometimes respond yes in absence of a signal. In the yes—no paradigm, there are two possible stimuli, either the tonal signal denoted s, or nothing present denoted n, and the two possible responses, yes or no. In this task one of four distinct outcomes occurs on each trial. These outcomes are delineated in Table 5.1. Given the tone, the observers must respond either yes or no, and so the sum of the probabilities in the top row of the matrix must be one. Likewise, given no stimulus, the observers must respond either yes or no, and so the sum of the probabilities in the second row of the matrix is also one. There are then only two independent probabilities in the table. Typically, the two that are used to describe the results are the probability of saying yes given s and the probability of saying yes given n. These are called the hit and false-alarm probabilities, respectively.

For convenience, responses do not involve the spoken word. Observers are seated in a soundproof booth in which there is a response box consisting of but-

TABLE 5.1
The Outcome of a Yes–No Task

		Response	
		Yes	No
Stimulus s		$P(Y/s)$ Hit	$P(N/s)$
	n	$P(Y/n)$ False alarm	$P(N/n)$

tons and lights. The subjects respond by pressing one button if they hear the tone and another if they do not, and a minicomputer collects the responses. A single trial of the yes–no procedure might proceed as follows: warning light (0.3 sec), pause (1 sec), observation interval (0.1 sec), pause (2 sec), answer interval (1 sec), pause (1 sec), feedback (0.4 sec), begin the next trial The observation interval contains the signal on half of the trials and the feedback indicates to the subjects whether their response was correct. From several hundred such trials we are able to estimate the probabilities indicated in Table 5.1. The estimate is based on the relative frequency of hits and false alarms obtained from the data averaging over trials (the responses on successive trials are assumed to be independent). In analyzing the data from a yes–no experiment, the researchers plot estimated probabilities of false alarms and hits on the x and y axes of a unit square as in Fig. 5.2.

Let us consider where a data point might lie in this square. Suppose first that the intensity of the signal is so low that nothing is actually heard. The subjects might respond no 100% of the time when the signal is present and will also respond no 100% of the time when the signal is absent, giving a hit probability of 0 and a false alarm probability of 0. This produces a point in the lower left corner of the square. However, if the subjects were told that false alarms were unimportant, but hits were very important, they might always respond yes (even though hearing nothing). This produces a point in the upper right corner of the square. At intermediate levels of bias, points could be produced interior to the square, but so long as nothing is heard, the subjects' performance will always lie on the diagonal connecting the lower left corner to the upper right corner. For

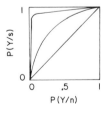

FIG. 5.2.   An ROC curve. The x axis represents the false-alarm rate and the y axis the hit rate. The diagonal line represents performance when nothing is heard. The arched curves represent performance for a larger stimulus value.

example, if the subjects guess yes on 50% of the trials, the hit probability will be 0.5, the false-alarm probability will be 0.5, and the data point will be centered on the diagonal.

It is easy to show that when the signal intensity rises so that it may be heard at least some of the time, then the observed data points will lie somewhere in the upper left quadrant of the square. In particular, at a given intensity a curve may be plotted for different instructional biases. This curve lies in the upper left quadrant and is termed the "isosensitivity" curve or the "*r*eceiver *o*perating *c*haracteristic" (ROC) curve and a set of ROC curves are diagrammed in Fig. 5.2. Note that all points on the curve represent the same sensory response. Different points on the ROC curve are produced as the subject's criterion or predisposition to respond yes varies. Sensory sensitivity is reflected in the position of the entire ROC curve used to fit the data: the closer the curve to the upper left-hand corner, the greater the sensitivity. As the subject's criterion moves, successive points on the same ROC curve are traced. Since we are mostly interested in the changes of sensory capabilities and not in differences in subject's criterion, the area under the ROC curve provides a useful measure of detectability since it ranges from 1 to 0.5. Another alternative measure of sensitivity is provided by the distance, d_e, from the positive diagonal to the ROC curve (measured along the negative diagonal). The interesting point about the area measure is that it can be shown to be the percentage correct in a two-interval forced-choice (2IFC) procedure, utilizing the same stimulus values.

Forced-Choice Paradigm

The 2IFC procedure is the simplest of the forced-choice tasks. In it, the subjects are asked to indicate which of the two observation intervals they thought contained the signal. The signal is presented with equal probability in either the first or the second interval. If the signal level is so low that the subjects are forced to guess randomly between the intervals, they will be correct half the time; if the signal is so loud that they always hear it, they will always be correct. Therefore, the 2IFC psychometric function has an ordinate ranging from 0.50 to 1.0. Under quite general assumptions, Green and Swets (1966) showed that the area under the yes–no ROC curve is the percentage correct in a 2IFC task. For a yes–no task, the ROC curve represents all possible outcomes for all possible decision criteria. The probability of a correct response, $P(C)$, in a 2IFC task provides the same information as the entire ROC curve. In short, the probability of a correct response in forced-choice tasks is a criterion-free measure of detection. Further, in practice it has been found that the 2IFC task is more efficient than the yes–no in the sense that the estimate of detectability can be found at the same level of reliability in fewer trials. Typically, the data of a single session can be used to estimate the percentage correct in a 2IFC task, whereas all of the data of several sessions are needed to generate the separate points on the yes–no ROC curve.

There are some additional considerations in forced-choice procedures. Researchers must be careful that subjects do not exhibit a bias for selecting a particular interval. In forced-choice tasks involving more than two intervals, certain combinations have a higher probability of correct response than do others. For example, in 3IFC procedures the signal is more readily detected in an (n, s, n) sequence than in an (n, n, s) or (s, n, n) sequence. This problem has been discussed (Pollack, 1968) and suggests that care must be taken in randomization and other aspects of experimental design in such tasks. In any event, the effect is quite small and some investigators (e.g., Swets, 1959) have concluded that performance, as measured by d', is comparable in 2, 3, 4, 6, and 8 IFC tasks.

Same—Different Paradigm

Forced-choice and yes—no paradigms are the principal psychophysical paradigms, although same—different tasks are sometimes employed. In the same—different paradigm, the subject is asked to indicate whether two observation intervals contain the same signal. Typically, the first of the two intervals contains an invariant signal, while the second may be the same or different from the first. Same—different tasks are most commonly used in discrimination studies.

Thresholds in Forced-Choice, Yes—No, and Same—Different Tasks

An analysis of the three paradigms in terms of the theory of signal detection leads to the conclusion that performance measured by a derived unit called d' should be larger by a factor of $\sqrt{2}$ in a forced-choice task than in a yes—no task, and d' for yes—no should be $\sqrt{2}$ larger than d' in a same—different task (Sorkin, 1962). The predictions of the theory of signal detection are not discussed in great detail. However, it is interesting to note for actual data that forced-choice d' exceeds yes—no d' by a factor slightly greater than $\sqrt{2}$ (Jesteadt & Bilger, 1969; Jesteadt & Sims, 1975). This superior than expected performance in 2IFC may be due to memory processes (Durlach & Braida, 1969). The main point is that it is not very simple to compare d' values obtained in 2IFC procedures with those obtained in yes—no procedures. In particular, it is not sufficient simply to multiply or divide the observed d' score by a $\sqrt{2}$ factor to obtain the expected d' value for the other paradigm.

The forced-choice, yes—no, and same—different procedures each can be examined using several methods. In the following sections we discuss two classical methods: the method of limits in which subsequent stimulus levels are dependent on the subject's response and the method of constant stimuli in which they are not.

METHODS

The Method of Limits

In the ascending method of limits, the stimulus intensity is set so far below threshold that it is never detected and is then increased in small steps of constant size until the subject detects it. In the descending method of limits, the stimulus intensity is set so far above threshold that it is always detected and is then decreased in small steps of constant size until the subject no longer detects it. In yes–no tasks, the threshold in the ascending series is taken to be midway between the signal level eliciting the last no and the first yes response. For the descending series, threshold is taken to be midway from the last yes and the first no. For example, if on a descending series the subject says "yes" at an intensity of 2.0 dB SPL (Sound Pressure Level) and "no" at an intensity of 0.0 dB SPL, his threshold for the series is 1.0 dB SPL. Ascending (up) and descending (down) series are alternated, and the mean of all the series provides an estimate of threshold. The mean is used since the ascending and descending thresholds differ, sometimes considerably. Because the signal level moves up and down, the method of limits is also referred to as an up–down procedure.

Since the stimulus level moves about systematically, the subjects are aware of the fact that the next stimulus will be louder (or softer) than the previous one. If the method of limits is used in a yes–no paradigm, it has been argued that, since the subjects know the schedule of stimulus presentation, they will exhibit one of two different response biases: some subjects will tend to respond the same way as on the previous trial (habituation), whereas others might exhibit a tendency to change their responses (anticipation). The error of habituation involves a predisposition to continue reporting yes in a descending series (since the signal was just audible) or no in an ascending series (since the signal was just inaudible). The error of anticipation involves a predisposition to report yes in an ascending series (since the signal is about to be audible) or to report no in a descending series (since the signal is about to be inaudible). Errors of anticipation and habituation are opposite tendencies, and their occurrence is not easy to spot.

Errors of anticipation and habituation are not the only problems with using the method of limits to find threshold in yes–no tasks. Remember that sensory effects may be separated from the subject's personal criterion by keeping track of both hits and false alarms. However, this cannot be done unless trials without signals are presented. Unfortunately, the method of limits is typically employed without "catch" trials (i.e., trials without a signal), so that the subject's criterion cannot be determined and may affect the data in an unobservable fashion. For this reason, it is a better technique to determine either d' or the ROC curve at each stimulus value. However, such a method is very time consuming, and it is,

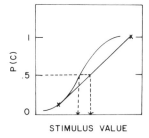

FIG. 5.3. A psychometric function and a possible approximation to it. Note that the function is approximated by points that are so far apart that an inaccurate estimate of threshold is obtained.

therefore, usually considered advantageous to utilize forced-choice tasks since these tasks circumvent criterion problems and do not require as many trials to achieve reliable estimates.

The method of limits may be used in forced-choice tasks. If it is, many observations are collected at each stimulus value. From the resulting psychometric function, an extrapolation to threshold is made. When the method of limits is used in forced-choice situations, errors of anticipation and habituation cannot occur, and the results may reflect the sensory system's capabilities. However, some nonsensory factors may come into play in up–down procedures. In a down sequence, for example, the subject has just heard the signal and that experience may serve as a cue assisting detection on the subsequent trial (see later sub-section Sequential Effects in this chapter). In forced-choice situations, therefore, it is preferable to randomize the order of presentation of the various stimulus values or to block together the trials at each stimulus value rather than use an up and down method (see the following discussion of the method of constant stimuli).

In using the method of limits, the step size must be carefully chosen. Suppose the step size is so large that it exceeds the width of the psychometric function (a width of 10 on the abscissa in Fig. 5.1). If so, threshold estimates could be grossly in error as shown in Fig. 5.3. Thus, in practice the step size is adjusted after preliminary data are collected.

Psychological or Psychophysical Effects on Threshold

Herrick (1967) and Pollack (1968) argued that the different psychophysical methods themselves cause divergent estimates of threshold values. They suggested that the variability obtained is due in large part to the procedures rather than to the subject's psychological inclinations. To parse out the effect of methodology from the effect of the subject's proclivities, it is possible to use a computer to simulate the psychophysical task as Pollack (1968) did for the method of limits. His main finding was that a so-called "error" of anticipation arises due to a purely mathematical factor and does not necessarily result from the subject's response bias. He showed that for the method of limits in which threshold is computed from the first reversal in the subject's report (i.e., as that stimulus value lying halfway between the last no and the first yes or the last yes and the first no), errors of anticipation arise from probabilistic consideration.

Pollack's results may be intuited quite easily. Consider the rule for determining the threshold using the method of limits discussed in the previous section (threshold is determined by the first no in a string of yes responses if descending or by the first yes in a string of no responses if ascending). Suppose that the omniscient experimenter knows the true form of the psychometric function and presents intensities corresponding to yes response probabilities of 1, 0.8, 0.6, 0.4, 0.2, and 0. In an ascending series, starting at the smallest stimulus value, the chance of claiming that threshold (i.e., the stimulus value corresponding to 0.50 detection) lies between the 0.2 and 0.4 point is 1 x 0.8 x 0.4 or 0.32. The chance that it lies between the 0.4 and 0.6 point as it should is 1 x 0.8 x 0.6 x 0.6 = 0.288. Thus, there is a greater probability of obtaining a threshold that lies below the actual threshold in an ascending series than there is of obtaining the actual threshold. Relative to the actual psychometric function, an error of anticipation is made. Similar arguments hold for the descending series: There is a greater probability of obtaining a threshold that lies above the actual threshold than there is of obtaining the actual threshold. Averaging the ascending and descending sequences tends to eliminate these errors and provides a consistent threshold as Pollack found.

This is only one of the interesting results that Pollack reported. His other results are of potential importance in understanding the adaptive techniques discussed later in this chapter. Pollack found that the obtained thresholds depend on the starting value of the stimulus, on the rules for termination, and on the step size. This leads to the conclusion that it is inadvisable to compare thresholds unless precisely the same psychophysical procedure and method is used. Further, the issue of the effect of rules for termination, the starting stimulus value, and the step size are of utmost importance in comparing results from adaptive techniques in which all three are varied. Of course, it is important to recognize that there is still a subject in the process. If the variability associated with the subject (i.e., internal noise, headset position) exceeds the variability due to the psychophysical procedure, then the effects of varying techniques may be small enough to be irrelevant. Some evidence supporting this view is discussed in later sections.

The Method of Constant Stimuli

In the method of constant stimuli the stimulus intensities are presented randomly rather than in a regular order. An attempt is made to select the levels so that the stimulus at the lowest intensity is never detected and the stimulus at the highest intensity always is. The stimuli are presented many times at each intensity; the order of presentation is random. From such data, it is possible to construct a psychometric function by keeping track of the proportion of correct responses at each stimulus intensity. Using linear interpolation, researchers can determine the 50% point in a yes–no task or the 75% point in a 2IFC task.

The main problem with this procedure is that in order to find threshold, the experimenter must know roughly where it is. Since the stimulus intensities examined in the method of constant stimuli are preselected, they must span the psychometric function. Besides this factor, the step size must be carefully selected so that the psychometric function is not spanned in too few steps (see Fig. 5.3).

A Critique of the Method of Limits and Constant-Stimuli Speed

The dependent variable in nearly all sensory research is the stimulus value needed for constant detectability or for constant discriminability. In 2IFC techniques the constant detection probability is usually fixed at 75%, in yes–no tasks at 50%. In either case it is the stimulus value that accompanies the constant detection probability that is of interest. The dependent variable is the stimulus value corresponding to one point on the psychometric function. The methods of limits and of constant stimuli provide more information than this; these methods trace the entire function. Unless the psychometric function itself is of interest, it is not necessary to determine the entire function in order to find a single point on it. With the advent of small real-time computers capable of controlling stimulus values, thresholds can be found without the necessity of tracing the entire psychometric function.

Since determination of the stimulus value at threshold is often the main aim of psychophysical methods, some variations of the classical procedures have been suggested in order to minimize the number of points on the psychometric function that need to be collected. One of these produces a two-point psychometric function in which a detection probability is determined at two stimulus values: one just below threshold and one just above it. A straight line can be

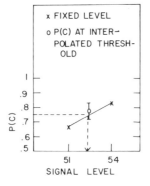

x FIXED LEVEL

o P(C) AT INTER-POLATED THRESHOLD

P(C)

1
.9
.8
.7
.6
.5

51   54

SIGNAL LEVEL

FIG. 5.4. A 2-point psychometric function for a 21FC task. The xs and the line through them were used to estimate a threshold of 52.3 dB. For a signal of 52.3 dB SPL, the $P(C)$ obtained from a 100 trial block was .78 (the circle). The standard deviation, $\sqrt{pq/N}$, is about 4% as indicated by the error bars. Thus, the 2-point estimate of threshold was reasonably accurate.

drawn between these points and the threshold value interpolated, or the points can be fitted with a cumulative normal ogive (Egan, Lindner, & McFadden, 1969) and the threshold value obtained. Although the procedure has pitfalls, it can be checked by collecting a third data point at the alleged threshold. The results are surprisingly good, as is seen in Fig. 5.4 (data from Yost, Penner, & Feth, 1972). The problem with the two-point psychometric function is in choosing the two stimulus values so that one lies below and one above threshold.

Another variation of the classical procedures was suggested by Raab, Osman, and Rich (1963). For a 2IFC procedure, they recommend a modified method of limits procedure in which the stimulus value decreases if the subject is correct 5 (83.3%) or 6 (100%) times out of 6 trials; if the subject is correct 4 (66.7%) times or less out of 6 trials, threshold is defined as being halfway between the last two stimulus values. By defining threshold as the linear average of the stimulus values corresponding to 66.7% and 83.3%, Raab et al. (1963) are simply performing a linear interpolation between the data points. In effect, they have determined two points on a psychometric function. One advantage of their technique, in addition to speed, is that the stimulus values are not determined before the data are collected. Instead, the subjects' responses, not the experimenter's guesses, determine the stimulus value.

The method of adjustment is one of the oldest procedures for finding threshold without determining the entire psychometric function. In its most typical form, the subject is instructed to adjust the stimulus until it appears equal to a comparison. Either the subject or the experimenter may control the actual levels, but the subject's responses determine subsequent levels, a strategy shared with computer-assisted methods. In our threshold example, the subject might be instructed to adjust the stimulus' intensity until it is "just barely audible," then to adjust it to be "just barely inaudible." The average intensity of these settings could be used as a measure of threshold. In the adjustment methods, the routine to find threshold may differ from subject to subject. Some subjects bracket their thresholds by increasing the signal level until it is clearly audible and then decreasing it until it is inaudible and then "splitting" the difference in settings as an estimate of threshold.

Adjustment procedures have several advantages. The primary one is that they are quite efficient; the time required for a threshold estimation is minimal. The major pitfall of adjustment techniques is that they are confounded with the subject's subjective report as are yes—no tasks. The stimulus values depend on the subject's report of what is heard. As such, the results of the adjustment technique are suspect. However, a preliminary estimate of threshold obtained by the method of adjustment is quite useful in determining the range of stimulus values in the method of limits and constant stimuli. This approach is recommended as a useful preliminary to any procedure, including the adaptive techniques discussed below.

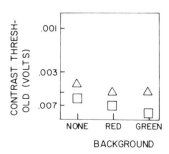

FIG. 5.5.   Contrast threshold required for detection of a grid superimposed on a background. The triangles represent the results from a forced-choice technique and the squares the results from the method of adjustment. There is no significant effect of background in the forced-choice technique, whereas using the method of adjustment, the background effect is significant.

A WORD OF CAUTION

In a recent visual study, McCall and Levinson (1977) reported an interesting conundrum. In this experiment, the detectability of a sinusoidal grating was measured. The grating was green and was presented by itself or superimposed on a background that was either red or green. Their data are presented in Fig. 5.5. From a methodological viewpoint, the main finding is that an up—down method in a forced-choice task did not result in the same trend as did a forced-choice method of adjustment. The data do not differ simply by a constant factor. In forced-choice techniques, there appeared to be no significant effect of the background on threshold. With the method of adjustment, the threshold in the presence of red and green backgrounds differs significantly. At present McCall and Levinson cannot pinpoint a sensory basis for the difference and so are arriving at the conclusion that the differences may be due to the psychophysical procedure. Since adjustment techniques are confounded with criterion problems, it is conceivable that such data might differ from those obtained from a 2IFC task in which criterion is not a factor. Nonetheless, it is mentioned here as a substantiation for the notion that the method may matter and should be carefully controlled.

Stationary Psychometric Function

In addition to the efficiency of modern adaptive techniques, there are a variety of assumptions made in the method of limits and constant stimuli that are important and may or may not be valid. The psychometric function is assumed to be invariant: It is assumed to be stationary over time so that there is no change in its shape or location during the course of a session or, if data are collected during the course of a few days, during the course of several days. The assumption of stationarity means that responses obtained from the subject are independent of each other and of the preceding stimuli. In fact responses are not independent. They exhibit sequential dependencies.

Sequential Effects

In the method of limits and constant stimuli, trials are treated as if they provide independent data. The results of all the trials are simply averaged without regard to the responses immediately preceding and following them. It has long been known that the judgments in psychophysical tasks are not independent. Preston (1936a, 1936b) provided data that demonstrated sequential response dependencies in psychophysical tasks, and his findings have been replicated. Senders and Soward (1952) presented a history of some old studies as well as some data of their own. In the vision area, there have been many studies showing that the observer tends to repeat his last response (Howarth & Blumer, 1956; Verplanck, Collier, & Cotton, 1952: Verplanck, Cotton, & Collier, 1953). In addition to simple repetition, it has been noted that some subjects tend to have streaks of correct or incorrect responses whose lengths exceed that expected by chance, raising the question of whether sensitivity or criterial changes occur. In auditory research, Shipley (1961), Day (1956), and Speeth and Mathews (1961) concerned themselves with this issue. Of course, the sequential dependency decreases as the length of the interstimulus interval decreases (Day, 1956). To the extent that sequential dependencies arise because the decision criterion is updated from trial-to-trial, then a number of models are plausible (Atkinson, 1963; Atkinson, Carterette, & Kinchla, 1962; Bush, Luce, & Rose, 1964; Dorfman & Biderman, 1969; Norman, 1964; Shoeffler, 1965).

Measurement of Sequential Effects

One of the simplest measures of sequential dependency was computed by Shipley (1961). She noted that, for her auditory-detection data in a 2IFC task, the probability of detection on trial n given that the subject has detected on trial n-1 is significantly larger than the probability of detecting on trial n given that the subject has not detected on trial n-1. The effect, although significant, is small. Averaged over all tonal and noise signals at two intensities, it is 2.4%. Other measures of dependency involve comparing the probability of detection in all trials with the probability of detecting given a detection response on the previous trial. In general, the magnitude of the sequential dependency depends on the task involved. It is typically small in auditory detection (Atkinson, 1963; Carterette, Friedman, & Wyman, 1966; Shipley, 1961), moderate in visual detection (Kinchla, 1964) and is smaller with than without feedback (Atkinson & Kinchla, 1965; Tanner, Rauk, & Atkinson, 1970).

Since sequential effects exist, it is certain that the psychometric function is not stationary (i.e., it changes over time depending on the previous responses). The question of whether the movement of the function is sufficient to cause threshold estimates to be in appreciable error is an empirical one and can be evaluated using adaptive psychophysical techniques.

ADAPTIVE PROCEDURES

An adaptive psychophysical procedure is one in which the stimulus value on any one trial is determined by the preceding stimuli and the subject's responses. This concept is not new: the method of limits, the method of adjustment, and the Raab et al. (1963) procedures are adaptive. What is new is that with the use of minicomputers it is possible to vary the step size automatically on a trial-by-trial basis depending upon the subject's responses. This ability has given rise to procedures in which the number of observations and the stimulus level are determined by the data (Taylor & Creelman, 1967; Wetherill & Levitt, 1965). Two of the most commonly used procedures are described in some detail in the following Subsection. It is helpful to be aware that the stimulus value may be the signal intensity, duration, frequency, or phase. All of these signal characteristics can be controlled by a minicomputer and adaptive procedures employed to measure the characteristic corresponding to some preassigned detection probability.

Transformed Up—Down Methods

One particularly useful method for determining the stimulus value needed for constant detectability was suggested by Wetherill and Levitt (Levitt, 1970; Wetherill, 1963; Wetherill & Levitt, 1965). Their extended technique is discussed after a brief digression to its origin. The simple up—down rule that is now discussed is different in a variety of ways from the final technique proposed by Levitt (1970).

A Simple Up—Down Rule

In the method of limits, the stimulus is intentionally presented at levels well above and well below threshold. In the simplest variant of this procedure (Dixon & Mood, 1948), a sequential technique was suggested for estimating the stimulus value, $V_{0.50}$ corresponding to a detection probability of 0.50, in a yes—no paradigm. An adaptive technique is defined as one in which the stimuli presented to the subject are dependent on the experimental data. On the first trial, Dixon and Mood suggested that the stimulus value be set at the best guess of $V_{0.50}$ available. If a positive (correct) response is obtained, the next observation is taken at a lower stimulus value. If a negative (incorrect) response is obtained, the following observation is taken at a higher stimulus value. The stimulus value is always varied in steps that are the same, constant size. A possible series resulting from this technique is shown in Fig. 5.6. A positive response is denoted by a plus sign, +, and a negative by a minus sign, -. If the estimate of threshold is made after n observations, and, if n is small, then so few runs (a run consists of a sequence of changes in stimulus level in one direction only) may be involved that

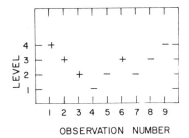

FIG. 5.6. A sequence of trials in a simple up–down method tracking $V_{0.50}$.

OBSERVATION NUMBER

a very inaccurate estimate of threshold is obtained. A safer procedure for small samples is to stop after a given number of runs have been completed. If the best guess of $V_{0.50}$ is not close to the true value, then many observations are required if the criteria for determining $V_{0.50}$ involves the number of runs.

From the data in Fig. 5.6, it is possible to estimate $V_{0.50}$ since the technique converges on some V such that the probability of increasing the stimulus value, p, exactly equals the probability, $1-p$, of decreasing the stimulus value. Some statisticians (e.g., Brownlee, Hodges, & Rosenblatt, 1953) advocate estimating $V_{0.50}$ from the average of all levels used from the second run to the level that would have been presented on the $n +$ first observation. Wetherill and Chen (1964) showed that a better estimate is simply to average the peaks and valleys for the sequence. In Fig. 5.6 there is one peak at Trial 6 and two valleys at Trials 4 and 7 so that

$$V_{0.50} = \frac{1}{3}[1 + 3 + 2] = 2$$

The preceding description of a transformed up–down method aimed at determining $V_{0.50}$ brings to mind some of the same problems that were observed in critiquing the method of limits and the method of constant stimuli. The step size is quite crucial. If many observations are to be collected, then small step sizes give very efficient placing of observations, although the first run may be very long if the guess as to where $V_{0.50}$ lies is not accurate. If few observations are collected, then a small step size coupled with an inaccurate estimate of $V_{0.50}$ may bias the estimate of $V_{0.50}$. After exploring a number of plans for adjusting step size, Wetherill (1963) suggested using 6 to 8 runs to estimate $V_{0.50}$ from the data collected. Threshold is not estimated after the first reversal: It is derived from 6 to 8 runs. After the first estimate, the sequence should be restarted near $V_{0.50}$ but using half the previous step size. A second division of the step size is possible after another series of 6 to 8 runs. Wetherill recommended an initial step size of about 1/6 the width of the range of stimulus values spanned by the psychometric function. If the initial step size is too large, efficiency is somewhat reduced but it can be horrendous if the initial step size is too small, since many trials may occur before $V_{0.50}$ is reached.

A Variety of Up–Down Rules

The simple up–down rule places observations in the region of $V_{0.50}$ and is therefore used to estimate the stimulus value corresponding to a 50% detection rate in a yes–no paradigm. Methods for estimating other points on the psychometric function are easily derived. Let us consider a popular alternative used in 2IFC paradigms.

Suppose that the following strategy is adopted. Whenever subjects are wrong (or respond negatively) the stimulus value increases; if they are right twice in a row (respond positively) at the same stimulus value, the value decreases; otherwise the value is unchanged. Let p be the probability of obtaining an increase in stimulus' level, when the stimulus' value is V_p. The probability of decreasing the stimulus value given that the stimulus is presented at value V on Trial n, depends on the results of the preceding two trials. The stimulus value is decreased if the subject has been correct on the last two trials at Level V and this happened with probability p^2. The procedure converges on some stimulus value, V, for which the probability of increasing V equals the probability of decreasing V or at which

$$p^2 = 1 - p^2$$

TABLE 5.2
Some Possible Thresholds That Can Be Tracked
Using Transformed Up–Down Techniques

Increase Level If	Decrease Level If	Condition at Convergence	Probability of a Positive Response at Convergence
− or	+	$p = 1-p$	$p = 0.5$
+ − or	+ +	$p^2 = 1-p^2$	$p = 0.707$
− −	− + or +	$p(1-p)+p=1-p(1-p)-p$ $p^2 -p+(1/2) = 0$	$p = 0.293$
+ + − or + − or −	+ + +	$p^3 = 1-p^3$	$p = 0.794$
+ + + − or + + − or + − or −	+ + + +	$p^4 = 1-p^4$	$p = 0.841$
− − − −	− − − + or − − + or − + or + or	$(1-p)^4 = 1-(1-p)^4$	$p = 0.159$

Solving for p, it is easy to see that $p = \sqrt{1/2} = 0.707$. Hence, the strategy converges on that stimulus level at which $p = 0.707$. A variety of up—down rules are presented in Table 5.2. The responses resulting in increasing and decreasing the signal values are labeled, and the level at which the procedure converges is listed. Having followed one of the rules in Table 5.2 (this table is close to that presented by Levitt, 1970), the next problem that naturally arises concerns the extraction of threshold from the data collected.

Data Analysis

Threshold Estimate.   In the simple up—down procedure, and for all transformed up—down methods, a run is defined as a sequence of changes in one direction only. Levitt (1970) recommends using the midpoint of every second run as an estimate of V. An even number of runs reduce the estimation bias. At the end of the block of trials, many experimenters simply average the midrun estimates to provide an estimate of threshold. In computing this statistic, any drifts over time in the location of the psychometric function are simply ignored. If the midrun estimates are not averaged, then a direct estimate of any gradual drifts in threshold can be obtained. If a drift occurs, it is not at all clear how to interpret it. If the drift is toward lower thresholds and is statistically significant, it might be argued that some learning to listen was involved, and so only the final asymptotic threshold values should be used in the determination of threshold. If the drift is toward higher thresholds and is statistically significant it might be argued that some fatigue was involved and so only the first few threshold values should be used in the determination of threshold. Whether or not a drift occurs, it is of use to have a measure of the variability of successive threshold estimates.

Approximate Error Estimate.   It is often useful to estimate the variance of the level or of the percentage point tracked. An obvious estimate of the variability in the level is provided by the standard error of the mean that can be found by simply computing the standard error of the mean for each midrun threshold value obtained in each run. If the number of runs are large, the standard error of the mean may be quite small: it is basically an estimate of how many observations the experimenter collected and is often so minute that its width is less than that of the data point that marks threshold on a graph of the results (Penner, 1977). A more useful measure of variability involves the width of the psychometric function. If two experimenters perform the same study and their threshold estimates are 2 dB apart, should they be alarmed? The difference of 2 dB is almost certainly statistically significant if sufficient observations have been collected so that the standard error of the mean is small. A more useful tool comparing the results from different studies involves the slope of the psychometric function. If it is fairly flat, then a 2 dB difference may not be alarming, if it is steep then a 2 dB difference may be of interest.

There are a variety of means to estimate the slope from the data in transformed up–down procedures. The simplest is to fit a psychometric function to the pooled data obtained across all runs. We may simply compute p for each stimulus value. Such a psychometric function has few observations at extreme probabilities (i.e., 50% and 100% in 2IFC) and many observations around the probability tracked (0.707 in our example). A lengthy procedure involves determination of two points on the psychometric function and is discussed in the next section. Whatever the procedure employed, it is often of more value to subsequent investigators to have estimates of the slope of the psychometric function than estimates of the standard error of the mean threshold value obtained.

Interleaving Up–Down Rules. Trials for two up–down rules may be interleaved at random if the points are symmetrically placed about the midpoint of the psychometric function. For example, in a yes–no task, the techniques tracing the stimulus values corresponding to the 70.7% and 29.3% points may be interleaved. One advantage of the mixing is that it insures that the subject cannot anticipate the rule used by the experimenter. The main benefit of tracking two values is that they can provide an estimate of the shape of the psychometric function. If the psychometric function is the integral of a normal distribution then an estimate of its standard deviation, σ, is simply obtained by subtracting $V_{29.3}$ from $V_{70.7}$ and dividing by 1.09 (as is easily seen by examining the tables of the normal distribution).

Example of the 0.707 Up–Down Rule. Some data obtained using the 0.707 response rule are presented in Fig. 5.7. The data are from a forward-masking study in which the signal, a click, follows the masker, noise. The paradigm is 2IFC. The first 20 trials are discarded to allow the stimulus level to approach the 0.707 level. The results from these 20 trials are not displayed. In the first trial of Fig. 5.7, the signal is presented with zero attenuation, the subject is correct twice in a row and so the signal is attenuated 3 dB; the subject is again correct

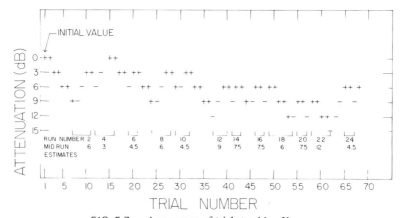

FIG. 5.7. A sequence of trials tracking $V_{0.707}$.

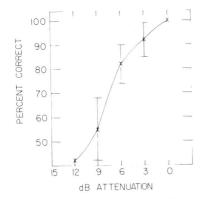

	Data	
Attenuation	P(C)	No. of Occurrences
0	1.00	2
3	.92	13
6	.81	26
9	.55	18
12	.43	7
15	0	1

FIG. 5.8.   The psychometric function for the data in Fig. 5.7. The probability of a correct response is displayed on the ordinate with the dB of
attenuation on the abscissa. It is constructed by pooling all the results in
Fig. 5.7. The error bars represent one standard deviation, as explained in
the text.

on two successive trials and so the signal is attenuated 3 dB more. On Trial 8, the
subject is incorrect, and so the signal attenuation decreases. The 3 dB step size is
somewhat larger than is recommended and is used for example only. The average
of each midrun estimate is as labeled in Fig. 5.7, and the final estimate of threshold is 6.5 dB of attenuation. The standard deviation computed from the 24
midrun estimates is 2.26 dB. A psychometric function for these data may also be
computed as is shown in Fig. 5.8. The threshold obtained using linear interpolation for the data in Fig. 5.8 is about 7.1 dB. The psychometric function spans
about a 10 dB range, and so its slope is about 5% per dB (i.e., 50% is spanned in
about 10 dB). A hypothetical 2 dB difference between two replications of this
condition corresponds to a 10% shift in the proportion of correct respones, a 10
dB difference would clearly be quite large in view of the slope of the function.

An estimate of the standard deviation of the percentage point tracked is also
included. Binomial variability is assumed so that the standard deviation is:

$$\sqrt{\frac{p(1 - p)}{N}} \qquad (1)$$

where p is the percentage correct at a particular stimulus value and N is the number of trials at that value. The deviation is typically ±5%. Translated into dB, our
threshold estimates are accurate within a range of about 2 dB.

As a final check on the procedures, it is a good idea to fix the level of the
signal at threshold and run 100 trials or so. This procedure may be time consuming, but is useful in verifying that the signal value did produce 70.7% correct
detection at the stimulus value that corresponds to the threshold.

In the transformed up–down methods, the step size is fixed when the data
collection begins. In the next technique that we discuss, the step size is allowed
to vary.

Parameter Estimation by Sequential Testing (PEST)

The second adaptive technique that will concern us is PEST. It was devised by Taylor and Creelman (1965, 1967) who, upon request, will furnish a computer program for running it. PEST differs from the transformed up—down methods in that it uses a variable step size which either increases or decreases depending upon the previous responses and signal values. PEST consists of rules specifying the size of the change of the stimulus value, the conditions under which the value should be changed, a criterion for ending a series of observations and used to estimate threshold, and a procedure for estimating threshold from the data collected. Before enumerating the particular rules that PEST applies, I will discuss some of the statistical considerations involved.

Statistical Considerations for Changing the Stimulus Value

Wald (1947) developed the concept of sequential sampling. In common statistical techniques, the sample size is preselected; in Wald's analysis samples are drawn one at a time and examined as they are drawn. For sequential-sampling techniques, it can be shown that the expected number of observations required to reach a decision is less than would be needed in order to make a decision on the basis of a single fixed-size sample. Of course, it may happen that the sequential procedure will take more observations than the fixed size one (although it is unlikely), and it may not always be convenient in practice to take samples one at a time but, by and large, sequential sampling is definitely an economical procedure.

An obvious place in which sequential sampling is feasible is in determination of the probability of a correct response that corresponds to some stimulus value, V. Suppose we are testing the null hypothesis, H_0, that the proportion of correct responses at a stimulus value, V, is p against the alternative, H_1, that the proportion is greater than p. Let $f_0(x_1)$ be the probability that the subject is correct if H_0 is true, similarly $f_1(x_1)$ is the probability that the subject is correct if H_1 is true. The joint likelihood of m correct observations if H_0 is true is:

$$P_{0m} = f_0^m(x_1) \qquad (2)$$

and the likelihood if H_1 is true is:

$$P_{1m} = f_1^m(x_1) \qquad (3)$$

Wald's test is to calculate p_{1m}/p_{0m} for each successive value of m and to continue testing as long as the ratio lies between two specified limits A and B ($A > B$). The process is terminated when for the first time $p_{1m}/p_{0m} > A$ or $p_{1m}/p_{0m} < B$. In the first case H_0 is rejected (i.e., the proportion correct at stimulus' value V is greater than p). If the ratio exceeds A, then the stimulus value should be decreased and testing continued. If H_0 is accepted, another test is needed to check the alternative, H_1, that the proportion is less than p. The likelihood ratio is again constructed, and another rejection region, as specified by A' and B', is defined.

The values of A and B and A' and B' are determined by the risks we are prepared to take in coming to one decision or another. Basically, the null hypothesis H_0 is accepted if after T trials the number of correct responses lies within a certain region. The region defines A, B, A', and B' and is expressed in terms of the power of the test. In Taylor and Creelman's formulation of Wald s notion, we do the following: If the number of correct observations at stimulus value V_p lies within the range E when

$$E = pT \pm W \tag{4}$$

then the stimulus value V_p is said to correspond to $p\%$ correct. The power of the test and the number of trials needed for convergence depend on W. If W is small then even a small deviation from the expected number of trials changes the stimulus level so that convergence is rapid. If W is large, the stimulus level does not shift rapidly and so convergence is slow, but the power of the decision is greater.

Taylor and Creelman recommend setting W equal to 1. With $W = 1$ and $p = 0.75$, a threshold estimate takes from 2 to 25 trials. As the target probability, p, decreases, a larger value of W is needed since the variability in the proportion of correct responses increases so that a wider range of E may be expected. If $E > |pt \pm W|$ then the stimulus value changes.

For each testing value, the experimenter (or the minicomputer as programmed by the experimenter) keeps track of the number of correct responses and the total number of responses at that value. After each trial, a test is made on the percentage or number of correct responses. If it exceeds some upper bound, the stimulus value is decreased; if it is less than some lower bound, the stimulus value increases. If the percentage lies between the bounds, the value is unchanged, and the test may be terminated. If the stimulus value is too high or too low then the experimenter may want to change it. The next problem then concerns the magnitude of the change.

Changes in Stimulus Value: The Step Size

If the current testing value is too high or too low, a step (i.e., a change) is made so that the stimulus is presented at a new value. The "appropriate" step size depends on numerous factors, and some of them are intuitive rather than mathematical. Very large step sizes are undesirable because subjects may be disturbed by overly large changes in the difficulty of the task or because the detection cue may depend on the stimulus value. A definition of "large" is not provided by Taylor and Creelman (1967) because the question is an empirical one depending on the slope of the psychometric function. In simple detection experiments, a psychometric function in a 2IFC task spans about 10 dB (see the preceding subsection) so that a 5% change in detectability results from a 1 dB change in stimulus level. If Wetherill's (1963) rule regarding step size were employed in the PEST procedure, then a step size of 1.7 dB is recommended corresponding to a 7% or 8% change in detectability. A step size of 1.7 dB may be quite reasonable when the procedure has converged to threshold but may be too small as a first step size, especially if the initial testing value is far removed from V_p. Although the first test value may be far removed from the actual V_p, it is clearly of some assistance to the experimenter if it is near V_p and if the slope of the psychometric function is known so that a reasonable step size may be picked. However, even if neither of these conditions are met, PEST can still converge on V_p if the following rules are followed.

1. If the direction of the step is changed, cut the step size in half (i.e., if one value is above and one value below V_p, try half way in between.)

2. If a second step is in the same direction as the preceding one, the step size is not changed. (If V_p is near target level, the sequential test is quite like to be wrong. It is better to check the previous decision than to halve the step size and check another point.)

3. The fourth and following steps in the same direction are double the immediately preceding step size. (V_p may be so far away from the current testing value that a very large step is required to get into the appropriate region.)

4. The third step size in the same direction is double the preceding one if the step before the most recent reversal did not result from a doubling. (This rule prevents "rocking" instability, a series of levels repeated over and over.)

If these rules for changing the step size are followed, the next question concerns the determination of threshold from the data collected.

Threshold Determination

A PEST run stops and an estimate of threshold is obtained when the rules call for a step of some predetermined size. The final precision of the estimate of the threshold is determined by this criterial step size. The estimate of V_p is that level called for by the last small step. No trials are actually run at this level so that no numerical transformation of the data need be made. Of course, it is possible to construct a psychometric function by computing the probability of a correct response for all stimulus values employed, as we did with the data from the transformed up–down procedure. Such a psychometric function, computed from the average of all or nearly all of the data collected assumes that the function is stationary. Since adaptive techniques do not necessitate this assumption, it may not be wise to calculate such a psychometric function even though it is feasible to do so.

We have just discussed two of the commonly used techniques for threshold determination. The immediate question that arises next concerns the comparison of the techniques with each other and with the older methods.

Comparison of Procedures

Comparison of the Method of Limits and Adaptive Techniques

In a computer simulation of the method of limits, Pollack (1968) found that the starting level, the step size, and the termination rule all affect threshold. Since transformed up–down methods and PEST vary all three of these, it is of immediate interest to compare thresholds obtained with these techniques. Mathematically, it seems obvious that a simple extension of Pollack's results imply that threshold estimates will be affected by step size, starting level, and the rules for changing value. However, thresholds and frequency difference limens (DLs) are nearly identical, independent of the psychophysical method employed (Wier, Jesteadt, & Green, 1976; Yost, Berg, & Thomas, 1976). The reason for the independence may be that the subject provides so much variability that the mathematical variability is swamped. Although it is up to the experimenter to demonstrate that threshold is independent of technique, near independence has been verified in numerous laboratories. Note that it is near independence of method, not paradigm, that is obtained.

Evaluation of the Transformed Up–Down and PEST Methods

PEST employs variable step sizes. In transformed up–down methods, the step size may change initially, but it should be fixed during the trials used to calculate the mid-run estimates of threshold. If the psychometric function is stationary throughout the experiment, then fixed or progressively smaller step sizes are sensible if they can be chosen so that the subject is not confused. If there is a gradual drift in the shape or location of the function during the test, then with a fixed step size, many trials may be required to move to the changed threshold position. Since PEST allows for increases and decreases in step size, it stands a better chance of capturing threshold in fewer trials than do the transformed up–down methods if the psychometric function shifts position, and if the step size changes do not greatly alter the nature of the observer's detection cue. The optimum strategy for increasing or decreasing the step size must depend on the type of changes that occur, and, since this is not always known, an optimum strategy is not possible.

To evaluate PEST quantitatively, Taylor and Creelman, (1965) considered the trade off between the number of trials to obtain a threshold estimate (speed of the estimate) and its accuracy: The slower the speed, the greater the accuracy of the measure. The number of trials required for a given threshold estimate from an "omniscient" ideal experimenter is compared with the number required in practice. The omniscient experimenter begins testing at a signal level that corresponds to V_p and the program simulating the search for threshold is subject to lapses (conditions in which the whole psychometric function shifts). Herein lies the problem. To quantify the ideal procedures, a model for human behavior (i.e., "lapses") is needed as well. In the absence of a model describing the subject's psychology (including such factors as sequential effects, learning effects, and lapses), the number of trials needed by an ideal method cannot be computed. Nonetheless, a common sense comment can be made. If the psychometric function is not stationary or if the initial testing level is quite removed from threshold, then techniques with variable step sizes are more efficient if varying the step size does not confuse the subject.

I have discussed two of the new psychophysical methods. PEST is typically employed to track the 75% point in 2IFC paradigms. Transformed up–down techniques track a variety of thresholds (see Table 5.2). We are then immediately confronted with the question of whether it matters which point on the psychometric function is tracked.

The Stimulus Value Tracked

In classical yes–no paradigms, threshold is defined as that signal level corresponding to 50% correct detection to the signal level reported present half of the time. Suppose that a signal is detected half of the time in a 2IFC paradigm. The probability of correctly choosing the interval containing the signal is composed of the sum of two independent probabilities. First, the subjects will choose the interval containing the signal if they detect the signal. This happens with probability 0.5. Second, the subjects may choose the interval containing the signal if they do not detect it (which happens with a probability of .50) but still guess correctly (the chance of a correct guess is also .50 since there are two intervals). Hence, the probability of a correct response in a 2IFC paradigm to a signal that is detected half the time in a yes–no paradigm is $1/2 + 1/2 \cdot 1/2$ or 0.75. An easier way to see the correspondence is to note that the yes–no threshold is the stimulus value corresponding to a point halfway between the extreme detection probabilities of its psychometric function, halfway between 0 and 100%. Likewise, the 2IFC threshold is the stimulus value corresponding to a point halfway between the extreme detection probabilities of its psychometric function, halfway between 50 and 100%.

In the transformed up–down technique and in PEST, it is possible to find stimulus values corresponding to other points on the psychometric function. Indeed, in the example of the transformed up–down methods, $V_{0.707}$ not $V_{0.75}$ was tracked. Procedures for determining the stimulus value corresponding to

50%, 29.3%, 79.4%, 84.1%, and 15.9% detection were outlined in Table 2. In this section, the mathematical question of whether it matters which stimulus value is tracked is considered.

Obviously, it is necessary to track stimulus levels for which a unique detection probability exists. Since infinitely many stimulus levels result in 100% or 50% detection, these levels are of no interest as a dependent variable. We cannot compare thresholds obtained in various conditions if these thresholds are not unique. We must restrict our measures to stimulus levels that have a unique detection probability associated with them.

But there is a large range of stimulus values that do produce unique detection results. Is there any rationale, apart from historical precedents, for picking one of them? At first glance, considering the slope of the psychometric function might seem to provide an answer. At the 50% point in yes–no or the 75% point in 2IFC paradigm, the slope of the psychometric function is steepest. For these percentages, if the signal level changes by some small amount, there is a maximal change in the corresponding detection score. Thus, if different experimental conditions (signal durations for example) result in different detection scores, we would observe a maximal change in the stimulus value at the steepest part of the psychometric function.

This logic would be impeccable were it not for the fact that there is variability in measuring the detection probability $P(D)$. If there are N trials used to estimate $P(D)$, then the standard deviation of the $P(D)$ is about $\sqrt{P(D) \times [1 - P(D)]/N}$. It is easily seen that the standard deviation is a maximum when $P(D) = 0.50$ in yes–no tasks or 0.75 in 2IFC. It follows that we are most susceptible to error in tracking the detection probability if we are tracking either of these detection scores, since we are least able to know when these probabilities have occurred.

Let us define the optimal preassigned response probability, $P(D)$, at which to estimate the physical stimulus value as one at which we are best able to spot a change in $P(D)$ for a given, fixed change, ΔV, in the stimulus value and for a fixed number, N, of observations. Phrased this way, the problem is recognizable as statistical in nature.

Basically we have two samples: N_1 observations at V_1 resulting in $P_1(D)$ and a standard deviation s_1 and N_2 observations at V_2 resulting in $P_2(D)$ with a standard deviation S_2. We are required to find the $P_1(D)$ for which

$$t = \frac{P_1(D) - P_2(D)}{\sqrt{\dfrac{S_1^2}{N_1 - 1} + \dfrac{S_2^2}{N_2 - 1}}} \qquad \text{if } N \text{ is small} \tag{5}$$

or

$$z = \frac{P_1(D) - P_2(D)}{\sqrt{\dfrac{S_1^2}{N_1 - 1} + \dfrac{S_2^2}{N_2 - 1}}} \qquad \text{for large } N \qquad (6)$$

is a maximum. Let $P_1(D)$ be represented as the integral of a density function $f(x)$ so that

$$P_1(D) = \int_\infty^c f(x)\, dx \qquad (7)$$

where $f(x)$ determines the form of the psychometric function. If it is the normal probability density function, then the psychometric function would be the integral of a normal distribution. A change of $P_1(D)$-$P_2(D)$ or ΔP in detection probabilities can be represented as

$$\Delta P = \int_{-\infty}^{c+\Delta} f(x)\, dx - \int_{-\infty}^{c} f(x)\, dx \qquad (8)$$

The variance of $P(D)$ is

$$\tilde{\sigma}_1^2 = [F(c)]\,[1 - F(c)]/N \qquad (9)$$

and the variance of $P(D) + \Delta P$, σ_2^2, is similarly defined. The change in detection score, ΔP, divided by the standard deviation $\tilde{\sigma}(\tilde{\sigma} = \sqrt{\tilde{\sigma}_1^2 + \tilde{\sigma}_2^2})$ is the critical statistic. That is, for fixed N and ΔV, the value of c, for which $\Delta P/\sigma$ is a maximum, determines the preassigned response probability for which we are best able to spot a change in the probability of detection.

The optimal $P(D)$ cannot be found without assuming the form of $f(x)$. For a normal ogive, in a 2IFC task, the maximum occurs for $P(D) = 0.75$. This means that for a fixed N and ΔV, we will be best able to spot a change in the percentage correct if we track the 75% correct detection threshold. To the extent that other stimulus levels are traced, the ability to notice a change in detection probability when one in fact occurs is reduced. In statistical terms, the chance of making a Type II error is minimal if the 0.75 detection probability is tracked. If the change, ΔV, is large then it will be detected even if V_p corresponding to a probability other than 0.75 is tracked. Another advantage of tracking the 0.75 point is that the problem of random noise — coughs, movement in the booth, mistaken button pushes — do not contaminate measurement of the 0.75 point as they do the points at the extreme probability of 1.0. The probability, p, corresponding to the stimulus value tracked, V_p, is not of major importance unless the effect on p of changes in the simulus value is small. In the final section of this chapter we discuss some of the benefits of any adaptive technique and some potential changes that may be employed to make any technique more efficient.

ADDITIONAL CONSIDERATIONS
IN CHOOSING ADAPTIVE TECHNIQUES

The Necessity of Adaptive Techniques

Some areas of research are of interest precisely because the threshold is known to change rapidly over time. One of the most common characteristics of all sensory systems is a reduction in sensitivity following an exposure to a so-called adapting stimulus. During or following the presentation of the adapting stimulus, threshold may be rapidly changing, and its alterations may be traced using adaptive procedures. Suppose, for example, that we wish to track the threshold of a 4000 Hz tone after a fatiguing 120 dB, 500 Hz tone is presented for 3 min. The threshold of the 4000 Hz tone is to be tracked for 10 min. Since the adapting tone is long, as is the 10 min during which the test tone threshold is traced, we would want to make a series of measures each time the adapting tone is presented. If we restricted ourselves to one threshold measure per one adapting tone presentation, it would take too long to collect the data. How can more than one threshold be collected? Using an adaptive procedure, it is quite possible to trace threshold in 10 trials, and if each trial takes 3 sec, we could trace recovery by presenting the threshold obtained in blocks of 30-sec intervals.

Adaptation and fatigue are two areas for which adaptive techniques are particularly well suited. Another area concerns learning to listen to extract the relevant detection cues in an experimental setting. Suppose that subjects are not given an opportunity to hear the signal clearly and are required to learn the cues for auditory discrimination. In such circumstances, it would be essential to estimate thresholds in as few trials as possible. For such tasks, adaptive psychophysical techniques are ideal (see Gundy, 1961, for an example of the research on this problem).

The Advantage of Adaptive Techniques: Speed

Perhaps the most salient characteristic of an adaptive procedure is its speed. Let us exclude the method of adjustment from our discussion on the grounds that it may lead to data confounded with the subjects' criteria and compare the older psychophysical techniques with the adaptive ones.

Penner, Leshowitz, Cudahy, and Ricard (1974) published data gathered in a 2IFC paradigm using an up–down method. The signal level was varied in eight steps over a 21 dB range. There were 140 trials per block with 10 observations at the extreme signal levels and 20 observations at all other levels. Four blocks were combined for each threshold reported, so that there were 80 observations per point, with 40 observations at the extremes. Psychometric functions were fitted to these data by a least squares technique (Egan, Lindner, & McFadden, 1969). There were then 560 observations per subject. At 3 sec per observation, this is a total of 21.47 hours of observing per subject. Suppose that we were to replicate the experiment using an adaptive technique with 100 observations hovering about threshold rather than spanning the psychometric function. A total of 3.83 hours of observing per subject would be required. In addition to tremendous time savings, the 100 observations would probably provide as many as 20 estimates of threshold, whereas the up—down procedure provided only 4. In these time calculations, only the actual time spent observing was included. Since subjects have "breaks" in between runs, the actual discrepancy in time spent gathering the data is far greater than 17.64 hours.

Additional time-saving devices may also be used. Instead of fixing the length of the response interval, the computer may be programmed to end the interval when the subjects' responses have all been collected. The "warning" light that typically lasts 400 msec and signals the start of the next trial can be eliminated. In the Penner et. al. (1974) study, a simple elimination of the warning light would save 2.86 hours of the subjects' time.

NEW DIRECTIONS IN ADAPTIVE PROCEDURES

Selecting a Step Size

One of the main problems with the adaptive procedures is choosing the next testing level. Time may be wasted in initially converging on threshold because steps are too small; the testing level sometimes marches away from threshold because the steps are too large. There are some potential solutions to these problems. The first and most compelling approach, is to yoke procedures: Begin with the method of adjustment, then proceed as usual given an estimate of threshold and measure of the width of the psychometric function.

Another more ingenious, and also more complicated approach, could be provided by accepting two responses from the subject on each trial. The first could be a judgment concerning the interval containing the signal; the second a confidence rating. The first judgment would be used to decide on the direction of the change in stimulus level, as already prescribed, in the PEST or transformed up—down methods. The confidence ratings could be used to decide on the step size. A high confidence rating would result in a larger step size than would a low rating. Of course, the stopping step size in PEST would not depend on the confidence ratings, so that data analysis in PEST is unchanged. For transformed up—down techniques, however, in the circumstances described, the midrun estimates could not be used since the steps vary in size. Two choices are apparent: Either a psychometric function could be fitted to the data to estimate the stimulus value resulting in some proportion correct, or the confidence ratings could be used in the first set of preliminary data in order to establish the region containing threshold, and then the typical fixed step size runs begun. The confidence ratings would be especially useful in the first series of trials when little is known about the location and the width of the psychometric function. The experimenter could, of course, cease to collect confidence ratings whenever he chooses.

Complex Strategies

Neither transformed up–down techniques nor PEST make any assumptions regarding the shape of the psychometric function, nor do they require any complicated mathematical curve fits in order to select the subsequent testing level. If sophisticated instrumentation is available then more complex adaptive strategies can be used. Such complexities do not provide the "optimum" testing procedure. Each technique has its own merits and demerits. Very efficient techniques tend to place greater reliance on assumptions concerning the shape of the psychometric function. In psychophysical experiments that are of limited duration, the validity of these underlying assumptions are often suspect, and so a case can be easily made for utilization of techniques that are not heavily dependent on testing procedures. Keeping these comments in mind, let us consider some complex testing strategies.

The first point of note about PEST and transformed up–down techniques is that they utilize the past 2 to 8 trials to set the subsequent testing level. The reason for utilizing so few trials is a belief that the underlying psychometric function may be drifting so that what is desirable is a glimpse at the momentary threshold rather than the threshold obtained over long time periods. If the drift is nonexistent or small, then information is lost by discarding previous testing information. If the alteration in threshold is not large, then using all but the last few trials to estimate the subsequent testing level is not optimal.

There is a remedy to this criticism. Suppose we assume a shape for the psychometric function – a logit or a cumulative normal will do – and use the assumed shape to fit nearly all the data obtained in the run. A "nearly all" rule is suggested because the first 10 to 20 trials may be learning trials, trials in which the subject is learning to spot the detection cue. Having fitted the function, we interpolate to obtain an estimate of threshold and use this estimate as the next testing level. This analysis is easy to implement on a minicomputer and eliminates the problem of choosing rules for selecting the step size since the next testing level always is the best guess of the signal's threshold value. The procedure could be coupled with PEST or the 0.707 transformed up–down rule: the major difference is only that selecting a step is no longer a problem.

There are disadvantages to this suggestion. If the psychometric function shifts rapidly, then it is not a good idea to utilize very much of the past to predict the future. If the underlying psychometric function is not closely approximated by the function chosen, the procedure suggested will not produce testing levels close to threshold. The latter objection is of less weight than the former since fairly large deviations from the assumed shape would be unlikely. Hall (1968) has suggested a similar procedure. Using on-line calculations from a digital computer, he places each observation at the maximum likelihood estimate of the target value derived from all the data collected. These and other more complicated strategies are available. The production of methods for efficiently estimating threshold is recent and is enabled by the existence of minicomputers.

CONCLUDING COMMENTS

In this chapter we have reviewed some modern experimental situations used in the study of sensory psychology. Forced-choice and yes—no techniques are the two principal paradigms in studies of detection, recognition, and discrimination. Whatever the paradigm, a method must also be selected. In the least efficient psychophysical techniques, step sizes are fixed and stimulus values are independent of the observer's previous responses. Inefficient techniques employ deterministic strategies to trace the probabilistic pattern of human response. Although the older methods are clearly inefficient, there is no generally optimum testing procedure. Each technique has its own advantages and drawbacks. In fact, there is no way to compare a given technique with an "optimal" one since any optimal strategy must be knowledgeable enough to model human behavior accurately. Despite the inability to delineate the characteristics of an ideal psychophysical method, adaptive methods in which the present stimulus values depend on the subject's responses and the preceding stimulus values are more efficient than the classical up—down method or the method of constant stimuli. The two adaptive techniques discussed in this chapter, the transformed up—down methods and PEST, have become the principal means of determining thresholds in modern psychoacoustic laboratories.

ACKNOWLEDGMENT

This work was supported, in part, by Grant No. 5 ROI NS13 673 from the National Institute of Health.

REFERENCES

Atkinson, R. C. A variable sensitivity theory of signal detection. *Psychological Review*, 1963, *70*, 91–106.
Atkinson, R. C., Carterette, E. C., & Kinchla, R. A. Sequential phenomena in psychophysical judgments: A theoretical analysis. *IRE Transactions of Information Theory*, 1962, *8*, 155–162.

Atkinson, R. C., & Kinchla, R. A. A learning model for forced-choice detection experiments. *British Journal of Mathematical and Statistical Psychology*, 1965, *18*, 183–206.

Brownlee, K. A., Hodges, J. L., & Rosenblatt, M. The up-and-down method with small samples. *Journal of the American Statistical Association*, 1953, *48*, 262–277.

Bush, R. R. Estimation and evaluation. In *The handbook of mathematical psychology* (Vol. I). New York: Wiley, 1963.

Bush, R. R., Luce, R. D., & Rose, R. M. Learning models for psychophysics. In R. C. Atkinson (Ed.), *Studies in mathematical psychology*. Stanford: Stanford University Press, 1964.

Carterette, E. C., Friedman, M. P., & Wyman, M. J. Feedback and psychophysical variables in signal detection. *Journal of the Acoustical Society of America*, 1966, *39*, 1051–1055.

Day, W. F. Serial non-randomness in auditory differential thresholds as a function of interstimulus interval. *American Journal of Psychology*, 1956, *69*, 387–394.

Dixon, W. J., & Mood, A. M. A method for obtaining and analyzing sensitivity data. *Journal of the American Statistical Association*, 1948, *43*, 110–116.

Dorfman, D. D., & Biderman, M. A learning model for a continuum of sensory states. *Journal of Mathematical Psychology*, 1969, *6*, 487–496.

Durlach, N. I., & Braida, L. D. Intensity perception I. Preliminary theory of intensity resolution. *Journal of the Acoustical Society of America*, 1969, *46*, 372–383.

Egan, J. P., Lindner, W. A., & McFadden, D. Masking level differences and the form of the psychometric function. *Perception & Psychophysics*, 1969, *6*, 209–215.

Green, D. M., & Swets, J. A. *Signal detection theory and psychophysics*. New York: John Wiley & Son, 1966.

Gundy, R. F. Auditory detection and an unspecified signal. *Journal of the Acoustical Society of America*, 1961, *33*, 1008–1012.

Hall, J. L. Maximum likelihood sequential procedure for estimation of psychometric functions. *Journal of the Acoustical Society of America*, 1968, *310*, (A).

Herrick, R. M. Psychophysical methodology: Comparison of thresholds of the method of limits and of the method of constant stimuli. *Perceptual and Motor Skills*, 1967, *24*, 915–922.

Howarth, C. I., & Bulmer, M. G. Non-random sequences in visual threshold experiments. *Quarterly Journal of Experimental Psychology*, 1956, *8*, 163–171.

Jesteadt, W., & Bilger, R. C. Frequency discrimination near masked threshold. *Perception & Psychophysics*, 1969, *6*, 405–408.

Jesteadt, W., & Sims, S. Decision processes in frequency discrimination. *Journal of the Acoustics Society of America*, 1975, *57*, 1161–1168.

Katsuki, Y. Neural mechanism of auditory sensation in cats. In W. A. Rosenblith (Ed.), *Sensory communication*. Cambridge, Mass.: MIT Press, 1961.

Kinchla, R. A. A learning factor in visual discrimination. In R. C. Atkinson (Ed.), *Studies in mathematical psychology*, Stanford: Stanford University Press, 1964.

Larkin, W. D., & Norman, D. A. An extension and experimental analysis of neural quantum theory. In R. C. Atkinson (Ed.), *Studies in mathematical psychology*. Stanford: Stanford University Press, 1964.

Levitt, H. Transformed up–down methods in psychoacoustics. *Journal of the Acoustics Society of America*, 1970, *49*, 467–477.

McCall, M., & Levinson, J. Linearity of low-level chromatic adaptation — A fly in the ointment. Supplement to *Investigative Opthamology and Visual Science*, 1977, p. 160.

Norman, D. A. Sensory thresholds, response bias, and the neural quantum theory. *Journal of Mathematical Psychology*, 1964, *1*, 88–120.

Penner, M. J. The detection of gaps in noise as a measure of the decay of sensation. *Journal of the Acoustics Society of America*, 1977, *61*, 552–557.

Penner, M. J., Leshowitz, B., Cudahy, E., & Ricard, G. Intensity discrimination for pulsed sinusoids of various frequencies. *Perception & Psychophysics*, 1974, *15*, 568–570.

Pollack, I. Computer simulation of threshold observations by the method of limits. *Perceptual and Motor Skills*, 1968, *26*, 583–586.

Preston, M. G. Contrast effects and the psychometric judgments. *American Journal of Psychology*, 1936, *48*, 287–303. (a)

Preston, M. G. Contrast effects and the psychometric functions. *American Journal of Psychology*, 1936, *48*, 625–631. (b)

Raab, D. H., Osman, E., & Rich, E. The effects of waveform correlation and signal duration on detection of noise bursts in continuous noise. *Journal of the Acoustics Society of America*, 1963, *35*, 1942.

Shoeffler, M. S. Theory for psychophysical learning. *Journal of the Acoustics Society of America*, 1965, *37*, 1124–1133.

Senders, V., & Soward, A. Analysis of response sequences in the settings of a psychophysical experiment. *American Journal of Psychology*, 1952, *65*, 358–374.

Shipley, E. F. Dependence of successive judgments in detection tasks: Correctness of the response. *Journal of the Acoustics Society of America*, 1961, *33*, 1142–1143.

Sorkin, R. D. Extension of the theory of signal detectability to matching procedures in psychoacoustics. *Journal of the Acoustics Society of America*, 1962, *34*, 1745–1751

Speeth, S. P., & Mathews, M. V. Sequential effects in the signal-detection situation. *Journal of the Acoustics Society of America*, 1961, *33*, 1046–1054.

Swets, J. A. Indices of signal detectability obtained with various psychophysical procedures. *Journal of the Acoustics Society of America*, 1959, *31*, 511–513.

Tanner, T. A., Jr., Rauk, J. A., & Atkinson, R. C. Signal recognition as influenced by information feedback. *Journal of Mathematical Psychology*, 1970, *7*, 259–274.

Taylor, M. M., & Creelman, C. D. *PEST: A rapid technique for finding arbitrary points on a psychometric function.* Paper presented at the meeting of the Psychonomic Society, Chicago, Month 1965.

Taylor, M. M., & Creelman, C. D. PEST: Efficient estimates on probability functions. *Journal of the Acoustics Society of America*, 1967, *41*, 782–787.

Verplanck, W. S., Collier, G. H., & Cotton, J. W. Nonindependence of successive responses in measurements of the visual threshold. *Journal of Experimental Psychology*, 1952, *44*, 273–282.

Verplanck, W. S., Cotton, J. W., & Collier, G. H. Previous training as a determinant of response dependency at threshold. *Journal of Experimental Psychology*, 1953, *46*, 10–14.

Wald, A. *Sequential analysis.* New York: John Wiley & Sons, 1947.

Wetherill, G. B. Sequential estimation of quantal response curves. *Journal of the Royal Statistics Society*, 1963, *B25*, 1–48.

Wetherill, G. B., & Chen, H. Sequential estimation of quantal response Curves II, A new method of estimation. (Technical Memorandum). Bell Telephone Laboratories, 1964.

Wetherill, G. B., & Levitt, H. Sequential estimation of points on a psychometric function. *British Journal of Mathematical and Statistical Psychology,* 1965, *18*, 1–10.

Wier, C. C., Jesteadt, W., & Green, D. M. A comparison of method-of-adjustment and forced-choice procedures in frequency discrimination. *Perception & Psychophysics*, 1976, *19*, 75–79.

Yost, W. A., Berg, K., & Thomas, B. Frequency recognition in temporal interference tasks: A comparison among four psychophysical procedures. *Perception & Psychophysics*, 1976, *20*, 353–359.

Yost, W. A., Penner, M. J., & Feth, L. L. Signal detection as a function of contralateral sinusoid-to-noise ratio. *Journal of the Acoustics Society of America*, 1972, *51*, 1966–1970.

6 Minicomputers and Vision Research

Robert Sekuler
Cresap Neuroscience Laboratory,
Northwestern University

INTRODUCTION

Work in vision and visual perception requires good control over stimulus geometry, luminance, and temporal characteristics (Boynton, 1966). Long before the advent of computers, vision scientists had developed sophisticated optical techniques for producing stimuli of virtually any desired complexity. Simply inserting a transparency at the right place in an optical system gives the experimenter virtually unlimited display capability. A carefully made transparency on fine-grain photographic substrate can contain upward of 10^{12} bits of stimulus information (Campbell, 1967). Obviously, to produce a similar, flicker-free display using electronic means would require both incredibly fast throughput and gargantuan memory, exceeding by several orders of magnitude that normally found on minicomputers.

Although the computer cannot compete with such optical systems in making stimuli of high-information density, the computer does offer advantages in the temporal domain, because of its unrivaled ability to produce any arbitrary complex temporal modulation (e.g., pattern of motion or flicker). In fact, the more complex and varied the stimulus temporal waveform, the more the minicomputer is the laboratory instrument of choice. As Campbell (1967) put it, "from a communications standpoint, a Boeing 707 filled with high resolution photographs has fantastic 'bandwidth'; and the equivalent number of bits processed by a high speed, high resolution enlarger is enormous; but the flexibility as well as the complexity of the possible transformations is limited [pp. 14–15]."

This paragraph provides a roadmap to the territory over which this chapter roams; the map should make the chapter more predictable and useful. I shall start by considering some of the special hardware needed for computer-controlled vision research. This hardware includes the delivery device (usually a cathode ray tube) and computer memory to match. The bulk of the remaining space in the chapter is concerned with various applications. Since only a restricted set of applications could be accommodated, I have chosen those that best illustrate the range of ways in which vision research is likely to be influenced and helped by minicomputer usage. The applications run from standard visual psychophysics to clinical work in vision and visual neurophysiology. Afterwards, a brief treatment is given to another kind of hardware: dedicated electronic devices that may be useful in hybrid, digital–analog vision research systems. The chapter concludes with some observations on the promise and dangers attendant to service of a minicomputer in sophisticated psychophysical methodology.

STIMULUS DISPLAY HARDWARE

I shall ignore, for the moment, the use of minicomputers to control the elements of standard optical systems (e.g., Maxwellian view systems) and consider schemes by which computers produce stimuli by electronic means in real time. To produce a stimulus, three fundamental subsystems are required: a display device such as a cathode ray tube, a stored representation of the desired display, and an interface or controller capable of transferring the stored representation to the display device. Each of the three subsystems may take many different forms and, although we may speak of each subsystem as separate and distinct from its partners, they are very much interactive. The characteristics of each limit the system designer's choices as to the other subsystems. Good discussions of these design complexities already exist; the reader would be well advised to examine the literature on computer graphics for the basics. In addition, the volume by Newman and Sproull (1973) and a number of recent articles in the new journal *Computers and Graphics* offer particularly good ideas for systems designers (Eastman & Wooten, 1975; Entwisle, 1977; Jarvis, 1975; Potts, 1975).

There are several major kinds of display devices available for computer created stimuli, including several types of cathode ray tube (CRT) displays: random-access storage, refreshed random-access and raster displays (van Gelder, 1972). Before considering each of the CRT types, let me offer some general caveats.

Here are some things to check. First, when not being swept across the tube, the display's beam should produce as narrow a point on the CRT as possible. This will permit the experimenter to produce stimuli containing spatial frequencies as high as necessary. Second, the size of the point should remain invariant regardless of where on the CRT it is imaged. Third, the accelerating potential of the electron beam should be as high as possible. Other things being equal, the maximum achievable luminance varies with the square root of the accelerating potential. Fourth, the spot luminance should be invariant across the face of the

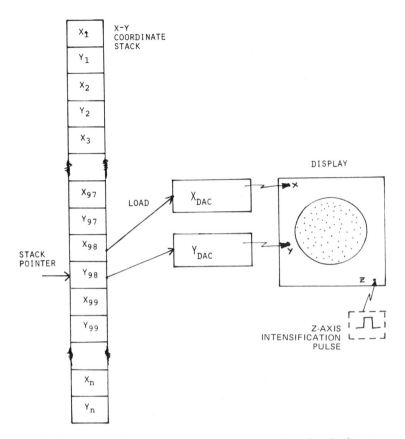

FIG. 6.1.   Block diagram of significant components for point-plotting on an $x-y$ display monitor. Coordinates of the to-be-plotted points are stored in stack prior to plotting. Successive pairs are accessed and loaded into x- and y- D-to-A convertors. After proper settling times have elapsed, a one-shot delivers an intensification pulse to the z-axis input of the display.

CRT (or as nearly so as possible). Some commonly used CRT displays (e.g., Hewlett Packard's 1332A display) suffer from variation of luninance with CRT position that is an inherent part of the CRT beam-spreader circuitry. When one tries to produce a uniform raster on such devices, a 1-cm diameter circular dim region appears in the center. This dim region could have disastrous consequences for experimenters using the display. Unfortunately, you can rely on neither catalog nor salesman necessarily to warn you of such deficits. Finally, my general advice is: before purchase, get a loaner if at all possible. This will allow you to see whether the device is actually suitable for your purposes and will give you some idea of how well the actual CRT display meets the manufacturer's specifications (often these are fiction). Nota bene: purchase of even the highest quality

CRT does not absolve the experimenter of the need for careful calibration and constant recalibration (Sperling, 1971a).

From the programmer's viewpoint, the simplest type of CRT display is the random-access storage display. Stimuli are created by intensifying an appropriate set of points on the tube. Of course, the desired stimulus must have previously been reduced to a set of points on Cartesian coordinates. As Fig. 6.1 shows, the corresponding x- and y-coordinates are accessed, each loaded into a digital-to-analog converter (DAC), and an intensification pulse (z-axis) delivered. The x- and y-axis DACs control the corresponding deflection amplifiers in the CRT display, thereby moving the electron beam to the desired location.

The beam does not write directly on the tube's phosphor but instead produces a charge on a fine, wire-grid just behind the screen of the CRT. The spatial pattern of charges on this grid is stored and transferred to the CRT screen by a continuous stream of electrons that floods the wire-grid uniformly. Electrons are repelled by regions of the wire-grid that have not received the positive charge, and local regions that have been charged (by the computer-controlled writing beam) allow the electrons to pass through, striking a phosphor-coated screen in front of that charged-region, thereby producing a bright spot.

With a direct-view storage tube in the CRT display, once the complete stimulus had been written on the tube, it may remain visible for an appreciable period (e.g., an hour) without significant spatial degradation and without requiring further action by the computer. This ability to store the stimulus, once it has been presented, is the strong suit of the storage display because it frees the Central Processing Unit (CPU) for other, more important experimental tasks. Unfortunately, there are some drawbacks to such a display. One cannot use it for temporally modulated stimuli. In order to alter the displayed pattern, one must erase the whole pattern and then start anew. The erase signal, in most displays, produces a bright flash lasting several hundred msec. Subjects in experiments usually find this flash disturbing. In addition, these displays offer relatively poor spatial resolution.

A second, more flexible display device is the nonstorage random-access CRT. In these devices the electron beam is positioned by x- and y-deflection amplifiers, and the intensified electron beam writes directly on a phosphor-coated screen. With most of the phosphors used to paint the CRT screens, the intensified region of the screen quickly loses brightness, and if a static display of some duration is required, all the points must be replotted (refreshed). Each refresh constitutes one temporal display frame. Most vision researchers purposely choose phosphors (P-4, P-15, P-24, or P-31) that have minimum persistence. This gives the greatest flexibility for temporal modulation. For example, if between one-frame of the display and the next, each stored x-value were incremented by some constant, the displayed pattern would appear to drift smoothly in a horizontal direction. Incrementing only the y-values instead would produce the appearance of vertical movement. In order to produce smooth movement in some other direction (e.g., $\theta°$), increment each x by $\cos(\theta)$ and each y by $\sin(\theta)$. Other geometric transformations can be achieved by applying the appropriate operators to x- and y-values between successive frames. In each case, rapid decay of the phosphorescence minimizes the chances that ghosts of previous display frames will haunt the current frame. Sperling (1976) has a good discussion of these techniques. I should note that when using data from CRT manuals, many experimenters describe the temporal decay of their stimuli in a way that is interesting but psychophysically meaningless. Such descriptions take this form: the phosphor decayed to 10% of its initial luminance within 1 msec. Unfortunately, this kind of statement completely ignores the possibility that, because the initial luminance was high, the phosphorescence might continue to be clearly visible for very much longer than 1 msec.

There are several problems associated with a nonstorage display as a method of creating stimuli. Since it is the most frequently used type of computer display in vision research, I shall devote extra attention to it. An obvious problem is that the display cannot approach in one frame the information content achievable with high-quality transparencies. Although the critical value varies with many parameters (Sperling, 1971b), as a rough guideline we can assume that all the points in one frame must be plotted within 30 sec if the observer's visual system is to be fooled into seeing all the sequentially plotted points as simultaneous. Good DACs have a settling time of 500 to 1000 nanosec; intensifying before they have settled will add disturbing comet-like "tails" to the points. [In some devices (e.g., Digital Equipment Corporation's VT11 Display Processor), the DAC settling times are nearly an order of magnitude longer than state-of-the-art. In such devices the time required to output a pattern from the computer memory is strongly limited by the settling time of the DACs.] Under most conditions, only 2000 points could be plotted per frame without flicker. When planning a computer-driven display system, several high-speed DACs of 12 bits or more are quite important. If such DACs are coupled with a good Direct Memory Access (DMA) device, display throughput can reach 60,000 points/sec on a 4096 x 4096 addressable grid. Of course, this is still a far cry from 10^{12} bits, but it is adequate for many good research purposes.

Let us consider an additional difficulty of the $x-y$ refreshed display. Vision research requires the control of stimulus luminance. The refreshed, random-access CRT display presents one obstacle to that control: Luminance will tend to vary with the number of points being displayed. The luminance of any point will depend upon the phosphor, the accelerating potential of the electron beam, and the time that elapses between successive intensifications of that point. The larger the number of points that must be plotted in a given frame, the longer will be the interval between successive refreshes of any point, and the lower the luminance. The inexperienced CRT user may not recognize this possible confound until too late. Fortunately, there are several ways to prevent the confound. Let us consider a complicated one first.

Calibration devices (e.g., Virsu & Lehtio, 1975) ought to be available for measuring the function that relates luminance to refresh rate. If that function is known, it is a relatively simple matter to compensate for variation in the number of points being plotted. One particularly attractive expedient, available on CRT displays with differential z-axis input, is to apply a variable "bucking" voltage to the minus z input, with the constant size intensification pulses going into the plus z input. Of course, with displays lacking differential input the same effect can be achieved by using a fast operational amplifier to mix the two signals before applying the sum to the single z-axis display input terminal. Another complicated solution is to vary the plotting rate as a function of the number of points per frame. This method, which requires careful attention to the execution times of program-display loops, would usually be the least desirable.

The simplest solution requires variation in neither the luminance signals to the CRT display nor variation in program timing, just the plotting of some imaginary points. Erlebacher and Sekuler (1974), in several of their studies of geometric illusions, used a computer controlled display to present standard and comparison figures. The nine different standards were presented in random order, each accompanied by a comparison line. On each trial the observer indicated whether the comparison line was longer or shorter than the accompanying standard. The computer noted the observer's response and, the next time that particular standard was presented, adjusted the comparison-line length appropriately, reducing it if it had been judged too long, incrementing it if judged too short. In this way, nine interleaved staircases (Cornsweet, 1962) were run, each homing-in on the point of subjective equality for a particular illusion-producing stimulus. To prevent covariation between luminance and the length of the comparison line, Erlebacher and Sekuler always plotted a constant number of points, regardless of the line length. This number was greater than that which would be required to plot even their longest line. To the array of points (pairs of x- and y-values) that would produce the desired line were added dummy values, which if plotted would address a point of the CRT display that was off-screen and, hence, invisible to the observer. By plotting a constant total number of points, some on-screen and the off-screen dummies, Erlebacher and Sekuler were able to vary line length independently of luminance. Mayzner and Greenberg (1971) also employed this technique.

Raster Displays

A third kind of CRT display uses a raster principle. Instead of randomly accessing x- and y-points to create the display, the beam of the CRT scans sequentially, line-by-line across the tube. Modulating the beam as it scans produces the desired luminance distribution. This approach has been implemented on three different kinds of instruments: television monitors (e.g., Mezrich & Rose, 1977), oscilloscopes (Tynan & Armstrong, 1977), and $x-y$ displays (Wilson & Giese, 1977). The television monitor offers special advantages. In particular, it allows the highest achievable luminances at the lowest cost, and color stimuli can be produced (Gourlay, Uttal, & Powers, 1974).

A stored frame of the stimulus consists of only the z-axis information; the x- and y-axis are scanned under the control of an external time base. The time base may either be intrinsic to the display device itself (e.g., oscilloscope), may be provided by the computer itself, or may be provided by an external device triggered by the computer. Such a device might be a chip capable of producing a ramp of the appropriate frequency and amplitude. For the case of the usual $x-y$ display monitor such as Hewlett Packard 1332A or Tektronix 604 or 606, provisions must be made for controlling both the x- and y-axis scans. Synchronization between the computer's output of the z-axis information and the moment-to-moment position of the CRT beam is crucial if one is to get the desired stimulus. With such a display one should think of the computer as producing the stimulus by temporally modulating the z-axis; spatial positioning is handled separately.

If the computer is to produce stimuli approaching an actual broadcast video signal in information content, it would have to have fantastic memory. For each frame, broadcast video signals would require 512 x 512 bits to be sorted for a 1-bit intensity modulation (any picture element, either black or white). Thus, in a machine with 12-bit words, nearly 22K words would be required to store a single frame of even this highly impoverished video image (assuming 1-bit bytes). An image with an appreciable tonal range (e.g., 16 grey scale levels) would require four times as much memory (assuming 4-bit bytes). Various manufacturers have made such memories available for microcomputers at quite reasonable cost.

But there is another difficulty with this implementation. Recall that the computer has stored the temporal waveform of the z-axis signal; x- and y-coordinates are implicit rather than explicit. The appropriate corresponding x- and y-coordinates are not stored along with the z-signal information; only the *position* of the z-axis information in the potential output queue, along with some knowledge of the x- and y-scanning procedures, would enable prediction of the output image. This means that for any but the most elementary possible geometric transformations from one frame to the next, simple matrix operators could not be used to update the memory. Since the intensity data are stored in a single, 1-dimensional vector, corresponding appropriate $x-y$ coordinates would have to be computed or the data rearranged into a 2-dimensional matrix before transformation operators could be applied. Needless to say, this requirement (1) obviates some of the advantages of the raster display and (2) would require substantial computational time between frames if a real-time display is required. The computations might be made manageable by the use of analog elements capable of taking the 2-dimensional coordinates as input and outputting a voltage proportional to the corresponding subscript (position) in a 1-dimensional vector.

Let us now consider some applications of raster-scan displays in vision research. With the growing importance of linear systems approaches to vision, many researchers have found it necessary to produce grating patterns of various sorts. Although optical techniques do exist for producing such gratings (Freeman, Mitchell, & Millodot, 1972; Fry, 1969), computer-generated and controlled gratings offer several experimental advantages. Primary among these is the ability to produce any arbitrary luminance profile and to vary that profile easily and rapidly. In a typical use, the digitized intensity profile of a 1-dimensional grating is stored as sequential items in a list. While the oscilloscope runs at a frame rate of 100 to 300 Hz, a high-frequency (100 KHz to 1 MHz) triangular waveform is impressed on the vertical axis. The result is that the oscilloscope beam is swept up and down quite rapidly, covering the entire vertical extent of the screen at the same time the beam sweeps horizontally. The effect is to create a uniform raster. Note that the frame rate of the scope is sufficient to prevent perceptible flicker. While all this is going on, the computer can read out successive items from the list of digitized waveform and, with the intervention of a DAC, modulate the intensity of the oscilloscope beam appropriately. At any one moment, then, the intensity of the oscilloscope trace is determined by the number that the computer has transferred to the z-axis. Since the transfer rate is slower than the signal going into the scope y-axis, the oscilloscope will sweep the entire vertical extent of the tube at least once before a new number is taken from the list and transferred into the DAC.

Two things are required. First, the time base of the oscilloscope should be synced to the list readout. To produce a steady grating on the face of the oscilloscope (i.e., one whose spatial phase does not vary randomly) any given word in the list should be accessed and input to the DAC when the oscilloscope beam is at the exact same horizontal position on each sweep. This synchronization is best achieved by having the computer trigger the sweep. The alternative approach, having the computer sense the oscilloscope's start of sweep, is less desirable because it requires more of the computer's attention.

The second sine qua non for a stable grating is to adjust the speed of the list readout and z-axis modulation so that the time taken to go through the entire list corresponds at least approximately to the duration of the scope sweep. Minor mismatches are not fatal. Assume the sweep speed is 100 Hz; the sweep duration is therefore 10 msec. If the list readout is completed in more than 10 msec, elements from the tail end of the list will not have any effect, since they will output on the DAC after the sweep and while the scope is waiting for another trigger signal. If the list readout is completed in less than 10 msec, grating will occupy less than the full horizontal extent. The tail-end of the display will be unmodulated (uniform). For most human psychophysical purposes, assuming normal rather than very large display screens and usual viewing distances the list should consist of at least 512 items. This means that the waveform will have been digitized into a large enough number of points to insure that even patterns with high spatial frequencies will be within the capability of the computer-controlled display. Of course, in order to present the grating for more than 10 msec (one sweep duration), the list would have to be repetitively outputted.

Unfortunately, like other display schemes, this one produces an unacceptably heavy overhead for the CPU. Let us take some ballpark numbers and see how heavy the overhead is: for example, a 100 Hz frame rate and a z-axis list 512 elements long. Items would have to be output at a rate of 512/10 msec or one point every 19.5 μsec. Since the tightest display loop would require about 8 μsec to access and plot a point, not much time would be left for anything else. The most obvious things that one might want to do while the display is being created include calculating the list for the next frame (if the display is to be altered) or recording some dependent measure that requires synchronization with the display (the observer's eye position). Obviously, then, some means should be found to free the CPU for these other tasks. We shall return to some solutions later.

Plasma Displays

Another storage device, the plasma screen, will get increasing use in the future although very little use has been made of it to date in vision research. At present, this device is undergoing rapid technological evolution, so the brief description that follows will be out of date by the time this chapter appears; this means, of course, that the utility of the plasma screen for vision research may be considerably enhanced over what this description implies. The plasma panel has two major advantages over the direct-view storage tube: First, it is capable of selective erase; second, the image quality does not degrade with passage of time. In the plasma panel, a set of glow discharge sites (e.g. in a 512 x 512 matrix) is created by two sets of parallel gold wire electrodes. The two sets of wires are orthogonally oriented to one another and are separated by a very thin space that is filled with neon-like gas. Each set of wires is covered with an insulating material. With an appropriate signal applied to one wire in each of the two orthogonal electrode sets, the gas in the region of the intersection of the two wires acts like a capacitor, storing the charge and lighting up. The entire matrix of wires is constantly subjected to a 50 kHz A.C. voltage that causes previously excited cells to light again; cells not previously excited are unaffected by the A.C. sustaining voltage and remain unlit. If the sustaining voltage is lowered momentarily at the intersection of wires in each of the two electrode sets, that cell will return to the unexcited (unilluminated) state.

Note that the frequency of the sustaining voltage is high enough to allow one cell to be turned on or turned off every 20 μsec. Unfortunately, at present plasma displays have only two brightness levels: on or off. Jarvis (1975) described a graphic display system based on a plasma panel. His illustrations of sample output, most notably the simulated half-tone picture he presented, gives a dramatic demonstration of the good-quality stimulus-generation capability of even present-day plasma-screen technology. The 512 x 512 matrix in a standard plasma panel covers about 8 1/2 x 8 1/2 inches.

In Jarvis's (1975) application, a PDP 11/20 had 18 address lines to the plasma panel. The lines included 9 bits for x-axis, 9 bits for y-axis, and lines for control of write, selective erase, and bulk erase functions. Jarvis addressed a problem that is central for most computer-based research in vision, not just research that uses plasma panels: How can the overhead on the CPU be minimized? To produce a new lit point on the plasma screen, the computer must transfer x- and y-coordinate words to registers connected to the plasma panel (note that in contrast to CRT displays, no digital-to-analog conversions of x- and y-words are required since the plasma screen addressing is done digitally). A simple program loop to achieve this would also involve two tests: (1) Is the plasma panel ready to receive information? (2) Has the end of the display list been reached?

The general difficulty with driving the plasma display with this simple program loop is that considerable time would be required for each pass through the loop, leaving very little time to construct or reconfigure the display list (pairs of x- and y-coordinates to be illuminated). Jarvis (1975) used a standard block, direct memory access (DMA) interface module from the computer manufacturer. Essentially, the DMA device is told by the CPU how many pairs of words (x- and y-values) are in the display list and where the display list is stored in memory. The DMA device accesses the proper number of $x-y$ pairs sequentially from memory and passes them to the plasma screen. When the output list is exhausted, the DMA device stops and acknowledges this condition by producing an interrupt. In order to implement line-drawing routines based on incremental commands (i.e., in which x- and/or y-values could be changed by 0, +1 or −1). Jarvis's DMA configuration is somewhat more complicated than I have described.

At the rate of 20 μsec/point (fixed by 50 kHz sustaining voltage), it would require 5.24 sec to plot every point on the 512 x 512 matrix. This is, of course, very far from "real-time" display; but to produce more typical (by vision research standards) displays of 1000 points would require only 20 msec, a quite acceptable figure. The possibility of parallel addressing would speed up display times appreciably on the plasma screen (Newman & Sproull, 1973).

Memory for Vision Displays

Other approaches that would speed up display rates on refresh display devices require that the digitized version of the to-be-presented image be stored in memories that allow faster throughput than does conventional computer memory. One such device is the videodisk (Mostafavi & Sakrison, 1976) that is capable of storing either 415 static monochrome television frames or 105 color images. In this particular application, the stimuli (pseudo-random patterns) were created, spatially filtered off-line and written by minicomputer onto the videodisk for subsequent use in experiments.

An alternative, less exotic storage device for a recycling memory is described by McCracken, Sherman, and Dwyer (1975). Their system took advantage of the availability of very long shift registers (1024 bits) organized in to a complete memory of 524 Kbits. This permitted storage of images containing 256 x 256 elements with 8 bits of tonal information per picture element.

The oscillator frequency of the shift registers (5 MHz) make it possible to create each display point in 200 nanosec on a television monitor. The mean luminances Mostafavi and Sakrison (1976) achieved (greater than 500 cd/m^2) is reminiscent of another advantage of using video monitors: luminances well into the photopic range. Incidentally, one nicety of the Mostafavi and Sakrison experiments is that the images written on the videodisk were compensated for the nonlinearity of the monitor's luminance response. The hardware alternative to this approach would require the construction of a box that compensated for the nonlinearity and would be inserted between computer and monitor. Similarly, large nonvolatile shift registers in the form of bubble memory have recently been introduced by Texas Instruments and could offer appreciable cost advantages over other memory types (Helmers, 1977) as the basis of recycling image-containing memories.

A Clinical Research Application

Minicomputers have been used in several settings which I feel are particularly creative and noteworthy. Let us consider the first of these in some detail because it represents what I believe to be a large class of potentially important clinical applications of minicomputers in vision. As anyone who has ever spent time performing clinical tasks knows, there is a good deal of art to many diagnostic procedures (Gans, 1971). For example, I once observed an ophthalmologist try to measure the acuity of a 75-year-old man. At issue was whether the man needed new glasses. The ophthalmologist began by projecting an enormous letter E on the wall and asking the man whether he could see it. The man looked in the direction, blinked and asked, "Why? Is there a letter there?" He claimed he could not see it. Someone unskilled in dealing with older patients might have stopped at this point and given the man the thickest glasses available. But this ophthalmologist, through a combination of kibitzing and cajoling, managed to get the man to acknowledge that he did in fact see the E. The doctor turned then to a process he called "walking the patient down the eye chart." He projected smaller and smaller letters on the wall; each time the man protested that he could not see anything and each time the ophthalmologist managed to get him to make a guess. The result? The man ended up with 40/20 in his poorer eye, good acuity for a 75-year-old.

Obviously, some kind of intelligent standardization would be helpful for many diagnostic tasks, particularly those that are time consuming and where a time saving might be effected. One obvious candidate for computer-based automation is perimetry, the assessment of visual-field function. This process, which in our laboratory often accompanies some of our research measurements, is a natural for automation (Safir, 1976).

There are two basic forms of perimetry: kinetic and static (Aulhorn & Harms, 1972). The two kinds correspond to the quick and dirty (but often quite adequate) and to the thorough (but usually too time consuming). In the kinetic mode, a stimulus of a particular size and luminance is moved slowly in from the far periphery of the field until it can just be seen. The stimulus is then returned to the periphery and again moved toward fixation, this time along another meridian. Once again, the point at which the stimulus becomes visible is determined. This process is repeated along each of perhaps 12 or so meridia and then, sometimes, repeated all over with a probe of a different size or luminance. The data are then represented as a contour (on polar coordinates) that represents the locus of points at which a stimulus of particular size and luminance became visible. Of course, different luminance and size stimuli produce different contours.

In static perimetry, the threshold of visibility is determined at each of many points throughout the field, using a stimulus of fixed size but variable luminance. This procedure, which takes a good deal longer than kinetic perimetry, usually gives a more detailed picture of the visual field, areas of integrity and area of functional loss. Heijl (1977) and others have developed a variety of computer-controlled perimeters. Heijl's work is of particular interest as it would be the easiest for nonclinicians to implement since it is not a projecting system and does not require the expensive hemisphere found in many perimeters. For reasons that need not concern us here, Heijl concentrated all 64 test points over a region 25° from fixation. The test points consisted of light emitting diodes (LEDs) mounted in holes in a black plastic board, the front of which was covered by a thin semitranslucent plastic film.

With appropriate front lighting to provide a constant uniform illumination, the LEDs were invisible unless lit. The luminance of any LED could be varied, under computer control, by varying the frequency of the pulse train used to energize the LED. Since all the pulse trains energized the LED above the critical flicker-fusion frequency, the Talbot-Plateau law tells us that the LED would appear unflickering at a luminance equal to the time-average mean of the flickering light. Any LED could be presented for 500 msec at any one of 16 levels, differing by 0.3 $\log_{10}$ units. A staircase procedure was used to measure the threshold at one randomly chosen point in the perimeter field; after threshold had been determined, that same level was used as the initial value of a track run at a neighboring point. Here, Heijl took advantage of the likely correlation of sensitivity

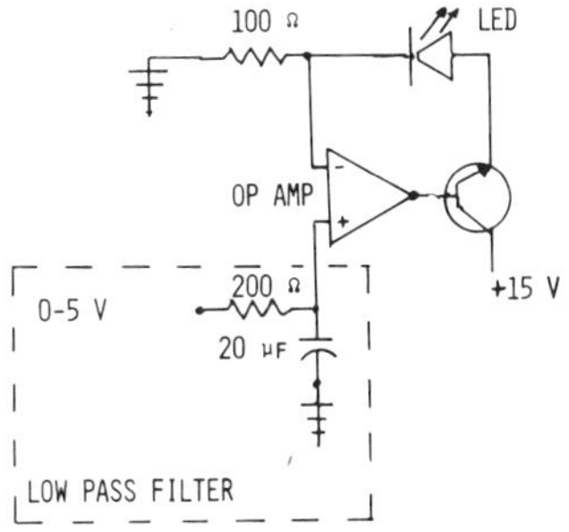

FIG. 6.2.   Voltage-to-current convertor used to drive light-emitting diode (LED). Maximum current and voltage are 50 mA and 5 V, respectively. The input to the operational amplifier is noninverting (0 to +5V) and derives from a D-to-A convertor that operates under computer control. The low-pass filter is down 3 dB at 50 Hz. In our application, the operational amplifier was a 741, the LED a Monsanto MV5222, and the transistor 2N474. Substitutions can be made quite easily.

between neighboring points in the field. The text proceeded until all 64 points had been tested. With slight modifications of the testing regime to take account of the peculiar field losses associated with glaucoma, Heijl was able to design a special test procedure that required only 4 min/eye as part of a glaucoma screening pilot project. Heijl carefully documented the claim that the computer-controlled perimeter is at least as good as, if not better than, routine manual perimetry performed at his clinic.

It should be pointed out that superior methods for controlling LED luminance are available. Since LED technology is rapidly making these devices into virtually ideal devices for vision research, I will comment briefly on one better method used at Northwestern. LED luminance is linear with current; unfortunately, because of large impedance changes, current is not a linear function of impressed voltage. Consequently, some compensation is required between a DAC driver and LED. One simple and reliable voltage-to-current converter, used in our laboratory is shown in Fig. 6.2 (Graeme, Tobey, & Huelsman, 1971). This particular converter incorporates a low-pass filter (3 dB down at 50 Hz), which smooths out the step-like character of discrete changes in LED luminance.

MINICOMPUTER AS BREADBOARD

The description of yet another clinical use of minicomputers in vision research will allow me to make another, more general point about one major advantage of such computers: The ease of programming and pilot testing with a full-scale minicomputer system makes the system into a natural, convenient, and sophisticated breadboarding device. Research ideas can be quickly turned into reality and tested. This possibility means that at any one moment the minicomputer system will be performing trivial tasks in the laboratory, tasks that in principle *could* be transferred to small-scale microcomputers or even less intelligent, single chips. But to focus on the triviality of the computer's task is to miss the point.

Of course, for many of the experimental tasks the computer does, there are cheaper alternative hardware implementations. But to go directly from hypothesis to hardware implementation without extensive pilot testing is often risky and likely to be a long-term waste of time. The minicomputer allows us to try things out in software that, after all, is more easily changed than is most hardware. (For an early application of this technique, see Mayzner, Tresselt, & Helfer, 1967.)

The ability to breadboard with software depends upon the programming aids available to the researcher. In our lab we have enough core and mass storage to let us program in a high-level language, FORTRAN. Our programs are linguistic hybrids, with the overall logic and complex calculations written in FORTRAN, and display and peripheral service routine coded in machine language. The advantage of the hybridization is that FORTRAN coding facilitiates revision of the overall logic, though at the cost of significant overhead time in execution; machine language code, although more difficult to debug and revise, maximizes display throughput.

On a number of occasions in our laboratory and elsewhere, we have been thankful for the capability that a minicomputer provides of convenient successive approximations to the right method and parameters for investigating a particular phenomenon. This can be demonstrated by considering some research that Eugene Levinson, Paul Tynan, and I did some years ago (Sekuler, Tynan, & Levinson, 1973). We started out to look for a visual analog to some auditory effects that Richard Warren had reported some time before.

Warren and his colleagues (Warren, Obusek, Farmer, & Warren, 1969) took four sounds of different kinds (buzz, beep, whistle, click, etc.) and repeated them one after another cyclically (e.g., buzz, beep, whistle, click, buzz, beep, whistle, click, etc.). Each sound was long and clear enough so that subjects had no difficulty in hearing each one but were unable to report the order of the sounds. We wondered whether this might be a general problem in the processing of temporal order information and set out to find an analog in vision. The important thing is not the outcome but the fact that, with our computer-controlled display, we were quickly able to set up and try several different approaches to the research problem.

We first wrote a program to display four letters of the alphabet, one after another, each briefly flashed. The letters were created with standard software on a 5 x 7 matrix. Sitting at a teletype in front of a CRT, subjects hit the space bar when they were ready. The computer then randomly selected four letters and presented them sequentially in the same place on the CRT screen. After observing several repetitions , the subjects typed in the order, and the computer responded with the correct order on the teletype. Unfortunately, subjects got all the orders right. Since it was very easy to name each letter as it appeared, subjects were able to store the labels for later output. So long as the letters were visible, subjects had no problem.

Once we discovered this obvious flaw, it took about 10 min to correct. We then programmed the letters to appear in different spatial positions (each letter had its own characteristic spatial position and temporal position in the sequence). Now the subjects watched the recycling letters jumping around the screen and, after 10 cycles of four letters each, typed in what they though the sequence was.

We quickly discovered that this arrangement produced an interesting and consistent illusion: When two temporally adjacent letters happened to be presented on opposite sides of the CRT, one right and one left, the left one usually appeared to precede the right one (even when their temporal order was the reverse). We subsequently ran about a half-dozen experiments to follow up this observed temporal order error (Sekuler, 1976).

One other point should be emphasized: It is vital to ensure that the display actually has the temporal and spatial characteristics you thought you had programmed. After we had first discovered the temporal order error, we stopped experimentation for 2 days and did nothing but verify our stimulus in every way we could think of. It has been our experience that one has to be extremely careful, particularly with complex stimuli being generated and plotted at very high rates. This is particularly important when one is using devices (some display processors) that may impose subtle orderings of their own on the programmed stimuli.

BREADBOARDING FOR RAPID CONTRAST SENSITIVITY MEASUREMENTS

There is another demonstration from our laboratory of the minicomputer's breadboardability. Increasingly, vision researchers have recognized the need to characterize the spatial-transfer characteristic of the eye-brain system more completely than simple acuity measures permit (Sekuler, 1974). This need can be satisfied by measuring the spatial contrast sensitivity function (CSF). This function relates the contrast at which a target grating is just visible to the spatial frequency of the grating. Contrast is defined as the difference between the maximum and minimum luminances divided by the space-average luminance.

The CSF, if it is to be well defined, requires 45 min to an hour since a large number of spatial frequencies must be tested. Typically, measurements are made at each of 12 to 15 different, logarithmically spaced frequencies for a well-defined curve. Besides its basic import for vision research the CSF has been shown to have considerable potential in the clinic for identifying visual-system pathology (Bodis-Wollner, 1976). For both reasons, it would be good if the CSF could be measured rapidly enough to make it feasible for standard clinical application. Unfortunately, 45 min to an hour is far too long.

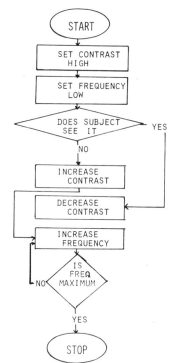

FIG. 6.3.   Flow chart for computer program that runs the tracking procedure for contrast-sensitivity function measurement.

Paul Tynan and I (Tynan & Sekuler, 1977) set out to adapt von Bekesy's audiometer (1947) for vision. Our goal was to develop an easily administered, rapid method for determining a patient's CSF. The most convenient way to implement the procedure was to use our minicomputer as a breadboard. Our aim, once the implementation was trial-proven, was to transfer the system to an easily portable, microprocessor-based device. But here let us focus on the original setup.

In Bekesy's (1947) system, a swept-frequency tone was presented to the listener, whose task was to maintain the tone at the threshold of visibility. When the listener depressed a switch, the intensity of the tone diminished; when he released the switch, intensity increased. In this way, the intensity of the swept-frequency tone tracked the locus of threshold values for a large range of frequencies. This procedure has been proved easy for virtually all listeners to perform, another attractive feature from our point of view.

The display was based on a Tektronix 7000 series oscilloscope since its high electron-beam accelerating-potential, coupled with a P31 phosphor, ensured high mean luminance (about 100 cd/m^2). An internal time base (ramp) produced a frame rate of 140 Hz. The y-axis signal, a 100 kHz triangle wave, provided a uniform raster by sweeping the beam up and down. The sinusoidal z-axis modulation was taken from a function generator operating in tone-burst mode. This means that (1) a sine wave was available at the output as long as we kept the proper input on to the function generator, and (2) the sine wave output always started in the same phase. The tone-burst feature makes it easy to present stable gratings: Turning the tone burst on with the x-axis signal insures that the z-axis modulation is phased-locked to the x-axis sweep on the oscilloscope.

But where does our breadboarded minicomputer enter into the picture? The computer had several tasks. First, it had to provide two time bases: one, for the logarithmic sweep of spatial frequency over the range of 0.5 to 30 cycles/degree; second, for the contrast sweep in response to the subject's switch closures and releases. Spatial frequency was swept by a variable voltage output by the computer to the frequency modulation input of the z-axis function generator. Contrast was swept by a computer input to the amplitude modulation of the same function generator.

Note that these two time-bases are interactive. If, for example, the contrast swept too slowly relative to changes in spatial frequency, our CSFs would be distorted by hysteresis; if contrast swept too quickly the variance in subjects' performance would be unacceptably high. Also, if the spatial-frequency change occurred too fast for subjects to keep up with, our CSFs would also be distorted. The computer made it easy to try various combinations of the two time bases, finally hitting on one that was comfortable for subjects and, at the same time, seemed to provide valid CSF. Figure 6.3 shows the program flow for the CSF tracker.

The computer sweeps over our spatial frequency range in 6 min whereas the subject-controlled contrast sweeps at 4 dB/sec. Contrast sensitivity function is graphed online on an $x-y$ plotter. A typical plot is shown in Fig. 6.4.

After plotting the raw track, the computer determines the midpoints of peaks and troughs and fits a curve to the data by convolving the midpoints with a smoothing function. This smoothed form of the track helps to summarize the data and brings its important features out of the noise.

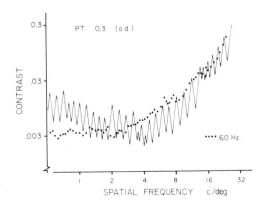

FIG. 6.4.   Typical data from the swept-frequency measurement of contrast sensitivity. Jagged line gives data for one observer and a stimulus that flickers slowly (0.3 Hz). Dots give midpoints of similar data collected from same observer but with more rapidly flickering stimulus (6.0 Hz). Note the change between the two sets of data at low spatial frequencies.

Sensing the state of the subject's switch and adjusting the amplitude modulation and frequency modulation DACs is a trivial use of a full minicomputer system. But being able to breadboard on the system did let us arrive quickly at a quasi-optimum set of parameters for transfer to a less flexible but less expensive, portable microcomputer.

The computer also helped us deal with the fact that the relationship between CRT contrast and modulating (Z) voltage varied with spatial frequency. Such variation is quite common and needs to be factored out of the data. We measured the voltage-contrast relationship over the range of spatial frequencies of interest and fit a polynomial of high order to the data. This polynomial was incorporated into the computer program that ran the CSF track. The amplitude-modulating signal from the computer to the z-axis function generator compensated for the expected variation in CRT response with Z-axis frequency. When the program was to produce a spatial frequency at which we know the CRT response would otherwise be diminished, we boosted the amplitude modulation to increase the CRT response. This insured that when we wanted a certain contrast, that contrast would actually occur, regardless of the CRT frequency response.

We validated the CSFs obtained using this continuous, Bekesy method by asking subjects to perform a similar task but without swept spatial frequency. For 30 sec only a grating of one spatial frequency appeared. During this period subjects used their computer-connected switch to control the contrast of the grating, keeping it at threshold. Measurements were made at nine different spatial frequencies, spanning the entire range of interest. We began with the lowest spatial frequency and worked up to the highest. Then, to measure test–retest reliability, we returned to the original, low spatial frequency once again.

Two outcomes are noteworthy. First, the thresholds defined by this discrete procedure were superimposable upon the contrast thresholds obtained using the swept frequency method; second, there was poor correspondence between the original run with the low spatial frequency grating to its subsequent retest. The observers almost always ended up with retest thresholds that were higher than the original. The cause was simple: Observers who had been tested with an ascending series of spatial frequencies were not expecting the sudden switch. As a result, they did not see the low-frequency grating until it had reached quite high contrast.

I will return to other, similar effects of stimulus uncertainty in computer-controlled vision research later. For the moment, it is sufficient to note that when subjects were told to expect a low-frequency grating at the end of the sequence (and were reminded of its impending presentation by a distinctive tone), test–retest reliability became quite satisfactory, suggesting that the method was not subject to any serious nonstationarity.

MINICOMPUTERS AS SOURCES OF CONTROLLED NOISE

The detection of a signal presented against a noisy background is a fundamental task observers are asked to perform in various areas of vision research. By manipulating the relationship between the characteristics of the noise and the to-be-detected signal, researchers can learn a good deal about the sensitivity and tuning of the mechanisms responsible for detection. The analytic power of this paradigm can be enhanced by having a computer tailor the noise to suit a particular purpose. One such example has already been mentioned (Mostafavi & Sakrison, 1976); let us consider several others here.

The first is an application from the laboratory at Northwestern. Karlene Bell and I have been using reaction times to determine the character of human motion-sensitive mechanisms. This effort was stimulated by the success of Pfingst, Heinz, Kimm, and Miller (1975) in using reaction times to measure supra-threshold as well as threshold auditory-sensitivity functions.

We wanted to measure sensitivity to movement using random dot patterns as stimuli. To avoid contamination by the presence of particular orientation components, we wished to use isotropic patterns, patterns that had equal energy along all meridia. Since they are members of a generally useful stimulus class, let me offer some comments about these patterns. Each point to be plotted requires two pseudo-random numbers, one for the x- and one for the y-coordinate. If the patterns are to be truly isotropic, there must be no correlation between: (1) x- and y-coordinates of the points; (2) x-coordinate of one point and x-coordinate of another; and (3) y-coordinate of one point and y-coordinate of another. The routines that generate these random numbers can be tricky, leading to non-zero correlations. In fact, we once discovered that as an artifact of the number used to seed the random-number generator, a nonisotropic pattern was produced. This lack of isotropy would have distorted our results had we not discovered the nonisotropy in the optical Fourier transform of the pattern. Using a photographic transparency of the pattern, it is a relatively simple test to carry out (Lipson, 1972).

Having verified the isotropy of our random-dot patterns, we first determined that subjects responded with equal latency regardless of the direction in which the dots moved. On each trial the pattern appeared first as a stationary set of dots and then, without warning, instantly accelerated to $4°/\text{sec}$. The movement, in which all dots appeared to travel as though rigidly connected on a sheet, continued until subjects hit a telegraph key, signalling that they had detected the motion.

We next measured reaction times to the same motion following various kinds of directional noise. In the simplest kind of experiment, the stationary pattern in the foreperiod was replaced by one that underwent a real-time 2-dimensional random walk. In this stimulus, the dots appeared to move randomly (again, spatially linked) from frame to frame. As before, without warning, the dots stopped their random oscillation and accelerated instantaneously to $4°$/sec.

The substitution of this random-walk foreperiod stimulus for the stationary pattern increased reaction time by about 50 msec (a 25% increment). This random oscillation contained noise uniformly distributed over all possible directions, forcing the observers to detect the uniform motion in the presence of noise. Under normal circumstances outside the laboratory, observers must discriminate the movement of objects from the retinal image movements caused by changes in eye position. Since the eyeball is constantly in motion, the observers' task outside the laboratory is much like that faced by our subjects: to discriminate steady, unidirectional motion from random oscillations.

Before going on to describe the experimental use of this noise, let us consider how it is generated. To begin, a pseudo-random number generator is used to get the initial coordinates of 512 spatially random dots; the coordinates are stored in a table as pairs $x_1, y_1, x_2, y_2, \ldots, y_{512}$. A second table also computed before the actual display was received, contained a set of 512 pairs of x- and y-increments. The increment values were computed by a routine that converts from polar coordinates to Cartesian. For each pair of increments, a pseudorandom number, θ, in the range 0 to 2π, was generated and passed as an argument to the conversion routine. Letting x_i be the ith x-axis increment and y_i be the ith y-axis increment, the routine computed

$$x_i = A \cos (\theta)$$

and

$$y_i = A \text{ sine } (\theta)$$

where A is the amplitude of the desired displacement of the dots plotted in the ith frame. In our experiments the value of A was held constant at a value that would produce instantaneous velocities (frame-to-frame) of 4 deg/sec, the same as the velocity of the to-be-detected unidirectional motion. In each frame, 512 dots were plotted at a rate of 33 msec/frame.

Before any dot was plotted, an x-increment was added to its x-coordinate and a y-increment to its y-coordinate. In each frame a constant pair of x- and y-increments were used to displace all the dots; but from frame-to-frame the pair changed, being selected from the previously stored table of 512 increment pairs. The effect was a 2-dimensional random walk. The the subjects, the stimulus looked as though someone had picked up the CRT and was shaking it violently, rapidly, and randomly in a frontoparallel plane.

Note that since our increments from the random walk came from a table of fixed length, the actual random walk would, after the entire table was exhausted, repeat. This repetition was never noticeable to our observers, since in most of our experiments the random walk was only presented for 1 to 2 sec, and it would have taken 16.9 sec to exhaust the table completely and begin again (i.e., 512 frames of dots at 33 msec each requires 16.9 sec).

One other comment about this display. By slightly modifying the plotting routine, we could generate two different versions of random walks In the one described above, we had a random walker who suffered from amnesia. The increment pairs were always added to the original, starting position of the dots. This caused the walk to be noncumulative; on any frame the position of each dot was uncorrelated with its position on the preceding frame. An alternative procedure, more strictly a true random walk, would have cumulated the steps taken by the dots. This cumulative random walk could be created in a variety of ways. Here is one which would execute the fastest: Let the table of increments be computed as described earlier but now, before any dots are displayed, perform the additional calculation of cumulating x- and y-increments. Again, letting x_i be the ith x-axis increment and y_i the ith y-axis increment, substitute the sum

$$x_1 + x_2 + x_3 + ... + x_{n-1} + x_n \quad \text{for } x_n$$

and

$$y_1 + y_2 + y_3 + ... + y_{n-1} + y_n \quad \text{for } y_n$$

After this set of substitutions has been carried out for all 512 pairs of increments, the stimulus display can proceed as before. Although this cumulative random walk is consistent with the traditional definition of a 2-dimensional random walk, it has some statistical properties that are undesirable for some of our experimental purposes. But I will indicate what they are in a moment.

With either cumulative or noncumulative random walks, on the average, the pattern is just as likely to oscillate in one direction as in any other. This, of course, was achieved by using random numbers uniformly distributed over the interval 0 to 2π to produce the table of increments.

We next wanted to determine how the detectability of unidirectional motion would be altered if the observer had to discriminate it, not from a true random walk but from a restricted walk. In the domain of spatial frequency, Stromeyer and Julesz (1972) found that only noise within a limited band around the test-grating frequency could mask the grating. We wondered whether a similar result might hold for visual motion: Would the detectability of upward motion, for example, be affected only by the upward components of the oscillating pattern? This question is important for theoretical reasons since an affirmative answer would permit us to apply the concept of the critical band (Fletcher, 1940) or tuned filter to the study of visual motion.

In one set of experiments, reaction times were measured to upward moving dots (4°/sec) following a foreperiod in which the subject viewed the same dots in oscillation. This time, however, restrictions were placed on the oscillations, reducing the amplitude of those oscillations that went in certain directions. Suppose, for example, we wished to reduce oscillations in a band of directions

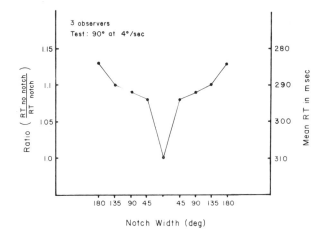

FIG. 6.5. Mean reaction times to onset of unidirectional movement following a quasi-randomly oscillating dot pattern. Test movement was upwards; increasing notch width implies that oscillations were prevented in an increasingly broad band of directions around upward. As the energy of the oscillations in the band around upwards decreases, reaction times also decrease.

around upward ($\pi/2$ in radians); assume that the desired band of reduced amplitudes is k radians in width. Instead of using random numbers in the range 0 to 2π to compute the table of increment values, we would replace any random numbers in the interval from $[(\pi/2) - (k/2)]$ to $[(\pi/2) + (k/2)]$ with numbers from outside this interval. This replacement ensures that the dot pattern, using the restricted table of increments, will oscillate randomly but with diminished amplitude in the band of directions around upward. Incidentally, forced-choice experiments have shown us that the presence of this restriction on the random oscillation is very difficult to detect until the restricted band gets quite large (i.e., $\pi/2$ radians or larger). Ball and I (1977) measured reaction times to upward motion following the random length foreperiods in which oscillations were presented in bands of various width, centered about upward. Figure 6.5 shows the outcome for three observers. As the band of reduced amplitudes covered an increased set of directions and the power of the oscillations in the band of directions around upward diminished, the reaction time decreased. This general approach has produced good measurements of the directional tuning of human visual mechanisms sensitive to different directions. In addition, we have been able to relate the differences in tuning to the discriminability of changes in the direction of motion.

Incidentally, the drawback to using a cumulative restricted-random walk is that the entire pattern undergoes a systematic drift in the direction opposite the center of the band of forbidden directions. This systematic drift would allow subjects to recognize the presence of the forbidden band; since the rate of drift would depend upon the width of the forbidden band, subjects might also be able to use rate of drift as a cue. Use of a noncumulative random walk eliminates the drift.

Without too much difficulty, the same basic stimulus can be used in another line of research. Ball and I have developed a method for allowing each dot to follow an independent trajectory rather than move in a manner that preserves the spatial-phase relationships among all the dots. The basic experiment requires the observer to detect a set of dots that tend to move in the same direction in the midst of a larger set of dots that undergo independent 2-dimensional random walks. The two sets of dots, the directional and the random, are spatially interspersed, and the aim of the research is to identify the parameters that control the detection of coherence. Julesz and Tyler (1976) have done analogous experiments on the detection of coherence in dynamic random-dot stereograms.

Two separate tables of increments are computed, one to be used for the undirectionally moving dots and the other with the randomly moving dots. The plotting program cycles, alternating one frame of undirectional movement with one frame of random movement. The alternation is sufficiently fast that the two sets of dots appear to be on the screen simultaneously and moving without flicker. [Tynan and Sekuler (1975) temporally interleaved plotting from two tables to create some of their spatially complex moving patterns.]

Here, just the technique for plotting the two components of motion is considered. As before, a table of x- and y-increment pairs is set up. But now, instead of using a constant increment pair for all the dots in one frame, a different pair is used for each dot. If we wish each dot to move along a constant path (although different from paths of its fellow dots), a fixed increment pair is associated with each dot. Statistically, this is a peculiar kind of randomness since, following any one dot's path over frames, the movement is not random; any dot follows a fixed path. The randomness resides in the aggregate, in the relationship of one dot's path to that of its fellows.

If we wish to have each dot undergo its own independent random walk, we allow the increment pair added to any dot's starting x- and y-coordinates to vary from frame-to-frame. A simple way to achieve this, while preventing the observer from detecting the repeating association of particular $x-y$ starting coordinates and $x-y$ increment pairs, is to make the table of increment pairs very much longer than the table of $x-y$ starting coordinates and to make sure that the length of the increment table is not an even multiple of the starting coordinate table's length (e.g., 4000 vs. 512). This way, if the plotting program sequences through the tables, two-starting coordinates and two-increment coordinates per point, each point will undergo its own independent random walk, and the paths will not repeat until very many frames have been plotted.

Note that by biasing the values of the angles used as arguments for the routine that generates the increment table, we can control the statistics of the random movement. This gives us the capability of producing any desired approximation to randomness, ranging in graded fashion from the case of complete randomness (paths of various dots are randomly distributed in a uniform fashion over all directions, 0 to 2π) to the case of extreme nonrandomness (all dots following identical trajectories). Incidentally, another dimension for variation can be produced by making A, the amplitude parameter for the random walk, itself a random or quasi-random variable.

In another use of computer-produced noise, Sperling (1976) presented a brief description of some preliminary experiments designed to isolate subclasses of motion detectors. Complex temporal luminance waveforms were presented at each of two different locations. If the locations were reasonably close together and the temporal waveforms identical except for a small phase shift (e.g. one display always lags slightly behind the other), we would have an extension of the usual study of 2-point stroboscopic movement

As Sperling (1976) points out, his method can produce sequences in which the luminance waveforms at a number of different points in the field would be uncorrelated for all but particular temporal and spatial separations or bands of separations. One could, of course, also vary the amplitude of the uncorrelated (noise) signals at the other locations. This sort of complex, computer-driven display would be quite easy to implement, either with a large array of LEDs or an x–y CRT display. Although as of this writing Sperling has not published any of his results, I would expect that his method could provide sensitive tests of a number of models of human-movement detectors. By logical necessity, all of these models are basically reducible to schemes for detecting temporal cross-correlations. [See Sekuler, Pantle, and Levinson (1978) for a general discussion of these models.] Using simple, computer-controlled two-frame random-dot displays, Lappin and Bell (1976) have verified the correlational character of the detection of coherent movement in the midst of uncorrelated noise. Related observations have been reported by Pollack (1972). It remains to be seen whether the simple principles that emerged from Lappin and Bell's two-frame paradigm are easily extrapolable to an extended train of frames approximating everyday motion.

As a final example of the use of noise in connection with computer-controlled vision research, I shall consider the elegant experiments of Srinivassan and Bernard (1977) with the common housefly, *Musca domestica*. The computer produced a vertically oriented moving square-wave grating on an $x–y$ CRT display. The grating which could be moved either to the left or right, was summed with visual noise by means of a differential input to the $x–y$ display. The stimulus-induced optomotor response of a tethered fly was measured by means of a force transducer. The noise was generated offline, under computer control, and recorded on tape for later use. If the noise were presented alone on the display, it would have appeared as evanescent, vertical, dark and bright bars of random width; this pattern would have changed from frame-to-frame (raster rate of 60 Hz).

The computer provided three signals to the CRT: a slow ramp x-sweep, a high-speed ramp (via a triggered function generator to the y-raster), and a square-wave modulation to the one side of the differential z-input. Taking advantage of the fly's poor acuity, Srinivassan and Bernard (1977) used a raster consisting of only 256 vertical lines (spatial separation of 21 min of visual angle).

To measure *Musca's* threshold for detecting motion, Srinivassan and Bernard (1977) recorded the optomotor response in the presence of increasing noise amplitudes. As the noise grew stronger, the optomotor response first remained constant and then fell off sharply, allowing the threshold to be estimated quite cleanly. In the main experiments, the fly was able to detect motion whose amplitude was only one-eighth that of the noise to which it was embedded. A pilot experiment with a human observer yielded approximately the same level of sensitivity.

Srinivassan and Bernard's (1977) description of their procedure for making the moving square grating sounds surprisingly unsophisticated: "Moving gratings are produced by depositing the content of each location into the appropriate neighboring location immediately after it is read . . . This procedure is more efficient than shifting the contents of all locations after completing a raster [p. 610]." There are a variety of alternative procedures that would have reduced the number of data transfers and, perhaps, enabled the computer to play some role in the measurement of the optomotor responses or enabled the generation of a spatially more dense raster. This latter capability would have helped convince me of the comparability of measurements made on *Musca* and *Homo sapiens*. The excellent visual acuity of the latter species makes me wonder about the assumption that the sparse raster in these experiments can produce comparable visual effects for the two species. The comparability is further jeopardized by the different indicator responses used with the two species: optomotor with *Musca* and a conscious, verbal description of the detected pattern with *Homo*. But these are only minor criticisms of an otherwise excellent paper one that certainly makes creative use of noise in conjunction with a computer-controlled display.

SELECTED USES OF MINICOMPUTERS IN VISUAL PHYSIOLOGY

Minicomputers have assisted widely in the determination of the receptive fields and trigger features of single neurons at various stages of the mammalian visual system. These applications have involved a number of approaches; I shall consider a few. Spinelli (1967) used an $x–y$ CRT display to map receptive fields. In some of the experiments from Spinelli's laboratory, mapping was done using single, computer-controlled moving dots. One notable feature of this approach is that the computer also generates easily interpretable plots of firing rates as a function of the dot's position in the field. Unfortunately, there has been some question about the relationship between field maps produced by this method and those produced by conventional means (Barlow, Levick, & Westheimer, 1966).

There has been a growing recognition of the possibility that manual mapping of a receptive field may be biased by the experimenter's expectation of what the field should look like; that expectation may influence the choice of stimuli to be tested and, consequently, the ultimate map that is produced (Stryker & Sherk, 1975). As a result, the availability of sophisticated and convenient computer-controlled mapping systems is to be welcomed.

In at least two laboratories, at M.I.T. (Stryker & Sherk, 1975) and the University of Rochester (Emerson & Gerstein, 1977), sophisticated computer systems are now being used routinely to map receptive fields, to process and summarize data in theoretically interesting and informative ways. For example, once a single cell has been clearly isolated and several basic manual assessments made (e.g. general location and size of field), the M.I.T. group uses a minicomputer to determine the cell's orientation "preference," response to stimulus length variation at the most preferred orientation, response to light and dark moving edges, and response to various kinds of stationary flashes (Schiller, Finlay, & Volman, 1976a). The important things to emphasize are: (1) the ease with which this battery of computer-run tests can be made; (2) the objectivity that can be programmed into the procedures; and (3) the possible theoretical gain that accrues.

The computer programs used to assess the cells' characteristics enable stimulus conditions to be presented in random order. For example, orientation specificity could be measured and the optimum orientation identified by moving a bar across the receptive field in a number of different orientations, presented in random order. Schiller, Finlay, and Volman (1976a) point out that such randomization is crucial because of the inherent short-term variability of cortical neurons' responses.

Although a number of laboratories are working on mammalian cortical visual physiology, there is no agreement on the best set of stimuli to probe the system, nor is there agreement on the relationships, if any, among the various possible measures that people have taken. Because of the availability of the computer, Schiller and his colleagues have been able to study more than 1000 neurons in the monkey striate cortex and, with each neuron, to collect substantial data from a large number of tests. The availability of the various dependent measures allowed Schiller, Finlay, and Volman (1976b) to determine whether the various measures were sufficiently correlated to suggest that they might be nonindependent. In addition, Schiller et al. were able to apply multivariate discriminant analysis (a rarity in neurophysiology) to develop improved differentiation on the basis of a linear sum of several different dependent measures of simple and complex cortical cells.

Finally, the work of Wurtz and his colleagues (e.g., Wurtz & Mohler, 1976) deserves citation as an important, sustained, and creative use of minicomputers. Much of Wurtz's work with awake, behaving monkeys is concerned with the effect of behavioral significance or attention on the response of single cells in cerebral cortex or superior colliculus. In a typical experiment, the computer is required to monitor the monkey's eye position, control the behavioral reinforcements, turn a fixation point on or off, and, at various times following a change in fixation point luminance, present a second visual target at a desired position away from original fixation. This second visual target might or might not fall in the previously determined receptive field of a cell from which Wurtz is recording. By making reinforcement contingent upon the execution of a saccade away from fixation to the new target, Wurtz can examine the change in the cell's response to the stimulus within its receptive field.

In one recent paper, Wurtz and Mohler (1976) found that, like cells in superior colliculus, visually driven cells in the frontal eye fields showed substantial and specific enhancement of response when the monkey used the stimulus as a target for a saccade. This enhancement was not present in the striate cortex, supporting the functional distinction between retinocortical and retinocollicular branches of the visual system. Although the superior colliculus is a poor analyzer of stimulus properties, its cells being less fussy in their response, the colliculus, according to Wurtz and Mohler (1976), does seem to "evaluate the significance of the stimulus to a remarkable degree. They [the cells] show a selective enhancement with eye movements directed toward their receptive fields ... and many cells also differentiate between stimulus movement resulting from an eye movement and those resulting from object movements in the environment [p. 772]." In this research, the minicomputer has been invaluable as a controller of complex stimulus and response contingenties; without the computer the work would simply have been impossible.

HYBRID SYSTEM: THE USE OF EXTERNAL HARDWARE

Because of the enormous bandwidth required to produce good computer-controlled displays for vision research, many investigators develop special hardware to reduce the otherwise impossible burden on the CPU. I feel that even when such a development is not absolutely crucial, burdens should be shifted from software and the CPU to hardware especially designed to accomplish specific and relatively limited tasks. The availability of such hardware makes the programmer's life more bearable and holds out the promise for increased computer capability. A similar attitude has been expressed in a different context by Arnold (1976). In the following discussion, I consider some selected and non-representative attempts to develop special-purpose hardware.

Gratings, of course, have become a major stimulus tool in vision research. Moreover, for a variety of theoretical reasons, experimenters often require the gratings to be temporally modulated or varied in phase, either discretely or smoothly. Various schemes for producing moving gratings under computer control (e.g., Srinivassan & Bernard, 1977) require that the computer run at full speed just to create the grating, leaving no time for any other function. One alternative is to construct a specialized analog computer (Arnett, 1976; Brown, 1977; Rogers, 1976; Shapley & Rossetto, 1976), but these stand-alone devices are often quite expensive and lack the inherent flexibility of the computer.

Tynan and Armstrong (1977) developed a system that combines computer software with a minimum of hardware construction. In fact, the only new hardware required cost less than $5.00. Figure 6.6 provides a function block diagram of their system. The display is produced on a standard, high-frequency oscilloscope, with a beam capable of being externally swept. The computer initiates a display frame with a sync pulse.

The sync pulse triggers a ramp generator that produces the CRT's horizontal sweep. The sync pulse also indirectly controls the function generator that modulates the CRT z-axis. Two one-shots introduce a computer-variable delay between the sync pulse and the activation of a function generator. The sync pulse causes the first one-shot to fire for a duration determined by a DAC voltage from the computer. The trailing edge of the one-shot's output triggers a second one-shot that fires for a fixed duration, slightly exceeding the duration of the horizontal sweep of the CRT. The output of this second one-shot turns on the z-axis function generator operating in tone-burst mode. In tone-burst mode: (1) the generator produces a sine wave whenever the second one-shot goes high; (2) the sine wave always starts in precisely the same phase; and (3) the sine wave stays on as long as the input is high. Since the delay between the start of the horizontal sweep and the onset of the sinusoidal z-modulation depends upon the DAC voltage, the computer can control the spatial position of the grating on the

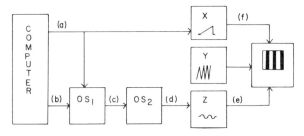

FIG. 6.6.   Block diagram of Tynan-Armstrong system for generating moving or oscillating gratings on an oscilloscope. See text for details.

CRT. To produce smooth movement, for example, the computer must increase the first one-shot's duration by a constant increment in each frame; after the grating moves one period the one-shot resets to its initial delay. This produces a grating that moves rightward. A leftward moving grating is produced by decreasing the first one-shot's duration from frame-to-frame. Of course, other forms of movement (square-wave or sinusoidal oscillations or various kinds of acceleration or deceleration) can also be produced. In addition, interleaving left and right movement produces counterphase gratings. In the system implemented by Tynan and Armstrong (1977), the frame rate is 140 Hz; this means that once every 7 msec, the CPU has to devote about 10 μsec to the display, leaving ample time for other tasks.

Vision experiments often require spatially partitioned stimuli. For example, it may be necessary to present different patterns in the center and surround of the field (Tynan & Sekuler, 1975). Or, it may be necessary to stimulate one circumscribed region of the field and allow that region to vary from trial-to-trial. Unfortunately, computer-controlled CRT displays do not easily lend themselves to this kind of partitioning. Suppose, for example, that one wanted to make a display of dynamic or moving dots on an $x-y$ CRT. Suppose further that one wanted to present the dots only in a circular region of the CRT, allowing the size of the region to vary between trials. Using software, one would have to calculate, before plotting any dot, whether the coordinates of that dot were inside or outside the allowable boundaries. Lengthy computations would be required to make this determination, making flickerless, real-time presentation of appreciable numbers of dots impossible. The CPU would have to take the coordinates, x_i and y_i, of the putative point, calculate $\sqrt{x_i^2 + y_i^2}$ and then check to see if the resulting value fell inside or outside the allowable, limiting radius.

Instead of this software approach, Tynan, Armstrong, and I designed and built a device that electronically partitions a CRT into several concentric circular or elliptical areas (Fig. 6.7). The heart of the device is an Intronix VM101 vector operator module. It continuously computes the square root of the sum of the square of the two voltages samples from the computer's x- and y-coordinate DACs. The module's output is an analog voltage that represents the distance of the CRT beam from a reference position on x- and y-inputs. By adding DC voltages to the x- and y-inputs of the module, one can easily change the location of the reference position (and hence the origin of the circular area to be plotted or blanked).

The output of the MV101 goes into a comparator. When this voltage exceeds some DC reference voltage (R_1), the comparator changes state, and a single-pole double-throw analog switch is activated. To blank the dots in some region of the CRT display, one input to the analog switch is the train of z-intensify pulses from the computer; the other input is a blanking voltage. If the coordinates of a dot are in the forbidden zone, the device switches the blanking voltage to the z-input of the monitor; otherwise, the train of intensify pulses is allowed to pass

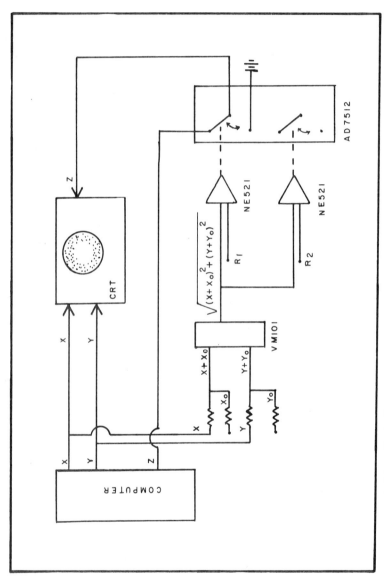

FIG. 6.7.   Block diagram of system for creating holes and patches in computer-controlled displays. Configuration shown assumes use of an x–y display monitor. VM101 is the Intronix vector module; R1 and R2 are a pair of reference voltages that feed into one input of comparators, NE521. AD7512 is a chip with two analog switches.

to the monitor. If we reverse the blanking and intensify connections to the analog switch, either of two complementary patterns can be produced: moving dots everywhere on the CRT *except* within some circular region, or moving dots *only* within some circular region with the rest of the CRT blank.

A second comparator and analog switch allows even more complex partitioning of the display. For example, the output of the first analog switch can feed into the second switch rather than directly into the z-axis of the monitor. If the comparator controlling the second analog switch has a higher reference voltage than the first, an annulus of moving dots can be produced, with the rest of the display blanked.

There are many variations on this basic operation. For example, threshold measurements have been made by attenuating rather than completely blanking dots in one zone of the screen. Also, one could implement 2- or 4-alternative spatial forced-choice procedures by varying the DC voltages that determine the position of the hole or patch with its radius. In principle, the same technique could turn a large screen display into a flexible, computer-controlled tangent screen for clinical use. In addition, continuously changing these voltages produces holes or patches that expand and contract or move in the frontal plane. We have used some of these capabilities to produce motion aftereffects (waterfall illusions) in the third dimension.

The partitioning device could also be used with raster type, grating displays (Arnett, 1976). Since the pattern being displayed is determined by the z-axis signal alone, several different gratings could be simultaneously presented in the center, annulus, and surround of the display. However, if the y-axis stroke rate exceeds 50 KHz, the frequency response of our inexpensive analog switches is exceeded, and the boundaries of display regions become fuzzy. This can be overcome by using switches with faster response times.

Uttal, Fitzgerald, and Eskin (1975) used analog elements in a hybrid minicomputer system in order to plot random dot stereograms in real time. As one might anticipate, the burden of computing the 2-dimensional projections of the 3-dimensional objects was carried quite well by the analog elements. The experimenter defined the general properties of the to-be-plotted stimulus: the size and depth position of some plane. Routines then computed the x–y and depth coordinates of dots that randomly covered the desired plane. The three values for each point were output via DACs to operational amplifiers. The op amps for x- and y-positions each had two inputs: one from the coordinate in question (x or y) and another from the depth signal. The depth signal conditioned the outputs of the x- and y-op amps to make them represent 2-dimensional projection of the pattern. In addition, a one-bit control voltage added to the x-axis signal determines whether the point would be plotted as part of the right eye or left eye view on the CRT. Basically, this was accomplished by adding the appropriate voltage to the x-axis input to the CRT, shifting the dot to one side or the other of the septum that isolated one eye's view from the other. This system was fast enough to compute and plot 12 dots per msec. The densest displays contained 50 points.

In many situations the speed of computation and display can be increased significantly if the CPU does not have to generate random numbers in real time. One solution, often impractical for reasons of storage limitations, is to reserve a large section of memory for a string of random numbers. The string can then be accessed using appropriate safeguards on sampling with replacement, etc. A second, preferred solution is to have hardware random-number generators like those used by Hogben, Julesz, and Ross (1976) and Ross (1976).

PSYCHOPHYSICS AND UNCERTAINTY

Because of some of the experimental capabilities they provide, minicomputers have had impact upon the methodology used in vision research. Since this volume contains an excellent chapter devoted exclusively to psychophysics (see Chapter 5), I shall keep my comments on the subject brief.

One obvious impact on vision research is an increased tendency to randomize and interleave testing with various stimuli. For example, studies of computer-controlled grating displays may interleave presentation of various spatial frequencies in an effort to run six or seven simultaneous tracks with a 2-alternative forced-choice procedure. Human nature being what it is, the more difficult it is to change spatial frequency (or some other analogous independent variable), the less likely experimenters are to randomize measurements with various frequencies. The computer, of course, makes it very easy to change the independent variable. We should be aware of the consequences of the experimental sophistication made possible by the minicomputer.

Computer-facilitated randomization may well reduce apparent sensitivity and do so in unpredictable and quite complex ways. Randomization produces stimulus uncertainty, a condition in which the detector has incomplete information about the to-be-detected target. Stimulus uncertainty reduces sensitivity, and the amount of the measured loss with randomization will depend on: (1) the character of the ensemble of potential stimuli; and (2) the presence of other sources of uncertainty that may swamp the effect of the randomization. Some of these effects can be quite large. For example, Karlene Ball and I (Sekuler & Ball, 1977) measured 2-alternative forced-choice detection of computer-controlled moving dots. At a particular luminance, when the dots always moved upward with a speed of 4°/sec, the subject could correctly identify the interval that contained the dots about 75% of the time. When the observer could not predict which direction the dots would move in — upward or rightward — although the luminance was the same as before, the subject could only identify the dot-containing interval 53% of the time. This drop in performance came about despite the fact that, in theory at any rate, the observer did not have to judge the direction of movement; the observer merely had to identify the interval containing dots. I am not arguing against randomization; I am merely proposing that we should be aware of the possible consequences. More of these are discussed by Cohn and Lasley (1974).

One final comment about psychophysical methodology and minicomputers. I am constantly surprised that the minicomputer has had so little impact on visual psychophysics. Basically, the methods that are used, even under the most innovative and sophisticated computer systems, do not represent any novel contribution that can be attributed to the advent of laboratory minicomputers. So let me suggest one line of development that may be fruitful. We all know that human observers can make responses that convey far more than one-bit; yet virtually all computer-oriented psychophysical procedures ignore this fact (e.g., PEST). Tracking procedure would be far more efficient if it were driven by responses of more than one bit.

At Northwestern, we have begun to develop such procedures. The basic idea is to use an adaptive procedure to home-in on the stimulus intensity or contrast that produces a particular response. Among the responses that our driver subroutines accept are reaction times and magnitude estimates. Consider one example of how the procedure works. Suppose that some study requires the generation of suprathreshold isosensitivity contours, the set of grating contrasts that for a variety of different spatial frequencies, all yield the same reaction time (it is already known that reaction time to grating onset varies with both contrast and spatial frequency). Using a very efficient search procedure, the subroutine would, for a given spatial frequency, first estimate reaction times produced by very high and very low contrasts. These reaction times would be less than and greater than the critical reaction time the routine was told to search for. In the simplest version of the subroutine, the dependent variable (reaction time) is assumed to be linear with the intensity or contrast dimension and, have estimated the reaction times associated with upper and lower points on the upper and lower portions of this linear function, the subroutine calculates new bracketing values of contrast that should approximate the desired reaction time.

Here is one way in which the search routine is used in a reaction time application. Assume that reaction time $(RT) = f(\text{stimulus contrast})$, where f is a decreasing linear function over some restricted contrast range of interest. Let C_t be the *unknown* contrast that would produce the desired, target reaction time, RT_t. Let C_H be a *known*, high contrast that preliminary testing has shown to produce a reaction time, RT_H, such that $RT_H < RT_t$. This inequality suggests that $C_H > C_t$. Let C_L be a *known*, low contrast that preliminary testing has shown to produce a reaction time, RT_L, such that $RT_L > RT_t$. This inequality suggests that $C_L < C_t$. Finally, C_n is the contrast used to test with on trial n; RT_n is the reaction time to C_n. On each trial we compute

$$C_n = C_L + \frac{RT_L - RT_t}{RT_L - RT_H}(C_H - C_L)$$

If, on any trial, $RT_n < RT_t$, we assume that $C_n > C_t$, and substitute $C_H = C_n$ before computing the new value of C_n. If, on any trial $RT_n > RT_t$, we presume that $C_n < C_t$, and substitute $C_L = C_n$, before computing the new value of C_n. The routine may be made to stop searching for C_t when either: (1) the value of RT_n is satisfactorily close to RT_t, (2) the variance of contrasts used over trials becomes satisfactorily low, or (3) when a sufficiently large number of trials has been run. In a typical reaction-time application, three reaction times are usually collected with the same contrast, the high and low reaction time is discarded, leaving the median reaction time to drive the search subroutine.

Of course, the search will take varying amounts of time depending upon the precision with which the experimenter needs to estimate the target value and the variability of the subject's responses. In addition, if the experimenter knows that the function relating the dependent variable to the independent variable is strongly nonlinear, the subroutine should be informed about the character of that nonlinearity. The subroutine could also be used to home-in on stimulus values that produce some constant level of magnitude estimate (i.e., "50"). By doing this for a variety of stimuli, one could generate families of suprathreshold isosensitivity functions for various response levels ranging upward from just above threshold.

The important thing is not so much the particular routine described here; it is merely an example. The important thing is that practicing psychophysicists should take greater advantage of both the minicomputer's potential for adaptive tracking and the real richness of the observer's responses.

MISCELLANEOUS USES OF MINICOMPUTERS

In addition to controlling various display devices, minicomputers have been widely used to control other devices in vision research, such as glow modulator tubes (Matin & Kornheiser, 1976), tachistoscopes, orientation of test gratings and position of density wedges in Maxwellian view systems (Brown & Black, 1976), slide projectors (Buckley & Gillman, 1973), and the $x-y$ position of a spot projected from a pair of orthogonally placed mirror galvanometers (Lisberger, Fuchs, King, & Evinger, 1975). This last application provided an interesting stimulus for the study of saccadic eye-movements. Gourlay, Gyr, Williams, and Willey (1975) used a computer-driven display to simulate the effects of various distorting and displacing prisms that have been used by other experimenters. This is one of several studies in which an on-line minicomputer allowed the observer's gaze position to be inserted into the stimulus loop (Estes, Allmeyer, & Reder, 1976; Shebilske, 1976). Finally, over the past several years, Mayzner and his colleagues (Mayzner, 1975; Mayzner, Tresselt, & Helfer, 1967) have used a computer-controlled CRT to explore many interesting spatio-temporal interactions among elements in a character display.

SUMMING-UP

Going back over several years' worth of vision and perception journals for this chapter convinced me that the minicomputer has really been an underachiever in the vision laboratory. Although a minicomputer need not be constantly used to capacity in order to earn its keep, most reported uses of minicomputers I came across were trivial at best. One difficulty is that for most vision research, a minicomputer and CRT is just not a match for a good optical system. But, of course, there have been some creative and fruitful uses of the minicomputer. These have been in research that uses the strength of the minicomputer: the ability to produce arbitrarily specified complex real-time temporal transformations of some stimulus. I believe this will continue to be the major vision research application for the foreseeable future.

REFERENCES

Arnett, D. Optical pattern generator for visual research. *Medical and Biological Engineering.* 1976, *14*, 532–537.

Arnold, J. T. Microprocessor application: A less sophisticated approach. *Science*, 1976, *192*, 519–523.

Aulhorn, E., & Harms, H. Visual perimetry. In D. Jameson & L. Hurvich (Eds.), *Handbook of sensory physiology* (Vol. VII/4). Berlin: Springer-Verlag, 1972.

Ball, K., & Sekuler, R. *Directional selectivity: Tuning functions and discrimination performance.* Paper presented at the meeting of the Psychonomic Society, Washington, D.C., November 1977.

Barlow, H. B., Levick, W. R., & Westheimer, G. Computer-plotted receptive fields. *Science*, 1966, *154*, 920.

Bodis-Wollner, I. Vulnerability of spatial frequency channels in cerebral lesions. *Nature*, 1976, *261*, 309–311.

Boynton, R. M. Vision. In J. B. Sidowski (Ed.), *Experimental methods and instrumentation in psychology*. New York: McGraw-Hill, 1966.

Brown, C. R. A digital technique for generating moving grating patterns on an oscilloscope. *Vision Research*, 1977, *17*, 299–300.

Brown, J. L., & Black, J. E. Critical duration for resolution of acuity targets. *Vision Research,* 1976, *16,* 309–315.

Buckley, P. B., & Gillman, C. B. The slide projector as a computer-operated visual display. *Behavior Research Methods & Instrumentation*, 1973, *5*, 104–106.

Campbell, S. Beyond symbolism: Imagery and the imagination. In F. Gruenberger (Ed.), *Computer graphics*. Washington, D.C.: Thompson Book Company, 1967.

Cohn, T. E., & Lasley, D. J. Detectability of a luminance increment: Effect of spatial uncertainty. *Journal of the Optical Society of America*, 1974, *64*, 1715–1719.

Cornsweet, T. N. The staircase method in psychophysics. *American Journal of Psychology*, 1962, *75*, 485–491.

Eastman, J. F., & Wooten, D. R. A general purpose, expandable processor for real-time computer graphics. *Computers & Graphics*, 1975, *1*, 73–77.

Emerson, R. C., & Gerstein, G. L. Simple striate neurons in the cat. I. Comparison of responses to moving and stationery stimuli. *Journal of Neurophysiology*, 1977, *40*, 119–135.

Entwisle, J. An image processing approach to computer graphics. *Computers & Graphics*, 1977, *2*, 111–117.

Erlebacher, A., & Sekuler, R. Perceived length depends on exposure duration. *Journal of Experimental Psychology*, 1974, *103*, 724–728.

Estes, W. K., Allmeyer, D. H., & Reder, S. M. Serial position functions for letter identification at brief and extended exposure durations. *Perception & Psychophysics*, 1976, *19*, 1–15.

Fletcher, H. Auditory patterns. *Review of Modern Physics*, 1940, *12*, 47–61.

Freeman, R. D., Mitchell, D. E., & Millodot, M. A neural effect of partial visual deprivation in humans. *Science*, 1972, *175*, 1384–1386.

Fry, G. Visibility of sine-wave gratings. *Journal of the Optical Society of America*, 1969, *59*, 610–617.

Gans, J. A. Consideration in the design of an automatic visual field tester. *Medical Research Engineering*, 1971, *10*, 7–11.

Gourlay, K., Gyr, J. W., Williams, S., & Willey, R. Instrumentation designed to simulate the effects of prisms used in studies of visual rearrangement. *Behavior Research Methods & Instrumentation*, 1975, *7*, 294–300.

Gourlay, K., Uttal, W. R., & Powers, M. K. VRS – A programming system for visual electrophysiological research. *Behavior Research Methods & Instrumentation*, 1974, *6*, 281–287.

Graeme, J. G., Tobey, G. E., & Huelsman, L. P. *Operational amplifiers*. New York: McGraw-Hill, 1971.

Heijl, A. Studies on computerized perimetry. *Acta Ophthalmologica*, 1977, Supplement Number 132, 3–42.

Helmers, C. This elephant never forgets. *Byte*, 1977, *2*, 6; 58–61.

Hogben, J. H., Julesz, B., & Ross, J. Short-term memory for symmetry. *Vision Research*, 1976, *16*, 861–866.

Jarvis, J. F. A graphical display system utilizing plasma panels. *Computers & Graphics*, 1975, *1*, 175–180.

Julesz, B., & Tyler, C. W. Neurontropy, an entropy-like measure of neural coorelations in binocular fusion and rivalry. *Biological Cybernetics*, 1976, *23*, 25–32.

Lappin, J. S., & Bell, H. H. The detection of coherence in moving random-dot patterns. *Vision Research*, 1976, *16*, 161–168.

Lipson, H. *Optical transforms*. New York: Academic Press, 1972.

Lisberger, S. G., Fuchs, A. F., King, W. M., & Evinger, L. C. Effect of mean reaction time on saccadic responses to two-step stimuli with horizontal and vertical components. *Vision Research*, 1975, *15*, 1021–1025.

Matin, L., & Kornheiser, A. Linked changes in spatial integration, size discrimination, and increment threshold with change in background diameter. *Vision Research*, 1976, *16*, 847–860.

Mayzner, M. S. Studies of visual information processing in man. In R. L. Solso (Ed.), *Information processing and cognition: The Loyola Symposium.* Hillsdale, N.J.: Lawrence Erlbaum Associates, 1975.

Mayzner, M. S., & Greenberg, J. Studies in the processing of sequentially presented inputs with overprinting paradigms. *Psychonomic Monograph Supplements,* 1971, *4*(4, Whole No. 52), 73–84.

Mayzner, M. S., Tresselt, M. E., & Helfer, M. S. A research strategy for studying certain effects of very fast sequential input rates on the visual system. *Psychonomic Monograph Supplements,* 1967, *2*(5, Whole No. 21), 73–81.

McCracken, T. E., Sherman, B. W., & Dwyer, S. J., III. An economical tonal display for interactive graphics and image analysis data. *Computers & Graphics,* 1975, *1*, 79–94.

Mezrich, J. J., & Rose, A. Coherent motion and stereopsis in dynamic visual noise. *Vision Research,* 1977, *17*, 903–910.

Mostafavi, H., & Sakrison, D. J. Structure and properties of a single channel in the human visual system. *Vision Research,* 1976, *16*, 957–968.

Newman, W. M., & Sproull, R. F. *Principles of interactive computer graphics.* New York: McGraw-Hill, 1973.

Pfingst, B. E., Heinz, R., Kimm, J., & Miller, J. Reaction-time procedure for measurement of hearing. I. Suprathreshold functions. *Journal of the Acoustical Society of America,* 1975, *57*, 421–430.

Pollack, I. Detection of changes in spatial position: Short-term visual memory or motion perception? *Perception & Psychophysics,* 1972, *11*, 17–27.

Potts, J. Computer graphics – Whence and hence. *Computers & Graphics,* 1975, *1*, 137–156.

Rogers, B. J. A technique for generating moving visual stimuli on a C.R.O. *Vision Research,* 1976, *16*, 415–417.

Ross, J. The resources of binocular perception. *Scientific American,* 1976, *234*, 80–86.

Safir, A. Computers in ophthalmology. *Investigative Ophthalmology,* 1976, *15*, 163–168.

Schiller, P. H., Finlay, B. L., & Volman, S. F. Quantitative studies of single-cell properties in monkey striate cortex. I. Spatiotemporal organization of receptive fields. *Journal of Neurophysiology,* 1976, *39*, 1288–1319. (a)

Schiller, P. H., Finlay, B. L., & Volman, S. F. Quantitative studies of single-cell properties in monkey striate cortex. V. Multivariate statistical analyses and models. *Journal of Neurophysiology,* 1976, *39*, 1362–1374. (b)

Sekuler, R. Spatial vision. *Annual Review of Psychology,* 1974, *25*, 195–232.

Sekuler, R. Seeing and the nick of time. In M H. Siegel & H. P. Ziegler (Eds.), *Psychological research*. Evanston, Ill.: Harper & Row, 1976.

Sekuler, R., & Ball, K. Mental set alters the visibility of seen movement. *Science,* 1977, *198*, 60–62.

Sekuler, R., Pantle, A., & Levinson, E. Physiological bases of motion perception. In H.-L. Teuber, R. M. Held, & H. Leibowitz (Eds.), *Handbook of sensory physiology* (Vol. VIII). Berlin: Springer-Verlag, 1978.

Sekuler, R., Tynan, P., & Levinson, E. Visual temporal order. *Science,* 1973, *180*, 210–212.

Shapley, R., & Rossetto, M. An electronic visual stimulator. *Behavior Research Methods & Instrumentation,* 1976, *8*, 15–20.

Shebilske, W. L. Extraretinal information in corrective saccades and inflow vs. outflow theories of visual direction constancy. *Vision Research,* 1976, *16*, 621–628.

Sperling, G. The description and luminance calibration of cathode ray oscilloscope visual displays. *Behavior Research Methods & Instrumentation,* 1971, *3*, 148–151. (a)

Sperling, G. Flicker in computer-generated visual displays: Selecting a CRO phosphor and other problems. *Behavior Research Methods & Instrumentation*, 1971, *3*, 151–153. (b)

Sperling, G. Movement perception in computer-drive visual displays. *Behavior Research Methods & Instrumentation*, 1976, *8*, 144-151.

Spinelli, D. N. Receptive field organization of ganglion cells in the cat's retina. *Experital Neurology*, 1967, *19*, 291–315.

Srinivassan, M. Y., & Bernard, G. D. The fly can discriminate movement at signal/noise ratios as low as one-eighth. *Vision Research*, 1977, *17*, 609–616.

Stromeyer, C. F., III, & Julesz, B. Spatial-frequency masking in vision: Critical bands and spread of masking. *Journal of the Optical Society of America*, 1972, *62*, 1221–1232.

Stryker, M. P., & Sherk, H. Modification of cortical orientation selectivity in the cat by restricted visual experience: A reexamination. *Science*, 1975, *190*, 904–905.

Tynan, P., & Armstrong, R. *Computer control of grating phase and movement.* Paper presented at the sixth conference on Use of Online Computers in Psychology, Washington, D.C., November 1977.

Tynan, P., & Sekuler, R. Simultaneous motion contrast: Velocity sensitivity and depth response. *Vision Research*, 1975, *15*, 1231–1238.

Tynan, P., & Sekuler, R. Rapid measurement of contrast sensitivity functions. *American Journal of Optometry and Physiological Optics,* 1977, *54,* 573–575.

Uttal, W. R., Fitzgerald, J., & Eskin, T. E. Parameters of tachistoscopic stereopsis. *Vision Research*, 1975, *15*, 705–712.

Van Gelder, P. CRT displays in the experimental psychology laboratory. *Behavior Research Methods & Instrumentation*, 1972, *4*, 102–103.

Virsu, V., & Lehtio, P. K. A microphotometer for measuring luminance on a CRT. *Behavior Research Methods & Instrumentation*, 1975, *7*, 29–33.

von Bekesy, G. A new audiometer. *Acta Otolaryngolica*, 1947, *35*, 411–422.

Warren, R. M., Obusek, C. J., Farmer, R. M., & Warren, R. P. Auditory sequence: Confusion of patterns other than speech or music. *Science*, 1969, *164*, 586–587.

Wilson, H. R., & Giese, S. C. Threshold visibility of frequency gradient patterns. *Vision Research*, 1977, *17*, 1177–1190.

Wurtz, R. H., & Mohler, C. W. Enhancement of visual responses in monkey striate cortex and frontal eye fields. *Journal of Neurophysiology*, 1976, *39*, 766–772.

7 The Minicomputer and Research in Hearing

Frederic L. Wightman
Auditory Research Laboratory (Audiology)
Northwestern University

INTRODUCTION

In the study of hearing, as in many disciplines, significant advances begin with the development of an idea or theory. Real progress however, is not represented by the theory itself, but by the research that it generates. Only through research can we actually learn about how things work and thus make progress. Progress in the study of hearing has been slow, and one important reason for this is simply that the research is hard to do. Experiments in hearing are heavily dependent on technology. As evidence for this, consider some of the history of the field.

The study of hearing, or hearing science as I will call it, is a relatively young discipline. While there can be no doubt about the monumental influence of the work of Helmholtz, Rayleigh, and others over a hundred years ago, systematic laboratory study of hearing began in the early part of this century. That this followed shortly after the development of the vacuum tube is no accident. It was the vacuum tube that made it possible for the first time to produce and control a pure tone, the stimulus that so much of hearing science has depended upon. Research conducted prior to this time suffered not from a lack of good ideas, but simply because it was not possible to generate a pure tone. In fact, it was not until 1938 that a source of high-quality pure tones (the Hewlett Packard 200-A audio oscillator) was available commercially. Research in hearing science made great strides forward in the 1920s, 30s, and 40s, although it was still a difficult and expensive business. The number of laboratories actively involved was small (Bell Telephone Labs and the Harvard Psychoacoustics Laboratory were two principal ones), and the research was still bound by the limitations of the available equipment. For example, at that time, it was still remarkably difficult to turn on and off a stimulus such as a pure tone in any sort of controlled way.

By the 1950s, hearing science had come into its own, and technological refine-
ments were in large part responsible. High-quality stimulus generation and control equipment was readily available at a cost bearable by a number of laboratories. The research, however, was still limited by the available technology; only
very simple stimuli (pure tones and noises) could be reliably produced. Whole
classes of experiments had to be deferred until the equipment could handle it.
For example, the production of multitone complexes, in which the amplitues
and phases of the tones could be individually adjusted, was beyond the capabilities of most facilities. Some years later, with the extensive application of
transistors, and in particular transistorized operational amplifiers, the situation
changed somewhat, but not dramatically. The equipment necessary to conduct
research in hearing became more reliable, smaller, and less expensive, but it was
basically the same equipment. Even the appearance of the digital computer on
many university campuses in the late 1950s did not have a significant impact on
hearing-science research. The principal function of the early computers was
data analysis, and hearing scientists needed much more help in gathering data than
in analyzing it.

The introduction of the first commercially available minicomputer by Digital
Equipment Corporation in 1963 marked the beginning of a revolution in laboratory research, particularly, in hearing research. It quickly became apparent that,
for reasons I hope to clarify shortly, the minicomputer could free the researcher
from the limitations imposed by conventional equipment. In spite of its high
cost (the first Digital Equipment Corporation PDP-8 systems cost over $20,000
in 1965), the minicomputer was immediately adopted as a principal research
tool by several hearing-science laboratories. In fact, the doctoral research of
several of my own colleagues, completed in the late 1960s could not have been
conducted without the minicomputer. Now, little more than a decade after they
were first introduced, minicomputers can be found in nearly all laboratories
involved in the study of hearing.

In order to understand the dependence of hearing science on technology and
to appreciate the tremendous impact of minicomputers, it may be useful to
review some of the basic principles that have guided research on hearing throughout its history. The long-range goal of this research is, of course, to understand
the processes of human hearing. In other words, we simply want to know how
the auditory system works. Since we are not at liberty to probe the inner work-
ings of an intact human auditory system, our research techniques must be
indirect. The most common approach has been to study input—output relations.
In this case, the input to the system is some acoustic stimulus, and the output is
a sensation. By carefully examining the relations between certain parameters of
the acoustic stimulus and features of the sensation produced by that stimulus,
we hope to reveal (and, indeed, we have to some degree) the rules governing the
operation of the intervening mechanisms. As in many areas of psychology, these
experiments amount to a search for invariance. We wish to know what transfor-

mation of the physical stimulus leave the response, a particular sensation, un-changed. To illustrate this point, consider just one attribute of auditory sensations, for example, loudness. We will know completely how the auditory system encodes loudness once we can write down all the ways in which an acoustic stimulus can be transformed and leave the loudness of that stimulus unchanged. In other words, the basic question in hearing science (and for psy-chology in general) is "what exactly is the stimulus?" or rather "what features of the physical stimulus are responsible for a particular sensation?"

This approach to the study of hearing, involving the study of relationships be-tween input and output quantities, is of course limited by the precision with which we can measure those quantities. Measurement of the output, auditory sensations, is a tricky business at best. Sensations are strictly private, covert events, and as such are not amenable to direct measurement. Indirect measures of sensations suffer from variability contributed by a host of uncontrolled fac-tors, such as bias, learning, attention, context. The search for techniques to reduce this variability has occupied generations of psychologists. In fact, one of the most influential developments in all psychology in the last quarter-century has been the application of a statistical technique (statistical decision theory) to separate the nonsensory variables that influence observer responses (bias, etc.) from the sensory variables (sensitivity) and hence to control variability. In spite of this, quantification of sensations remains a very difficult area, and the precision of even our best measures is questionable.

Measurement of the input to the auditory system (sound) is considerably more straightforward, since it is an observable, physical quantity; however, even these measurements are difficult and, for most of us, subject to considerable variabil-ity. The problem is that there are a great many interdependent factors that must be considered when making acoustic measurements, and although each one can be brought under control, it is often rather difficult to do so. For example, suppose we wish to measure the sound-pressure level (SPL) of various pure tones presented to a listener over headphones. What we would like, of course, is a measurement of SPL taken at the eardrum, but anywhere in the external ear will do. What is involved is the insertion of a small tube (probe tube) into the ear canal while the subject is wearing the headphones. The tube is connected to a microphone, amplifier, and voltmeter.

When making the measurements, however, or rather when attempting to con-vert voltmeter readings to sound-pressure level in the ear canal, several issues must be considered. Among these are the frequency of the tone, placement of the ear-phones on the listener's head, placement of the tube in the ear canal, the acous-tics of the tube, and the response of the microphone. Small changes in any one of these parameters can cause dramatic changes in measurement. Consequently, it is difficult to generalize from measurements of this sort; it is risky enough to try to generalize from one time to another on the same listener, let alone from one listener to another. This lack of generalizing ability, coupled with the sheer difficulty and inconvenience of making acoustical measurements, leads most of us in the field to perform relatively infrequent acoustic calibrations and to perform them in a highly simplified way (e.g., a standard coupler is used rather than a real ear). The voltage waveform measured across the headphone is taken as a direct reflection of the resulting acoustic stimulus. This is admittedly a significant compromise, and it potentially could introduce systematic bias into our experiments; however, there is no evidence that it has. In practice, the more serious problem appears to be the variability that is left uncontrolled by such procedures.

Specification of the input in terms of an electrical waveform certainly does not solve all of our problems. Although it is far easier to measure and control an electrical signal than an acoustic one, it is becoming clear that the precision and attention to detail that must be brought to bear in this area in order to conduct research in hearing is far greater than one might imagine. For example, consider a simple experiment in which we wish to measure the detectability of a tone burst. Obviously, the frequency, intensity, and duration of the signal are important and can readily be measured and controlled. But what about more subtle factors, such as starting phase and the details of the rise-fall envelope usually applied to prevent a "click" at onset and offset? In certain conditions these variables are quite important. The failure or inability to control the stimulus completely, at least in its electrical form, can have disastrous consequences, not only in terms of uncontrolled sources of variability, but also, potentially, in misinterpretations of experimental results.

To summarize, it can be said that hearing science involves a search for perceptual invariances through careful, detailed analysis of input- output relations. Precise measurement of the input, sound, and the output, sensations, is of paramount importance, and failure to control or measure sources of variability in those measurements can either obscure effects of potential interest or, worse, lead to systematic bias and misinterpretation of results.

Modern technology has provided hearing researchers with a degree of stimulus and response control that greatly expands the range of experiments that can be considered. The availability of high-quality, solid-state stimulus generation, measurement, and control equipment has had a great deal to do with this. It is the application of minicomputers in the research, however, that most recently has had the greatest impact. In the pages that follow, I describe several of the more important applications. Also a brief account of the essential theoretical considerations is included where appropriate. Most of the examples will be drawn from current practice in my own laboratory and, hence, is somewhat specific to that particular setting. Although this may not provide a complete picture of all the ways minicomputers are used in hearing-science research, it will probably give a representative sample. In many cases, when feasible, actual source listings of working programs are included. The point of doing this is primarily to emphasize the ease and simplicity of most of the techniques.

STIMULUS GENERATION

As soon as minicomputers were first used in hearing-science research, it became clear that one of the tasks for which they were ideally suited was stimulus generation. There are several reasons for this. First, the use of the computer for generation of experimental stimuli provides a degree of stability, flexibility, and precision simply not attainable by other means. Second, stimuli of almost arbitrary complexity can be produced relatively easily and individual parameters independently manipulated, usually with considerable speed and almost always with great precision. If a few simple rules are followed, computer generation of stimuli is quite trouble-free. In fact, it is so straightforward that I occasionally regret the fact that because none of my students has suffered the drudgery of daily calibration and adjustment of a dozen or so analog devices, they will probably never be able to appreciate the freedom provided by the computer.

Regardless of the complexity of the stimulus and the experimental use that will be made of it, the same general procedure is followed for getting a computer to produce it. First, an equation or a series of equations is written that defines the stimulus in some way, usually as a function of time. The equations are then translated into some kind of symbolic language that the computer can understand (in our laboratories this is FORTRAN). Since computers represent quantities in a discrete rather than continuous fashion, the equations written for the computer define the stimulus or "sample" it only at discrete, typically equally spaced instants of time. The next step is to have the computer evaluate the equations for as many time instants as may be required. For example, if the desired stimulus has a duration of 100 msec and (because of considerations to be discussed shortly) we decide that the stimulus should be defined every 50 μsec, then 2000 samples of the stimulus need to be computed and stored (either in the computer's memory or on a mass-storage device such as a magnetic disk.) Each sample is simply a number that represents the value (a voltage usually) of the stimulus at a particular instant of time. Finally, the list of numbers is transmitted to a device known as a digital-to-analog (D/A) converter that, as its name implies, converts each number to a voltage. The conversion (which is normally handled by a short subprogram) proceeds sequentially; the numbers are converted one after another, with a precisely timed interval (50 μsec in our example) between them. The output of the D/A converter is a voltage waveform that is a step-wise approximation to the desired stimulus waveform. Low-pass filtering, or smoothing, of the D/A output produces the actual stimulus waveform, which is subsequently manipulated (attenuated or amplified and then transduced to sound) just as if it had been produced by a conventional stimulus generator.

If the simplicity and generality of this approach is not obvious at this point, it might help to note that a FORTRAN program to generate a burst of a pure tone is no longer than a half-dozen lines. To expand that program so that the stimulus will consist of a sum of sinusoids of arbitrary amplitudes and phases requires the addition of only another half-dozen lines. Illustrations of both of these examples will be provided later in this chapter.

While the programming necessary for computer generation of stimuli is straightforward and easily mastered, there are a number of technical details that must be considered before production of stimuli is actually attempted. Complete understanding of the theoretical bases of these issues required considerable mathematical sophistication. Consequently, only a bare outline is presented here. The interested reader is referred to several of the excellent texts on the subject listed at the end of the chapter.

Sampling Rate

Conventional signal generators used in hearing research produce stimuli that are continuous functions of time. In other words, these generators "define" the stimulus at each and every possible instant of time. In contrast, a stimulus is represented in a computer as a sequence of numbers; each number "defines" the stimulus at only one instant of time, and between two successive instants (numbers), the stimulus is undefined. Thus, the computer representation is called *discrete* rather than continuous, and the individual numbers are called *samples* of the stimulus. The theory of sampling tells us that if a sequence of numbers representing equally spaced samples of a desired stimulus is converted to analog form (voltage in our case) at a particular rate (samples-per-second), and if the resulting step-like analog waveform is appropriately low-pass filtered, the result will be a stimulus that is indistinguishable from the desired sampled stimulus. The requirements for sampling rate and subsequent low-pass filtering are dictated by the frequency content of the desired stimulus waveform. It can be shown mathematically that if the highest frequency in the desired stimulus is f_H, then the sampling rate f_S must be at least $2 \times f_H$, and the cutoff frequency of the low-pass filter must be no higher than $f_S/2$. In practice, becauseof the limitations of both the devices used to convert the numbers to voltages (D/A converters) and low-pass filters, it is always desirable that the sampling rate be as high as possible. Higher sampling rates, however, obviously require more computation and more storage space for any given stimulus. Thus, some compromise must be sought. Sampling rates of $2.5 \times f_H$, with low-pass filtering of $0.4 \times f_H$ are usually adequate. For example, with a sampling rate of 20,000 points/sec, and low-pass filtering at 8000 Hz, frequencies as high as about 8000 Hz could be included in the desired stimulus.

The sampling theorem creates problems for hearing scientists using the computer to generate stimuli, because of the fact that the ear is sensitive to frequencies as high as 15 to 18 kHz. (Note that to produce a stimulus containing frequencies as high as 18 kHz, a sampling rate of over 40 kHz would be required). High sampling rates are often necessary, with the result that large numbers of computations need to be performed and large amounts of storage are required.

The latter is usually the more serious problem. For example, a 1-sec stimulus computed with a 40 kHz sampling rate would require storage of 40,000 numbers. This is beyond the memory capacity of most minicomputer systems. Generation of long-duration high-frequency stimuli is relatively straightforward, however, if some kind of rapid-access mass-storage device (disk or magnetic tape) is available. It is also common practice to effect certain efficiencies in stimulus storage by taking advantage of the fact that many stimuli of interest are periodic. If this is the case, only the numbers defining one period of the stimulus need be computed and stored. Then this sequence can be converted (D/A) repeatedly, as often as necessary. For example, to produce a 1 kHz sinusoid at a 20 kHz sampling rate, only 20 numbers (one period of 1 kHz, or 1 msec) need be computed and stored. Then, to generate a 1-sec sample of the 1 kHz tone, the sequence of 20 numbers is simply converted 1000 times.

The procedure is more complicated if the period of the desired stimulus is not exactly divisible by the sampling period (the reciprocal of the sampling rate). For example, suppose we wish to produce a 3 kHz sinusoid, using a sampling rate of 10 kHz. The stimulus period is 1/3000 sec or approximately 0.3333 msec, and the sampling period is exactly 0.1000 msec. As a result, to define one period of the stimulus, we would need to compute 0.333/0.1000 or 3 1/3 samples. It is obviously impossible to compute 1/3 of a sample. The problem can be solved in this case by computing three periods of the stimulus or 10 samples. The general rule is: to produce periodic stimuli by repeatedly converting a sequence of numbers, the sequence must define exactly one period of the frequency that is equal to the greatest common divisor of the sampling frequency and the fundamental frequency of the stimulus. In the example above, with a stimulus frequency of 3 kHz and a sampling frequency of 10 kHz, the greatest common divisor is 1 kHz. Hence a 1-msec (10 points) sequence was required. As another example, consider a stimulus consisting of the sum of the sinusoids at 900 Hz, 1200 Hz, and 1500 Hz, with a 10 kHz sampling rate. The fundamental frequency of the stimulus is 300 Hz, and the greatest common divisor of 300 Hz and the sampling frequency, 10 kHz, is 100 Hz. Thus a 10-msec (1/100 sec) sample (100 points) is required. Finally, if a long-duration stimulus of 8001 Hz is to be produced, at a 20 kHz sampling rate, then a 1-sec sequence (20,000 points) is required, since the greatest common divisor in this case is 1 Hz.

Quantization Error

Numbers in a computer and, hence, the stimuli that result from conversion of those numbers (D/A) to voltages are represented with a precision that is limited by the number of binary bits assigned to each number. In the computer itself, this limited precision is not usually a problem, since, with the use of multiple-precision and/or floating-point arithmetic, precision can be increased almost arbitrarily. For example, a double-precision floating-point number in a typical

TABLE 7.1
Highest Signal-to-Noise Ratio
Obtainable from D/A Converters

Number of Bits	Signal-to-Noise Ratio (dB)
8	50
10	62
12	74
14	86
16	98

16-bit (word length) computer (DEC PDP-11) has a precision of about 17 significant digits! The precision of D/A converters, however, is an issue of some significance. Most converters operate on binary (or BCD) coded integers of 16 binary bits or fewer. A typical D/A converter might accept 12-bit integers and convert them to voltages in the range −5V to +5V. Because of the limitation to 12 binary bits, only 2^{12} or 4096 different voltages are possible; the difference between adjacent voltages is thus 10/4096 or 2.44 mV. In general, with a converter that uses N bits, and a range of X volts, the difference between adjacent voltage levels is $X\,(\frac{1}{2}^N)$ volts. If, as a result of computation, a stimulus value is called for that lies between two adjacent voltages (quantization levels), it is usually rounded or truncated to the nearest possible voltage. This rouding to the nearest quantization level produces an error in the output stimulus. In many cases the effect of the error is equivalent to the addition of random noise to the desired stimulus. The root-mean-square (RMS) voltage of this equivalent noise is $1/\sqrt{12}$ times the voltage difference between adjacent quantization levels. In other cases, such as generation of periodic stimuli, the quantization error is reflected in harmonic distortion in the desired output stimulus. The highest signal-to-noise ratio obtainable from a D/A converter is usually defined as the ratio of the RMS value of the largest sinusoid that could be produced to the RMS value of the quantization noise. Table 7.1 gives this ratio (in dB) for D/A converters using various numbers of binary bits.

It should be emphasized that these signal-to-noise ratios are theoretical and, because of other, more subtle errors in the D/A conversion process, rarely achieved. It is usually the case, however, that for many hearing-science applications, D/A converters using 12 bits are adequate. For certain critical uses, converters using 14 bits or more are required.

Nonlinearities in D/A Conversion

In order to appreciate the capabilities of computer systems used for the generation of analog stimuli, it is clearly necessary to understand the theoretical limitations imposed by the sampling rate and quantization error issues previously discussed. It is also important to consider certain practical limitations.

One of these practical limitations is a result of the troublesome nonlinearities that appear in most D/A conversion systems. Ideally, conversion of a number stored in the computer to a voltage should occur instantaneously. In other words, during stimulus generation, as each number is delivered to the D/A converter (at precisely timed intervals, determined by the sampling frequency), the voltage at the output of the converter should change instantaneously and remain absolutely stable until the next number is delivered. Of course, such instantaneous changes of state cannot be achieved in any real physical system; however, in typical D/A converters, the change from one voltage to another does occur fast enough (within a few microseconds) that speed alone is not a concern. The real problem is that with most D/A converters each transition from one voltage to the next is accompanied by rather large overshoot. .

These undesirable transients, or *glitches* as they are often called, are usually very brief (less than 1 μsec) but are of such magnitude (often several volts) that they cannot be ignored. The most serious issue is that the amplitude of the transient that occurs at a D/A transition depends in a complicated, nonlinear way on the size of the transition. Thus, the glitches cannot be represented simply as an added periodic sequence of equal-amplitude pulses at a rate equal to the sampling rate. If this were the case, the effect on the stimulus could be represented as the addition of unwanted components in the stimulus spectrum at integer multiples of the sampling frequency. These components would simply be removed by the low-pass filter that always follows the D/A converter. Because of the nonlinear behavior of the glitches, the unwanted components appear in this spectrum at integer multiples of the fundamental frequency of the number sequence being converted. That is, if the number sequence used to generate a stimulus represents a 1-msec sample of the stimulus, and this sequence is repeated according to the scheme described earlier, the unwanted components introduced by the glitches will fall at multiples of 1 kHz. This is true whether the stimulus itself contains a 1 kHZ component. For example, if a 1-msec sequence is used to produce a 1 kHz sinusoid, the distortion components will occur at 1 kHz, 2 kHz, 3 kHz, etc. In this case they could easily be removed by further low-pass filtering. If, however, a 1-msec sequence is used to generate a 7 kHz sinusoid (as would be required if the sampling rate were 20 kHz), the components at 1 kHz, 2 kHz, etc. would be troublesome indeed.

Even the use of specialized sample-and-hold amplifiers (called *deglitchers* by the manufacturers) to suppress the D/A transients does not always prove totally satisfactory. These devices as well have certain nonlinear characteristics that contaminate the desired stimulus waveform. Even though the problem of nonlinearity is serious, with care and appropriate choice of components its effects can be reduced to a tolerable level. Well-designed D/A conversion systems can produce stimuli that are more than 70 dB higher in amplitude than the distortion components. It is difficult to achieve this level of precision with conventional analog equipment.

Speed and Timing Stability

This is another important practical issue involved in the D/A conversion process that must be considered in order that the quality of computer-generated stimuli approach the theoretical limits. It is fortunate that the requirements for speed and timing stability are relatively easily met in practice and present little difficulty for the experimenter.

The speed requirement can be summarized simply by stating that for most signal-generation applications in hearing, science, sampling rates of 10 kHz or higher are required, and rates of 20 kHz are typical. A sampling rate of 20 kHz means of course, that every 50 μsec, a relatively short time even in computer terms, a new number must be delivered to the D/A converter for conversion to analog form. The first and most obvious consequence of this is that most stimuli will not be produced in "real time." A time interval of 50 to 100 μsec is simply too short, in most cases, for the computation required to produce one stimulus value. Thus, the numbers necessary to produce a stimulus will not be computed as the stimulus is being presented but rather beforehand. They are then stored away and retrieved and converted when needed. This poses no significant problem since stimulus parameters can usually be defined well enough in advance to allow sufficient time for computation. In certain demanding applications, however, such as an experiment involving complex, adaptive changes in signal parameters from trial-to-trial, although speed may not be an issue, the amount of storage that must be reserved for the precomputed digital versions of stimuli is quite large.

The problems caused by the speed requirement can be alleviated somewhat by operating a D/A converter in what is typically called *direct-memory-access* (DMA) fashion. In this scheme, a separate hardware device controls retrieval of stimulus samples from the computer memory and delivery to the D/A converter, leaving the central processor free for other chores. The processor is involved only momentarily at the beginning (the DMA device must be told where in memory the stimulus samples are and how many there are), and sometimes at the end of conversion of a particular stimulus or portion of a stimulus.

The use of a DMA device to control D/A conversion also allows long-duration stimuli to be produced, without the necessity of storing all the stimulus samples in the computer memory. A programming trick known as "double-buffering" is used, and the sequence of operations is as follows. First, two successive segments of the stimulus sequence, say 5000 samples each, are loaded into two adjacent memory arrays (the entire stimulus sequence is presumably stored on disk or magnetic tape). Next, D/A conversion of these segments is initiated. As soon as conversion of the first is complete and conversion of the second is begun, a third segment of the stimulus sequence is loaded into those memory locations that previously held the first segment. Then, when conversion of the second segment is complete, the DMA device is directed back to the beginning of the first memory array where it now finds the third stimulus segment. As this third segment is converted, the fourth is loaded into the memory locations that previously held the second segment. This process is continued for as long as is necessary to generate the entire stimulus. In this way, stimuli as long as several sec or even min (2 min at 20 kHz sampling rate requires storage of 2,400,000 samples) might be generated.

The final technical issue to be considered here is that of the stability of D/A timing. In most systems, the timing of the interval between successive D/A conversions is handled by a separate hardware device (a clock). Obviously, in order that the stimulus actually generated is the same as that which was computed (i.e., the D/A output rate equals the sampling rate), this clock must be quite accurate. It must also be stable, since short-term variations in output rate introduce another kind of unwanted noise in the output stimulus. Neither requirement is difficult to meet. Commercially available clocks of the sort typically used for D/A conversion employ a crystal-controlled oscillator to establish a time-base. These clocks produce time intervals with an absolute accuracy of better than 0.01% and a short-term variability that usually does not exceed one part in 10^8.

EXAMPLES OF STIMULUS-GENERATION ALGORITHMS

The simplicity and generality of the procedures used for stimulus generation can best be illustrated with a few examples. In the next few pages, then, several working algorithms will be discussed. While some of the details of these algorithms are necessarily specific to the system for which they were written, the routines can easily be tailored to any minicomputer system having the necessary hardware and software capability. The examples are given in FORTRAN IV code, since most minicomputer systems now in use can handle this language. The subroutines necessary to drive the D/A converter are not included, since these would almost certainly be written in the assembly language of the specific computer involved.

The first example is a very simple one. Figure 7.1 gives the FORTRAN listing of a program that will generate a burst of a sinusoid of user-specified frequency, duration, and starting phase. The program assumes a sampling rate (RATE) of 20 kHz (thus, the highest frequency that could be produced is about 8 kHz), and a maximum duration (DUR) of 0.5 sec (the array IWAVE, which stores the computed samples, has 10,000 locations reserved for it). The starting phase (PHASE) is given in radians and is referenced to sine-phase (i.e., for PHASE = 0, the waveform will begin at a positive-going zero-crossing). The program includes no provision for specification of the amplitude of the stimulus. This is because it is always wise to take advantage of the full range of the D/A converter to maximize signal-to-noise ratio. Thus, in this case, the amplitude is set to 8191, the

```
C PROGRAM TO COMPUTE AND GENERATE A TONE-BURST. USER TYPES
C FREQUENCY, DURATION, AND STARTING PHASE. AMPLITUDE IS CON-
C TROLLED EXTERNALLY.  THE PROGRAM CALLS THE ROUTINE "CONVRT"
C WHICH IS AN ASSEMBLY-LANGUAGE ROUTINE WHICH ACTUALLY PRODUCES
C THE ANALOG VERSION OF THE TONE-BURST.
C
C
        DIMENSION IWAVE(10000)
C
C "IWAVE" HOLDS THE WAVEFORM POINTS
C
        RATE=20000.
C
C RATE IS THE SAMPLING RATE
C
C PARAMETERS ARE ENTERED HERE
C
        WRITE(7,100)
100     FORMAT(' TYPE FREQUENCY')
        READ(5,101) FREQ
101     FORMAT(F10.3)
        WRITE(7,102)
102     FORMAT(' TYPE DURATION IN MSEC')
        READ(5,101) DUR
        WRITE(7,103)
103     FORMAT(' TYPE STARTING PHASE')
        READ(5,101) PHASE
C
C COMPUTE THE TONE-BURST
C
        NPTS=RATE*DUR/1000.
        TWOPI=6.28318531
C
C THIS IS THE COMPUTATION LOOP
C
        DO 10 I=1,NPTS
            T=(FLOAT(I-1))/RATE
10          IWAVE(I)=8191.*SIN((TWOPI*FREQ*T)+PHASE)
C
C END OF COMPUTATION - FOR MORE EFFICIENT OPERATION
C THE "TWOPI*FREQ" STEP SHOULD BE OUTSIDE THE LOOP
C
C NOW OUTPUT THE BURST
C
20      CALL CONVRT(IWAVE,RATE)
C
C
        PAUSE 'TYPE CR FOR ANOTHER BURST'
        GO TO 20
        END
```

FIG. 7.1.   Listing of FORTRAN IV program to compute and generate a burst of a sinusoid.

maximum positive number that can be handled by the 14-bit converter (the converter accepts signed binary integers, so its range is from -2^{13}, or -8192, to $2^{13}-1$, or 8191). With many stimuli, such as the tone-burst in this example, it is a simple matter to adjust amplitude with an external attenuator (manual or computer-controlled). Of course, if a complex stimulus is to be produced, an external attenuator will only allow adjustment of the overall stimulus level. Control of relative amplitudes of individual components of the stimulus is in this case achieved in the program. An example will be presented later.

A photograph of an oscilloscope display of a tone-burst stimulus generated by the sample program is shown in Fig. 7.2. For this example the frequency was

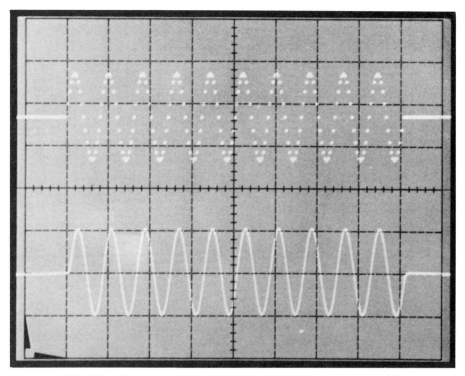

FIG. 7.2.   Photograph of an oscilloscope tracing of a burst produced by the program in Fig. 7.1. The upper trace shows the actual D/A converter output, a step-wise approximation to a sinusoid. The lower trace shows the same waveform after low-pass filtering.

1000 Hz and the duration 10 msec (starting phase = 0). The upper trace is the raw D/A converter output. Note that each cycle is represented by 20 discrete voltage levels. The lower trace shows the same waveform after it has been low-pass filtered at 8 kHz. The filtering smooths the waveform by attenuating the high-frequency energy present in the raw D/A output, thus producing a nearly perfect tone-burst.

For many experiments in hearing science, the simple tone-burst stimulus produced by the program in Fig. 7.1 is inappropriate. In certain conditions (high-stimulus level, low noise), the instantaneous onset and offset produce audible clicks. These "clicks" are not artifacts like the switching transients often introduced by conventional signal-gating devices. They are a necessary accompaniment to any stimulus that is turned on and off and are a result of the spread of energy at onset and offset to frequencies higher and lower than the stimulus. This energy (and hence the clicks) can be attenuated by bandpass filtering, or equivalently, by shaping the leading and trailing edges of the tone-burst, making onset and offset more gradual. For reasons of convenience, shaping has been the more popular alternative. The fine details of the shaping of any tone burst determine just how the energy of the stimulus will be distributed throughout the spectrum. Consequently, depending on the requirements of a particular experiment, the choice of a particular shaping scheme may represent an important procedural decision. Before the computer, most hearing scientists were forced to settle for an equipment manufacturer's decision about what constituted a good signal-shaping scheme. With analog equipment, shaping is rather difficult, and the results almost always leave a great deal to be desired. The computer not only makes it possible to shape a stimulus easily and well, but gives the experimenter complete freedom in the choice of the exact shaping function.

In programming terms, shaping is accomplished simply by multiplying the first few numbers (onset) and the last few numbers (offset) in the stimulus

```
C PROGRAM SEGMENT TO SHAPE A STIMULUS OF "NPTS" POINTS
C STORED IN ARRAY "IWAVE", WITH A "SINUSOIDAL" RISE-FALL OF
C DURATION "RFDUR" MILLISECONDS.  FOR THIS EXAMPLE "RATE" IS SET
C TO 20,000 PTS/SEC, "RFDUR" IS 10 MSEC, AND THE STIMULUS
C DURATION, "DUR", IS 50 MSEC.
C
C
        DIMENSION IWAVE(10000)
C
C ASSUME STIMULUS IS COMPUTED HERE AND STORED IN IWAVE
C
        DUR=50.
        RATE=20000.
        RFDUR=10.
        NPTS=RATE*DUR/1000.
        NPTSRF=RATE*RFDUR/1000.
        PI=3.14159265
C
C PUT ON RISE-FALL
C
        DO 10 I=1,NPTSRF
               T=FLOAT(I-1)/FLOAT(NPTSRF)
               FACTOR=.5*(1.-COS(PI*T))
C
C AS "I" INCREMENTS FROM 1 TO "NPTSRF", "T" GOES FROM 0 TO 1,
C AND "FACTOR" GOES "SINUSOIDALLY" FROM 0 TO 1.
C
  10           IWAVE(I)=FLOAT(IWAVE(I))*FACTOR
C
C NOW DO FALL TIME.  THIS COULD BE COMBINED IN RISE-TIME LOOP AND
C MADE MORE EFFICIENT.
C
        DO 20 I=1,NPTSRF
               T=FLOAT(I)/FLOAT(NPTSRF)
               FACTOR=.5*(1.-COS(PI*T))
C
C IN THIS CASE "FACTOR" GOES FROM 1 TO 0.
C
               J=NPTS-NPTSRF+I
  20           IWAVE(J)=FLOAT(IWAVE(J))*FACTOR
C
C STIMULUS IS NOW READY FOR OUTPUT
C
        END
```

FIG. 7.3.   Listing of FORTRAN IV program segment illustrating the implementation of one of the many possible shaping algorithms.

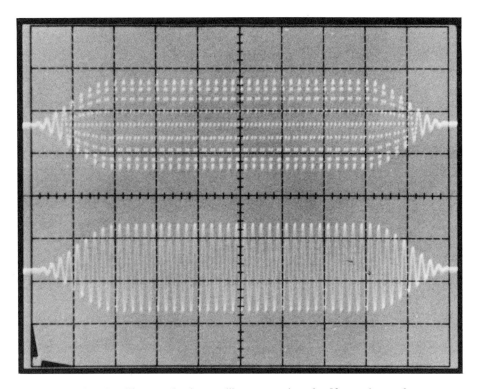

FIG. 7.4.   Photograph of an oscilloscope tracing of a 50-msec burst of a 1000 Hz sinusoid that has been shaped with the algorithm given in Fig. 7.3 (10 msec rise-fall time). The upper trace is the D/A output, and the lower trace is the same waveform after filtering.

sequence by functions. In the case of onset, the function begins at or near zero and ends at 1.0. For example, to give the 10-msec tone burst shown in Fig. 7.2, a 2-msec linear rise-decay time, we would simply multiply the first 40 entries in the stimulus array by the quantity $N/40$ (N is the index, or array entry number), and the last 40 entries in the array by $[(200 - N)/40]$. Figure 7.3 shows the FORTRAN code needed to implement a slightly more complicated (and for most experiments more desirable) shaping algorithm. In this case, the multiplying function is a half cycle of a sinusoid. Figure 7.4 shows the result when a 50-msec 1 kHz tone burst, produced by the program in Fig. 7.1, is shaped with a 10-msec "sinusoidal" rise-decay time.

The tremendous power of the computer as a stimulus generator is hardly evident in the previous examples. While there can be no doubt about the advantages of using a computer, such as precision, stability, and flexibility, its use could not be justified if the only stimuli of interest were pure tones. However, stimuli of almost arbitrary complexity can be produced almost as easily as pure tones

```
C PROGRAM TO COMPUTE A COMPLEX-TONE STIMULUS CONSISTING OF "N"
C COMPONENTS, THE FREQUENCIES OF WHICH ARE STORED IN "PARAM(1,K)",
C AMPLITUDES (MAXIMUM IS 1.0) IN "PARAM(2,K)", AND PHASES IN
C "PARAM(3,K)". A MAXIMUM OF 100 COMPONENTS IS POSSIBLE.
C THE WAVEFORM IS STORED IN "IWAVE"
C
C
          DIMENSION IWAVE(10000),PARAM(3,100)
C
          TWOPI=6.28318531
          PI=TWOPI/2.
          RATE=20000.
          DUR=250.
          RFDUR=30.
          NPTS=RATE*DUR/1000.
          NPTSRF=RATE*RFDUR/1000.
C
C ASSUME "N", THE NUMBER OF COMPONENTS, AND THE APPROPRIATE ENTRIES
C IN "PARAM" ARE DEFINED
C
C COMPUTE THE WAVEFORM AFTER INITIALIZING "IWAVE".
C
          DO 10 I=1,NPTS
   10             IWAVE(I)=0
C
C OUTER LOOP IN FOR "N" COMPONENTS.
C
          DO 30 J=1,N
              FREQ=PARAM(1,J)
              AMP=PARAM(2,J)
              PHASE=PARAM(3,J)
              AMPFAC=8191.*AMP/FLOAT(N)
C
C INNER LOOP IS TO COMPUTE EACH COMPONENT.
C
          DO 20 I=1,NPTS
              T=(FLOAT(I-1))/RATE
              VALUE=AMPFAC*SIN((TWOPI*FREQ*T)+PHASE)
   20             IWAVE(I)=IWAVE(I)+VALUE
   30     CONTINUE
C
C END OF COMPUTATION--NOW PUT ON RISE-FALL
C
          DO 40 I=1,NPTSRF
              T=FLOAT(I-1)/FLOAT(NPTSRF)
              FACTOR=.5*(1.-COS(PI*T))
              IWAVE(I)=FLOAT(IWAVE(I))*FACTOR
              T=FLOAT(I)/FLOAT(NPTSRF)
              FACTOR=.5*(1.+COS(PI*T))
              J=NPTS-NPTSRF+I
   40             IWAVE(J)=FLOAT(IWAVE(J))*FACTOR
C
C STIMULUS IS NOW READY FOR OUTPUT
C
          END
```

FIG. 7.5.   Listing of a FORTRAN IV program to compute a complex stimulus consisting of the sum of sinusoidal components of user-specified frequency, starting phase, and relative amplitude.

with the computer, and it is in this application that we may begin to appreciate its power.

For example, suppose we wish to produce a multicomponent complex-tone stimulus with the frequency, amplitude, and phase of each component individually specified. This is a simple matter, as the FORTRAN code in Fig. 7.5 shows. In this example, the frequencies, amplitudes, and phases are presumed to be stored in the array PARAM, the duration of the stimulus (DUR) is fixed at 250

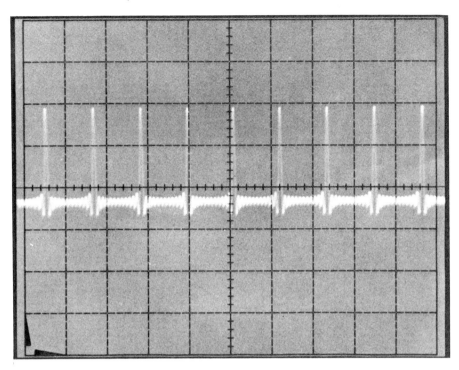

FIG. 7.6.   (a) Photograph of an oscilloscope tracing of a complex-tone stimulus computed with the algorithm given in Fig. 7.5. In the case shown here, the stimulus consisted of the first 12 harmonics of 200 Hz, all at the same amplitude, added in cosine phase. (b) Same as (a), but the components were added in random phase.

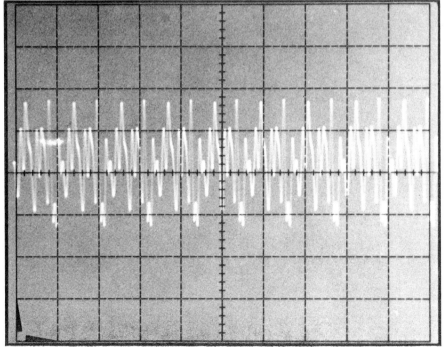

msec, with a 30-msec rise–fall time (RFDUR), and the sampling rate (RATE) is set to 20 kHz. All the stimulus parameters can, of course, be entered into the program in any of the usual ways, and can be readily changed.

Figures 7.6a and 7.6b show two examples of stimuli generated with the algorithm given in Fig. 7.5. In both cases the stimuli consist of 12 equal-amplitude sinusoidal components at harmonics of 200 Hz. In one case (Fig. 7.6a), the starting phase of all the components was 90° (cosine phase), and in the other (Fig. 7.6b), the starting phases were randomly assigned. Studies of pitch perception using stimuli of this sort have appeared frequently in the last 5 or 6 years (see, for example, Patterson, 1973). They could not have been undertaken without the availability of a computer to generate the stimuli.

A wide variety of useful stimuli can be produced using an algorithm of the sort shown in Fig. 7.5. In fact, Fourier's theorem tell us that virtually any waveform can be produced if enough sinusoids of appropriate amplitudes and phases are added together. Of course, the theorem formally applies only to periodic waveforms, but this is of relatively minor concern. The period of a complex stimulus produced by summing sinusoids is equal to the reciprocal of the greatest common divisor of all the frequencies (the fundamental frequency of the complex), and it can be made as long as required if the problem of periodicity is to be avoided. For example, if we wish to produce a 1-sec sample of Gaussian noise with a bandwidth of from 1 Hz to 10 kHz, all we need do is add up 1-sec samples of 10,000 sinusoids, spaced 1 Hz apart in frequency, from 1 Hz to 10 kHz, with amplitudes and phases chosen randomly. This waveform is not periodic within the 1-sec interval and, in fact, is undistinguishable, mathematically and perceptually, from a 1-sec sample of noise from a conventional noise generator (so long as it has the same frequency limits).

Although it may seem a waste of time to add up thousands of sinusoids just to produce a sample of noise, the use of computer-generated noise has some important experimental advantages. These are all related to the fact that from the experimenter's viewpoint, the noise is not random at all. Its characteristics (amplitude and phase at each frequency) are completely known and, thus, can be manipulated very precisely. For example, any desired spectral characteristic (band-pass, low-pass, "notch") can be built into the noise stimulus by appropriate choice of component amplitudes. Also, stimuli for dichotic experiments can be produced by generating two noises that are related in a specific way. A time delay can be introduced into one, for example, simply by adding the desired amount to the phase of each component sinusoid (for a time delay this amount would, of course, be proportional to the frequency of the sinusoid). Even more exotic relationships are possible. In a recent experiment reported by Grantham and Wightman (1978), listeners heard computer-generated dichotic noise bursts in which the interaural phase relationships were time-varying, such that the noises appeared to move about in auditory space. This stimulus could not have been generated by conventional means.

There is a significant disadvantage to the use of computer-generated noise that arises from the fact that a given noise stimulus is only one sample of the infinite number of possible samples of the noise process having the desired average characteristics. If, during the course of an experiment, this one stimulus is presented over and over to observers, their performance, regardless of the task, will almost certainly be affected by their "learning" of specific characteristics of that one noise sample. The problem can be avoided simply by presenting a different noise sample on each trial. This is usually accomplished by computing a number of different noises (20 to 30 is probably enough) with the desired characteristics ahead of time. The noises might differ, for example, in the phases of individual sinusoidal components. During the experiment, the stimulus to be presented on a given trial is selected randomly from this collection, thus preventing observers from "learning" the characteristics of any one stimulus.

Generation of complex stimuli such as noises can require substantial amounts of computing time, if the computation is performed by summing sinusoidal components. For example, in order to generate a single 1-second sample of wideband noise (10 kHz bandwidth, 20 kHz sampling rate), 20,000 waveform points need be computed for each of 10,000 sinusoids, and then these 10,000 waveforms need to be added together. This might involve evaluation of the SIN function (FORTRAN) 2×10^8 times. On a typical minicomputer system, these computations would take approximately 60 hours! Fortunately, there are alternative procedures available that effect remarkable efficiencies in computation by taking advantage of the redundancies inherent in periodic functions. For example, a close look at a sinusoid reveals that an entire cycle can be constructed by computing only those points necessary to define the first quarter cycle. The second quarter is simply a time-reversed version of the first, and the second half cycle is an inverted version of the first half cycle. Also, if more than one cycle of a sinusoid is to be included (in the noise example above this would be the case for every component except the one at 1 Hz), the points required to define the second and successive cycles can be obtained without computation simply by copying the points from the first cycle. These techniques can reduce the time required to compute complex stimuli by several orders of magnitude.

Perhaps the most widely used technique for generating complex stimuli is the so-called "Fast Fourier Transform" or FFT. This is a very efficient algorithm, developed in the late 1950s by scientists at the Bell Telephone Laboratories. Its sole function is (as its name implies) to evaluate the Fourier Transform of a list of numbers. While a complete discussion of the uses of the Fourier Transform, and of the FFT in particular, is well beyond the scope of this chapter, a few general remarks can be made. If the input to the FFT algorithm is a set of numbers that represents a stimulus waveform (a time function), the output is the spectrum of the waveform. This property makes the FFT very useful for computerized spectral analysis, as we will see later. Because of the nature of the Fourier Transform, if the input to the FFT is a list of numbers that defines the amplitude and phase of the sinusoidal components desired in a complex stimulus (a spectrum), then the output will be the points representing the stimulus waveform itself. Thus, the FFT can be used for stimulus synthesis as well as analysis. The algorithm is very fast. On a typical minicomputer the wide-band noise stimulus described earlier can be synthesized in about 10 seconds.

In order to operate efficiently, most versions of the FFT algorithm require that the number of input values and the number of output values be a power of 2. This is somewhat restrictive, since for some applications involving stimulus synthesis a transform of 4096 (2^{12}) points may not be big enough (e.g., the desired stimulus may be longer), but a transform of 8192 (2^{13}) points will probably exceed the memory capacity of most systems (an 8192 point transform requires 16,384 storage locations). In these cases, however, either the transform can be done in pieces or one of the many less-efficient non-power-of-two FFT routines can be used.

The FFT is an extremely powerful tool for stimulus synthesis. It has become so widely used (not only in hearing science, but in many fields) that now many special-purpose instruments (e.g., spectrum analyzers) contain hardware devices to perform an FFT. There is little doubt that in the years ahead, hardware FFT processors will become readily available at modest cost. Interfacing these devices to laboratory minicomputer systems could greatly simplify and speed up stimulus generation.

SYNTHESIS OF SPEECH STIMULI

Until recently, research on hearing was dominated by studies using simple stimuli, such as sinusoids or combinations of sinusoids. There are several obvious reasons for this. First, from the point of view of most hearing scientists who study input—output relations, the sinusoid is an ideal signal. Any complex stimulus can be represented as a combination of sinusoids, and if the auditory system behaves in a linear fashion, the sensation produced by a complex stimulus would be simply the sum of the sensations produced by the component sinusoids. Second, at least in the last 40 years, sinusoids have been relatively easy to produce and manipulate. Of course, it has been clear for some time that, in many ways, the auditory system is not linear; a given sensation is often a great deal more than just the sum of its component parts. It has also been clear to many hearing scientists that although our initial efforts might reasonably be directed at the "component parts" of auditory processing (e.g., frequency and intensity discrimination, absolute sensitivity, frequency selectivity, and masking), our long-range goal is an understanding of the more complex processes involved in the perception of speech and music.

There have been relatively few attempts to study complex auditory processes directly. One reason for this is that the stimuli of interest have been difficult to quantify and manipulate. For example, consider a simple speech stimulus, such as a word, and contrast this with the traditional tone-burst stimulus. The tone burst is completely defined by its frequency, intensity, and duration (and the details of rise—fall time). Also, a tone burst in one laboratory is identical for all practical purposes to the same tone burst produced by another laboratory. With the word, however, the problems of stimulus specification are severe indeed. Even if we disregard the issues related to meaning (context, word frequency, etc.), quantification of even the seemingly simple variables such as duration, intensity, and variability, both inter- and intraspeaker, presents enormous difficulty. Consider intensity. How do we specify the intensity of a word? Should it be peak sound-pressure-level, some kind of average pressure, or should we use an energy measure that takes duration into account? As an illustration of our relatively primitive development in this area, consider the fact that in most laboratories speech intensity is specified in terms of a subjective visual averaging of peak deflection on a VU meter. An even more serious problem faced by speech researchers is that of experimentally manipulating the speech signal. It is simply not possible by conventional means to alter the individual parameters of an utterance in any systematic way. Only rather gross manipulations have been feasible, such as filtering, amplitude distortion (peak-clipping, etc.), and time compression, and as a result, research with the speech signal has been quite limited in terms of the range of experimental questions studied.

The availability of laboratory minicomputer systems has had a profound impact on research with speech stimuli. Both problems mentioned above, those of stimulus specification and of stimulus control, are solved by having the computer actually generate the speech stimulus. In this way, since the stimulus exists as a sequence of numbers, decisions about specification and control are entirely in the hands of the experimenter. Virtually any scheme for measurement of the stimulus or for manipulation of its parameters can be carried out because the required operations are simply mathematical ones and can be performed with arbitrary precision.

Computer synthesis of a speech stimulus is somewhat different from synthesis of most other stimuli of interest to hearing scientists. The differences, however, are to be found only in the type of algorithm used to compute the desired number sequence. The rules about sampling rate, quantization error, and postgeneration filtering apply to speech stimuli as well as to the simple stimuli discussed earlier. Different synthesis algorithms are needed primarily because the parameters of the stimulus are time-varying. That is, they change during the stimulus itself. In real speech such changes are a result of the continuous movement of the articulators within the vocal tract during an utterance. Thus, in order to generate a stimulus that has speech-like properties, or one that sounds like real speech, it is necessary to model the effects of the moving articulators in the computational algorithms. In practice this is done by computing brief segments of the desired speech stimulus (the parameters are fixed for the duration of a segment) and then piecing the segments together. The duration of the individual segments is short (5 to 10 msec is typical), so that when they are pieced together, the parameter changes appear continuous, and, thus, the stimulus is a close approximation to a real speech sound.

The algorithms used to compute individual segments of a synthetic speech stimulus are based on a different principle than that used for generation of simple stimuli such as tones and mixtures of tones. Recall that the basic procedure for generating simple stimuli is to add sinusoids. This is a very general approach and theoretically could be adapted to the production of speech-like stimuli; however, it would be terribly inefficient and cumbersome. A large number of sinusoidal components would be involved, due to the complexity of the speech stimulus, and, hence, a list of perhaps 200 parameters (amplitudes and phase of each component) might be required to define each segment. A problem arises, in that it is simply not clear to researchers trying to generate a synthetic speech stimulus how such parameters as amplitude and phase of sinusoidal components relate to the acoustic–phonetic parameters with which they are much more familiar. For a number of important reasons, speech is usually described in terms of parameters related to production, namely, the fundamental frequency of voicing (if the speech sound in question is voiced) and the center frequencies, amplitudes, and bandwidths of the "formants" (natural resonances of the vocal tract). These are parameters that were originally derived from a kind of spectral analysis of speech sounds, known as spectrography.

The most widely used speech-synthesis algorithms are based on models of the human vocal tract. Synthetic speech is produced by taking the digital representation of a source waveform (this is a sequence of numbers that represents either the quasi-periodic glottal waveform, for a voiced speech sound, or a random noise, for an unvoiced speech sound) and processing it in a way that simulates the passage of a real source waveform through the vocal tract. For obvious reasons this process is known as "digital filtering"; the "filter" in this case is the vocal tract. The parameters that control the operation of these digital speech synthesizers are thus the parameters of the source waveform, and the parameters of the filter. These of course are the same parameters as are derived from spectrographic analysis, namely, fundamental frequency (for a voiced sound), and formant frequencies, amplitudes, and bandwidths. Typically, no more than 20 parameters are required to define a segment of speech synthesized with these algorithms.

A complete discussion of speech-synthesis algorithms is not our purpose here. A number of excellent sources are available for the interested reader (see list at end of this chapter), and the details, including FORTRAN listings of working programs, are enumerated there. A few general comments, however, are in order here. For research on hearing, the utility of digital speech-synthesis algorithms lies in the fact that they can be used to produce speech-like stimuli that can be readily specified and systematically controlled. Hence, the issue of whether the synthetic speech sounds natural is usually of less importance to hearing scientists than, for example, to communication engineers who are interested in speech synthesis as part of an efficient voice-transmission system. The hearing scientists' interest may be in the discriminability of small changes in the speech stimulus, or in the effect of some change in the stimulus on perception of a synthetic word. Research of this sort has only recently become feasible as a result of the development of the capability to synthesize speech stimuli with a computer.

SIGNAL PROCESSING

The emphasis of this chapter has thus far been on the use of minicomputers for stimulus generation. This is clearly the area of hearing science research in which computers have had (and will continue to have) the most profound impact. Generation of experimental stimuli, however, is certainly not the only function served by minicomputers. In the next few pages, a brief account is given of a few other applications of minicomputers in the general area of signal processing. In order to understand just what is meant by signal processing in this context, a brief description of two of the relevant research areas may be helpful.

Earlier in this chapter, hearing science was described as a study of input—output relations. As was suggested, the success of this approach depends on precise measurement and control of both input quantities (acoustic stimuli) and output quantities (sensations). The application of the computer to problems of stimulus generation has greatly extended our capabilities in terms of the input quantities; however, quantification of the output, sensations, has remained a difficult area. Most experiments still depend on some form of observer report for measurement of sensations, and in spite of efforts to reduce the variability in these measurements (by using highly practiced listeners, controlling for response bias, etc.), significant amounts of uncertainty remain. In an effort to reduce this uncertainty, some experimenters have begun to study techniques for measuring a response to acoustic stimulation that do not require an observer's report. These techniques involve measurement of the electrical activity evoked in an observer's nervous system by presentation of an acoustic stimulus. The measurements are made by recording the electrical potentials developed in small electrodes placed either on the surface of the scalp, in the external ear canal, or, in some cases, inside the middle ear. Although it is technically difficult to make measurements of this sort, and interpretation of the results is often somewhat subjective, the general concept is an attractive one. Techniques such as this are becoming increasingly popular, particularly for certain clinical applications, such as the assessment of the hearing status of very young children and others who for some reason are difficult to test using conventional means.

Measurement of auditory evoked potentials requires the use of a minicomputer, both because the potentials of interest are very small (less than 1 μV in many cases) and because they are contaminated by both electrical and physiological noise. In fact, this noise is often an order of magnitude or more greater than the signal. The computer is used to extract the signal of interest from the noise so that it can be subjected to further analysis and interpretation.

The first step in this process involves digitizing a segment of the amplified potentials from the electrodes. Thus, the voltage waveform is sampled, usually at equally spaced instants, and these samples are converted (with a hardware device called an analog-to-digital, or A/D, converter) into a sequence of numbers stored in the computer. This procedure is exactly the reverse of that used for stimulus generation (digital-to-analog conversion), and the same rules apply. The sampling rate must be at least twice the highest frequency in the analog waveform, and the resolution of the A/D converter (given by the number of binary bits used to define the output number) should be great enough to provide a sizeable signal-to-quantization-noise ratio (see Table 7.1). Once the potentials are in digital form, they can be processed in any number of ways to reduce the unwanted noise.

The most common signal-processing technique applied to auditory evoked potentials is simple averaging. This requires presentation of a large number of stimuli (thousands), collection of digitized versions of each of the resultant physiological potentials, and then averaging these potentials. Depending on the application, each digitized potential will represent a segment of from 10 to 100 msec of the potential developed after stimulus presentations. The digitized potentials are "time-locked" to the stimulus presentation. That is, sampling of each potential is started and stopped at the same time, relative to the stimulus delivery. This is the key feature of the averaging technique. When the digitized potentials are added, or averaged, since the "noise" in the potentials is presumably not related to the stimulus, and, thus, uncorrelated from one segment to the next, it will grow only at the rate of 3 dB per doubling of the number of segments added together. Whatever "signal" in the potential is correlated with the stimulus will grow at the rate of 6 dB per doubling of the number of segments added together. Thus, the signal-to-noise ratio will be improved by 3 dB for every doubling of the number of digitized segments added together. Other more sophisticated signal-processing techniques can also be used to extract the desired signal from the interfering noise. For example, if interference is introduced by a 60 Hz "hum" in the equipment, a digital filter (a simple computational algorithm) can be used to remove any 60 Hz component from the digitized potentials.

The use of minicomputers for processing physiological potentials is widespread and certainly not restricted to research on auditory evoked potentials. Only a brief outline of the principles involved and their application has been given here, since an entire chapter in this volume (Chapter 9) is devoted to this topic. The reader is directed there for a complete and detailed treatment of this important area.

A second signal-processing application of minicomputers in hearing science is in the general area of research with speech stimuli. The use of computers for speech synthesis was discussed earlier. In addition to synthesis, however, much of the research with speech involves analysis, and computers are an essential tool in this effort as well. It has been through analysis of naturally occurring speech sounds and subsequent experimentation with synthetic speech stimuli that researchers have been able to identify those features of the speech waveform that carry important information.

Analysis of speech is basically a spectral analysis; however, the special feature of speech analysis is that the *changes* in the spectral content of the waveform from moment-to-moment are of particular importance. Hence, the analysis that is necessary is called a short-term spectral analysis. The original research on short-term analysis of speech was carried out before the minicomputer era, and it was tedious work. A relatively gross spectral analysis was performed by passing the speech sound of interest (which was repeated by means of a tape loop) through a parallel bank of bandpass filters. The outputs of these filters were scanned sequentially, and the amount of energy as a function of time appearing at the output of each filter was recorded on paper. The result of such an analysis (which might take several minutes) was a graphical representation of the short-term spectrum, called a spectrogram. The abcissa of such a display represented time, the ordinate represented frequency, and the darkness of the pattern reflected the amount of energy. Measurements of the characteristics of speech sounds were then taken visually (with a ruler) from the spectrograms. Great care and long experience were necessary to reduce the error in those measurements to a tolerable level.

The use of minicomputers for speech analysis has brought a welcome measure of speed, flexibility, and precision to the area. The basic steps in the analysis are similar to those involved in the analysis of physiological potentials. First, the speech waveform is digitized with an A/D converter. A sampling rate of 10 kHz (provided the waveform is first low-pass filtered appropriately) with a 12-bit converter is usually sufficient for the purposes of analysis. Then, with the speech in digital form, any one of a number of signal-processing algorithms can be applied to extract the features of interest. If a simple short-term spectrum is needed, the FFT may be appropriate. If a plot of the formant frequencies as functions of time is desired, then either cepstrum analysis or linear prediction (Markel & Gray, 1976) would be used. A description of the variation in the fundamental frequency of the speech waveform might require yet another technique. Speech is a terribly complicated process, and no single analysis technique as yet seems to satisfy every need. Speech analysis is an active research area, and new procedures are continually being proposed. For our purposes here, the important feature of all these procedures derives from the fact that they are computer based. Development and use of any of these sophisticated speech-analysis techniques would not have been possible without the flexibility and precision provided by the computer.

In addition to evoked response recording and speech analysis, the signal-processing capabilities of minicomputers are beginning to be used for a number of other purposes in hearing science. In general, these other applications involve the use of the computer to perform some kind of digital filtering on a stimulus waveform. The specific details are too numerous and varied to summarize here, and, moreover, several excellent texts on digital filtering and its applications are available (e.g., Ackroyd, 1973). In order that the reader appreciate the tremendous potential of this area of minicomputer use, however, an elementary discussion of what is meant by digital filtering may be useful.

The purpose of digital filtering is the same as that of conventional analog filtering, namely, to modify a waveform in some way. It is convenient to think of filtering as a modification of the spectral content of the waveform (e.g., a low-pass filter attenuates the high frequencies in the waveform), but of course any modification of spectral content will be reflected in the waveform itself (e.g., low-pass filtering smooths the waveform) and vice-versa. Digital filters are usually implemented in the form of algorithms operating on the number sequence that represents a waveform rather than its spectrum. A complete understanding of how these algorithms work requires considerable mathematical sophistication; however, the general principle can be illustrated with a simple example. Suppose we take a sequence of numbers that represents a waveform and construct a new sequence in which each number (except the first) is the average of the corresponding number in the original sequence and the number preceding it. Thus, the new sequence is a "running average" of the original sequence. The averaging process is a simple kind of digital filtering, in this case low-pass filtering. The output of the filter (the new sequence) is a smoothed, or low-passed, version of the input.

Digital filters can be designed to satisfy an almost unlimited range of requirements. Their great advantages over analog filters are (1) that they can be made arbitrarily complex with virtually no concern about noise or stability, (2) that parameters can be manipulated independently (i.e., there is no problem of "impedance matching"), and (3) that they are completely free of drift and other variations. The only practical limitation in digital filtering is speed; as a filter is made more complex, the algorithms needed to implement it become more costly in terms of computer time. Few digital filters of interest to hearing scientists will run in real time.

DATA ACQUISITION AND CONTROL OF EXPERIMENTS

Up to this point, my discussion of the application of minicomputers in hearing science has been limited to coverage of techniques that, for the most part, are not feasible without a computer. The synthesis of complex stimuli, analysis of physiological potentials and speech, and digital filtering all require a computer. These however, are not the only uses, nor, perhaps the principal ones, to which minicomputers are currently put in hearing-science laboratories. It is important to note that minicomputers are only a little more than 10 years old and only recently have they become economically reasonable. Consequently, many (perhaps most) hearing scientists are just now becoming familiar with the computer as a laboratory instrument and are only beginning to learn the new techniques. For some disciplines such as the physical sciences and engineering, the move toward the use of minicomputers in the laboratory was a more natural one. In hearing science, however, it has been a slow process.

In many laboratories the computer functions as a "process controller." That is, its primary task is to run the experiments by turning on cue lights, controlling the presentation of stimuli (which are generated with analog devices), collecting responses from the subjects, and tabulating the data. In other words, the computer is used as a replacement for the racks of relays and solid-state switching and timing devices so common around hearing laboratories only a few years ago. While the use of a computer to control experiments may represent an underutilization of a powerful resource, the advantages are many. The flexibility and precision provided by the computer are as welcome and as needed in these tasks as in those described earlier in this chapter. A brief description of how the computer is used to control experiments, along with some simple examples, may help to illustrate this point.

In many cases in which the computer is used to control external devices, a simple on–off indication is all that is required (e.g., cue lights). In other words, the computer must send to the device a single binary digit (bit) of information; the status of that bit (0 or 1) is sensed by the device and used to determine whether the device is "on" or "off." If several devices are involved, or if one device can operate in a number of different modes, the necessary information can usually be transmitted in the form of a binary number consisting of several binary digits (e.g., n-bits can indicate 2^n different "functions").

The binary digits necessary for controlling devices are usually transmitted as voltage levels, produced by a so-called "interface" connected to the computer. A common convention is that a binary 1 is represented by +5V and a binary 0 by 0V. The status of any individual bit in the interface is controlled from a program or subprogram in the computer (usually written in machine language). Thus, to turn on a light, or to trigger an electronic switch, a command is issued from a program to set the appropriate bit in the interface to a 1. The voltage thus produced is transformed, if necessary, (a single transistor will often do the trick) to the voltage needed to perform the desired function. Most laboratory devices will accept the common +5V and 0V levels directly. To control more complicated devices, several bits in the interface are involved (e.g., to indicate an attenuation value to a computer-controlled attenuator).

Some equipment used in hearing research requires a variable control voltage rather than the binary +5V and 0V levels available from standard digital interfaces. Examples of this type of apparatus are voltage-controlled oscillators, $X-Y$ plotters, and display tubes. In these cases, D/A converters are used to generate the voltages required. These D/A converters are programmed in the same manner as for stimulus synthesis, except that in most cases there are fewer worries about sampling rate (e.g., a steady or relatively slowly changing voltage is often what is needed).

In order to run an experiment, the computer must be programmed not only for control of external devices, but also for data acquisition. The procedure involved in the latter task is simply the reverse of that involved in the former. Rather than providing voltages (in binary or continuous form) that activate external devices, the computer senses voltages produced by external devices. In hearing-science laboratories, the most common devices that the computer must sense are subject-response manipulanda. The voltages produced by these devices are either in binary form (this is the way a pushbutton might be wired: a 0 is output except when the button is pressed, at which time a 1 is output) or in continuous form (e.g., from a potentiometer or a joystick). Binary inputs are made accessible to a program by simple electronic modules in the computer interface. Continuous inputs must, of course, be converted to a digital form by an A/D converter.

Precise timing is needed both for device control and data acquisition. For example, in psychophysical experiments it is often necessary to have very precise control over the duration of stimuli, the time interval between stimuli, or the time between a stimulus and a response (as when reaction-time measurements are desired). It is always necessary to control the more gross time intervals in an experiment (duration of a trial, length of response interval, etc.). Both of these timing functions are handled by some kind of "clock" that is normally housed in the computer itself. This clock is usually programmable, in the sense that it will "tick" or count at selectable rates (e.g., 1 kHz, 100 kHz, 1 MHz), and these rates are precisely determined, usually by some form of crystal oscillator. Most clocks also have an automatic counting register that can be accessed from a program. Interval timing proceeds as follows. First, the counting register is loaded with a number, and the clock rate is selected. Next, the clock is started. The counting register automatically decrements by one at each "tick" of the clock. When the register reaches zero (register underflow condition), a signal is sent to the program. In this way, very precise timing is possible. For example, if the clock rate is set to 1 kHz and the number 1000 is loaded into the register, the time that will elapse between starting the clock and register underflow indication will be exactly 1 sec. If the clock rate had been set to 1 MHz, the elapsed time would have been 1 msec. Since the crystal oscillator in the clock is free running, the maximum error would be 1 count, 1 msec in the first example and 1 μsec in the second. By selecting clock rate and numbers of counts approximately, practically any time interval of interest to experimenters can be measured with great accuracy.

The simple experimental control and data-acquisition operations described in the past few paragraphs do not tax the capabilities of any laboratory minicomputer system. Neither the number of functions to which the computer must attend nor the number of responses it must collect is great enough to require more than a small fraction of the computer's time. Even so, some experimental paradigms are so complex as to be impractical without computer control. For example, consider the so-called adaptive paradigms, which are becoming increasingly popular in hearing research. These procedures require a decision to be made on every trial about what signal to present (its intensity or frequency, typically). That decision is based in some way on the observer's past response history and often requires a rather involved computation (see Chapter 5 for a more complete discussion). It is difficult to imagine conducting adaptive experiments without the assistance of a computer.

The advantages of computer-controlled experiments cannot be overemphasized. Perhaps the most important one is flexibility. A laboratory run by computer is not specifically tailored for one type of experiment. Changing from one experiment to the next usually involves little more than loading a different program into the computer and perhaps setting a few dials. Even the latter can be avoided if the computer is also used to generate the stimuli. This means not only that one laboratory can support a variety of research efforts but, more importantly, that a given experimenter is not committed, by virtue of the specific laboratory configuration, to one line of research. In the past, it has probably been the case all too often that experimenters have been limited in their experimental outlook by the available facility. Modifying that facility might involve too great an effort or expense, or both. The computer removes many of those limitations.

A second important advantage is accuracy. In simple terms, computers, unlike laboratory assistants, almost never make mistakes. A computer-controlled experiment will run the same way every time, and errors, if they do occur, can be easily traced to the computer program or to the few adjustments (e.g., attenuators, filters) that usually need to be made to external equipment. Although we will probably never be able to conduct research that is completely free of equipment problems, the computer greatly reduces the possibility of error from these sources.

The third advantage derives from the computer's speed and power. Because of the fact that the computer can do so much so rapidly, experiments can proceed very efficiently. Several subjects can be tested simultaneously, and many types of data can be gathered and analyzed from each one. This can often reduce the total time commitment for a complete experiment from several months to a few weeks.

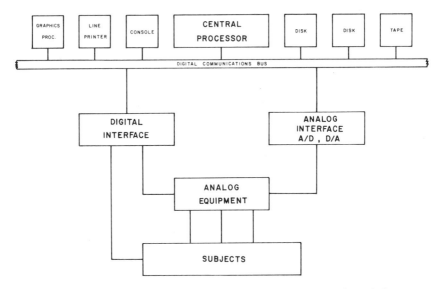

FIG. 7.7. Schematic diagram of the equipment configuration of the Psychoacoustics Research Laboratory at Northwestern University.

THE COMPONENTS OF A WORKING LABORATORY

My discussion of the applications of minicomputers in hearing science would not be complete without some consideration of the hardware itself. What follows therefore, is a list of the components of a working system and a brief outline of their functions and capabilities. In order to prepare this list, I have chosen the example I know best, which is my own laboratory. While this may not be a typical system, it is relatively complete, so the full range of components and their uses can be discussed. Also, the reader should keep in mind that even though most of this equipment is less than 3 years old, much of it is already outdated. Less costly and more effective devices are constantly becoming available.

A schematic representation of the entire laboratory system is shown in Fig. 7.7. The heart of the system is the computer, which in this case consists of a Digital Equipment Corp. PDP-11/40 central processor, with hardware arithmetic processor (fixed and floating point) and 64K 16-bit words of core memory. For random-access mass storage, there are two 1.25 Megaword moving-head cartridge-disk drives, and for serial mass storage, there is a 125-inch/sec, 9-track (1600 B.P.I.) industry compatible magnetic tape drive. Also connected to the computer are a 300 lines/min upper- and lower-case line printer, a 30 cps console terminal, and an interactive graphics processor with 17-inch CRT. Signals are produced with two independent 14-bit (delitched) D/A converters (maximum sampling rate 140 kHz), driven by a standard direct-memory-access interface, and signals are digitized with a single 12-bit A/D converter (140 kHz maximum sample rate) multiplexed to 16 input channels. Control of experiments and data acquisition are handled through a digital interface (commercially available) with 64 bits (4 words) of output and 64 bits of input.

The graphics processor is used extensively in signal-processing applications, such as speech analysis. Digitized speech waveforms can be displayed and edited, and the results of spectral analyses (and other analyses such as LPC or cepstrum) of the waveform can be viewed almost instantly (a 512-point FFT takes 400 msec). Much of the research that is now routine with speech stimuli is simply not feasible without such a display device.

The analog equipment includes a modest complement of filters, attenuators, amplifiers, and mixers for manipulating the signals produced by the computer, as well as all the familiar measuring instruments (countertimer, oscilloscope, RMS voltmeter, and wave analyzer) for checking signal intensity, timing, and spectral content. There are also 6 computer-controlled attenuators (one-quarter dB resolution, 128 dB range) for programmable intensity changes (e.g., on a trial-by-trial, or signal-by-signal basis). All the analog equipment is interconnected via a removable patchboard system, so that changing the laboratory configuration from one experiment to another can be accomplished in a matter of sec. The usable dynamic range of the analog system is about 85 dB, and the total harmonic distortion of most stimuli is less than .03%.

Stimuli are presented over matched TDH-49 headphones to subjects (typically three at a time) seated in a double-walled sound-isolated room. There is no measurable noise produced in this room by the computer system, which is located just outside.

Experiments are run under total computer control. The computer generates all the stimuli, controls their presentation, and collects responses from observers. Setting up for a given day's run is usually accomplished in a few minutes, since all that is required is mounting the appropriate patchboard, starting the computer program, and setting a few dials. Because of the excellent stability of the D/A converters and the internal clocks, calibration is only occasionally necessary. In many cases the subjects set up the experiments themselves. With the experimental parameters stored on disk, all the subjects need to enter at the beginning of a run is the name of the program and their name. Depending on their complexity or duration, stimuli are either pre-computed and stored on disk or magnetic tape, or are computed at the beginning of the experiment. Data are typically stored on disk and later transferred to tape for long-term storage; summary statistics are printed at the end of each run.

In any discussion of the hardware required in a computer-based hearing laboratory, cost is an important concern. This is important because while many researchers quickly recognized the potential of minicomputers soon after they appeared, only a few could find the financial support required to put together a working system. A modest system with the capabilities to synthesize stimuli and control experiments originally cost over $100,000. As a result, many chose the less desirable, but at the time less costly, alternative of a laboratory based on solid-state control circuitry and analog stimulus-generation equipment. The situation now is quite different. Over the course of their 10-year life, minicomputers have become bigger, better, faster, and considerably cheaper. At this point, the cost of a complete working laboratory system (less than $35,000) is within the reach of many hearing scientists.

CONCLUSIONS

Some might say that application of minicomputers has marked the beginning of a new era in hearing science. Perhaps so, but only in the sense that the research techniques are new. Most of the questions we are asking now about how the ear works are the same as those asked 50 or 100 years ago. Thus, although the computer has not helped us formulate better questions, it has allowed us to conduct research in a way that has a better chance of answering those questions that we do ask. In other words, the computer has simply made it easier to do good research.

The primary objective of the application of minicomputers in hearing science has always been to free the researcher from the limitations imposed by technology. As more sophisticated computer systems become available, this objective is more completely fulfilled, with the result that a wider range of experiments becomes accessible to the investigator. This freedom carries with it a great burden of responsibility. We must always be wary of the dangers inherent in the use of a research tool as powerful as a computer. For example, we must guard against the tendency to study a particular problem, conduct a particular kind of experiment, or gather data that are peripheral to the purpose of an experiment, simply to put the computer through its paces. The computer will be quite helpful in the hearing-science laboratory as long as the investigator assumes the responsibility for using it effectively.

ACKNOWLEDGMENT

Preparation of this manuscript was supported in part by Grant No. KO7-NS11072 from the National Institutes of Health.

SUGGESTED READINGS

These excellent texts are recommended for the reader who would like a more detailed or more advanced treatment of the following topics:

The Fast Fourier Transform
Brigham, E. O. *The fast Fourier transform.* Englewood Cliffs, N.J.: Prentice-Hall, 1977.

Digital Filtering and Signal Processing
Oppenheim, A. V., & Schafer, R. W. *Digital signal processing.* Englewood Cliffs, N.J.: Prentice-Hall, 1975.
Steiglitz, H. *An introduction to discrete systems.* New York: John Wiley & Sons, 1974.

Speech Analysis and Synthesis
Flanagan, J. L. *Speech analysis, synthesis, and perception* (2nd ed.). New York: Springer-Verlag, 1972.
Markel, J. D., Gray, A. H., Jr. *Linear prediction of speech.* New York: Springer-Verlag, 1976.

REFERENCES

Ackroyd, M. H. *Digital filtering.* London: Butterworth, 1973.
Grantham, D. W., & Wightman, F. L. Detectability of varying interaural temporal differences. *Journal of the Acoustical Society of America,* 1978, *63,* 511–523.
Markel, J. D., & Gray, A. H., Jr. *Linear prediction of speech.* New York: Springer-Verlag, 1976.
Patterson, R. D. The effects of relative phase and number of components on residue pitch. *Journal of the Acoustical Society of America,* 1973, *53,* 1565–1572.

8 A Survey of Computer Use in Cognitive Science

Richard B. Millward
Brown University

INTRODUCTION

There are three general ways in which the computer has influenced the study of cognitive science: It has been a tool for analysis of data and complex theories, it has provided precise control of stimulus material and allowed accurate response measurement, and it has served as a model for theory development. It would be a mistake to emphasize any one of these to the exclusion of the others, because it is the combination of the three that has produced a revolution in fields dealing with human cognition — psychology, linguistics, artificial intelligence, education, and philosophy. All three types of influence cannot be treated comprehensively within a few pages; hence, I shall sacrifice depth for breadth. Greater detail can be found in the references cited throughout this chapter. (See also Aaronson, Grupsmith, & Aaronson, 1976.)

DATA ANALYSIS AND NUMERICAL METHODS

In the cognitive sciences, computers were first used, and perhaps still are most extensively used, as a tool for data analysis and for the simulation of complex theories stated mathematically. Certainly psychology, with its heavy empirical emphasis, has needed computers to manipulate large quantities of data. Since the statistical methods used in cognitive science are essentially the same as those used in other fields, only a brief comment on particular topics directly related to cognition will be made here. Three topics are of particular importance: (1) parameter estimation and simulation of mathematically stated theories, (2) multidimensional scaling, and (3) translation of protocols into problem-behavior graphs.

A systems analysis of a complex process breaks the process into components, each of which can be analyzed more simply than the whole. Ideally, the components can be described with closed mathematical expressions. Unfortunately, even the simplest cognitive processes appear to involve a number of components (Sternberg, 1969), and usually these cannot be easily isolated from one another. Thus, the model of the process may specify a number of components, but the test of the model must consider all of them simultaneously. This usually involves a parameter-estimation process that requires hill-climbing or huge maximum-likelihood estimations. Even when closed expressions are available, the solutions are often rather complex (e.g., Millward & Wickens, 1974). Of course, in many cases no estimation procedures are known at all, and one must resort to simulation.

Perhaps one of the most original and useful analytical procedures developed to study how people organize their world is scaling. Historically, scaling began with factor analysis and related correlational techniques. In the cognitive sciences, however, simple linear-scaling techniques are inadequate because the relationships under investigation are usually not linear and because such techniques frequently assume more precise data than actually exist. That is, often only ordinal relations are measurable. Hence, these traditional approaches have, for the most part, been replaced by the recent developments in multidimensional scaling (Carroll, 1972; Kruskal, 1964; Shepard, 1962). Multidimensional scaling techniques depend on a computational algorithm that would be impossible without the computer. The combination of numerical manipulations with graphic output has meant that complex relationships among a set of data points can be literally "looked at." Since no mechanism has the analytical power of man himself, the interaction of the computer and the scientist provides a powerful analytic device. Chang (1973) has discussed a program for interactive graphics using multidimensional scaling; the combination of the powerful numeric computational technique and the graphics display reflects the growing sophistication of the tools now available for studying cognition.

Other scaling techniques make different assumptions about the underlying structure. INDSCAL (Carroll, 1972) assumes that individual subjects have different weights on a common set of variables. Hierarchical clustering looks for structures corresponding to a hierarchy instead of an orthogonal arrangement of dimensions. There are even programs that combine hierarchical clustering and orthogonal space (Degerman, 1970).

One final data-analysis technique has been less successful. In problem-solving situations, the description of the problem defines a task environment that can be translated into a search space (Newell & Simon, 1972). The experimental procedure is to ask a subject to talk out loud while trying to solve the problem. The theory assumes that the subject has a view of the problem corresponding to the task environment, and, when the subject tries one approach to the problem, he or she can be described as moving around in the search space. The difficulty lies in describing this path through the search space from the subject's verbal protocols. Because the subject cannot mention everything he or she thinks, there are gaps in the verbal record. If the theory is adequate, it should be possible to fill in the gaps on the basis of other evidence obtained later. The theory itself often consists of a large number of states plus transitions between these states. The analytical problem is to determine, from the subject's verbal protocols, the states through which he or she passed.

No simple numerical techniques are even conceivable for solving this problem. Furthermore, because of the incompleteness of the data, the computer must keep track of a large number of alternatives until further data are obtained. Analyzing protocols from problem-solving experiments is not yet a matter of running a computer program and may never become such, but the technique would be totally impossible without computer assistance. Although some demonstration protocols have been analyzed by hand, any productive use awaits a fully operational computer program. Further development depends on a good program that can understand natural language, a topic discussed later.

ON-LINE EXPERIMENTATION

The second influence of computers on cognitive science, the on-line control of experiments, is the area that makes the heaviest use of minicomputers. Because experimentation and data collection are particularly important to a developing science, this is a most important area. The relationship between the first influence mentioned and this second influence should be obvious: With computers running experiments, the amount and complexity of the data collected exceed the ability to process the results without a computer.

The development of all sciences has relied heavily on the apparatus available. Consider, for example, the importance of the telescope to astronomy, the microscope to biology, and the electromagnet to physics. Although some areas of psychology have reached a high level of sophistication without computers, the study of information-processing has depended crucially on them. The future will see even more imaginative uses of computers as cognitive scientists study the complex interactions of events within the organism. Perhaps a few comments on this last point are in order.

One of the obvious difficulties in studying human cognition is that almost all the events of interest occur within the organism. Although the behavioristic tradition emphasized a simple functional analysis involving only stimulus inputs and response outputs, today it is almost universally agreed that, except for a few simple systems, we must postulate internal mechanisms. The process of formulating models of internal systems and then testing these models requires elaborate experiments with a complex and/or highly controlled stimulus input as well as response measurements of the most general type.

Stimulus Control and Generation

Cognitive scientists deal with extraordinarily complex stimuli. Presented visually, a "simple" stimulus like the word *WORD* consists of 4 out of 26 possible letters arranged in a row in some kind of type font for some duration at some intensity in the context of some other set of words that may or may not be meaningfully related. The subject encodes it within 500 msec, producing a phonological internal code, a meaning, and perhaps even some associations or information about its state in the whole system (e.g., whether it is a word). The cognitive researcher is usually not very concerned with the luminance or contrast of the letters or exactly how large they are or whether the subject is looking at the *O* or the *R* when the word is presented. But these physical parameters of the stimulus cannot be completely ignored, because they do introduce variation in responses and make the detection of cognitive events more difficult.

One of the most useful devices for sensory work is a computer of average transients (CAT), a simple nonprogrammable computer. It is run by synchronizing the signal onset and the recording of the response, which is some continuously varying voltage. Although a single response wave is not detectably different from background noise, its consistency allows one to overlay responses repeatedly so that the signal-to-noise ratio is increased until the pattern is clearly evident. Continuous responses are not often recorded in cognition experiments, but the methodology for recording multiple discrete responses is conceptually very similar. A semantic-memory experiment may consist of a number of words to which subjects respond and to which their reaction time is recorded. A single reaction time tells the experimenter nothing. Only by averaging over a large and, unfortunately, noisy sample of words can patterns emerge. Thus, any additional noise in the system must be overcome by increasing the sample size.

An important trade-off for the cognitive researcher is flexibility vs. stimulus control. There are many different ways to deal with stimuli, and flexibility to introduce new procedures is important. However, a minimum degree of control is also necessary. A computer is ideal, because it allows for a great deal of variation with a high level of accuracy. The computer introduces its own problems, however, and its proper use requires an understanding of the total system.

An example will help to illustrate the point. For many experimental paradigms, a videoscope is ideal. There are two major types of scopes used for presenting stimuli. The first is a simple refresh oscilloscope in which the computer is programmed to present a single point on a screen. Some refresh scopes have character generators so that only the $x-y$ coordinates and the number representing the character need be sent. With these scopes, an experimenter knows precisely when each letter is displayed. The second type of scope is the TV raster scopes used as terminals to computers. These display scopes have internal buffers containing a code for each position on the screen. The programmer simply sends a character to some location in this buffer, and the control unit displays it for him. Although this procedure makes programming the scope easy, it also introduces a serious source of error. Like any normal television set, the scope is "refreshed" every 1/60 sec in synchrony with the line voltage. This means that, even though the computer is programmed to send the information to the scope at 1000 characters/sec, the experimenter does not know the exact time at which it is displayed. The display time can vary from the time sent by as much as 16.67 msec. (An analysis of this problem was made by Christian and Polson (1975) and deserves reading.) Although reaction-time differences between subjects can be as large as 100 msec, such large differences are usually compensated for by using within-subject designs. But the time error created by the TV display is an added noise component to the within-subject variance. It cannot be eliminated by experimental design but only by increasing the sample size so as to reduce the standard error of the mean.

Fortunately, a solution to this problem is available. Many TV raster scopes have a special control character that "tags" all the following characters so that they are displayed in special ways. These special ways may include blinking, graphic symbols, or half-intensity presentation. On our scope at Brown University, we are able to turn the half-intensity function into an "off–on" function so that tagged characters will be off, i.e., at zero intensity. Later, a single control character can be sent to turn all tagged characters on at once. We have also tapped the line-voltage signal that initiates the display sweep and use it to interrupt the computer. (Of course, we have built in a software switch to turn the interrupt off.) The programming procedure is to send all the letters of a stimulus to the TV raster buffer tagged for zero-intensity. When all the characters have been sent, the computer turns the interrupt on and waits for a signal indicating that the screen is about to be refreshed. Immediately after this signal is received, a single character sent to the video control will, in less than 50 μsec, switch the zero-intensity level to full intensity, thus displaying the letters.

Even this high degree of precision is not satisfactory for many vision experiments. The problem is that each character is still made up of a number of sweep lines, and each of these takes about 0.03 msec. Thus, a letter of 10 sweep lines take 0.3 msec to be displayed, top to bottom. Although this kind of noise is unimportant for cognitive research, it may cause trouble for extremely refined vision research. The point is that noise is relative to the problem and, at the cognitive level, increased flexibility often outweighs a small loss in precision. This example can be generalized to the whole range of stimuli-generating and response-measuring devices in use today: One must understand the limits of the system and know how precise the measurements must be in order to detect the effects of interest. For instance, the error introduced by the sweep rate of the TV raster was important in experiments using a masking procedure.

In this procedure, a word was presented for as short a period of time as 30 msec, after which it was masked out by displaying dollar signs over the letters. Then two letters were displayed, one above and one below one of the four letters of the word. The time constraints were such that, with 16.67-msec random time intervals between word displays, mask, and single-letter presentations, no effects could be observed. By adjusting the apparatus in the manner described above, however, we were able to get effects comparable to those obtained by using tachistoscopes. On the other hand, in a situation in which a sentence is presented to subjects and they are asked to respond yes or no to its truth value, the times involved are so gross compared to the 16.67-msec "error" that the error can safely be ignored.

A cognitive researcher needs to be able to present stimuli in a number of different ways. If pictures, rather than words, are to be displayed, new demands are placed on the system. Oscilloscopes can be used for simple line drawings, but a slide projector allows for a wider variety of stimuli. It is easy to interface random-access projectors to computers, but one limiting factor is the time between slides. Projectors have a maximum cycle time of around 3 sec, although, with fewer slides, one can get down to less than 50 msec between two adjacent slides. One trick here is to use two projectors and fire them in succession. Another advantage of two projectors is that the beams from them can be mixed with a beam splitter (Millward, Aikin, & Wickens, 1972). If the slides are made as negatives, then two slides projected simultaneously but made so as not to overlap where they are transparent will project together. With two projectors, there will then be 80 x 80 = 6400 slide combinations. Millward and Spoehr (1973) used this procedure in an experiment on concept learning.

Other potential variations come easily to mind for this dual-projector setup. If the beam splitter is rotated slightly, the image "bouncing" off the internal diagonal half-silvered mirror is projected at a different angle, but the image going through the mirror is not disturbed. Since the two projectors both pass through the beam splitter and bounce off the mirror inside it, two images are presented, one shifted to the left (or right) and the other displayed straight ahead. This arrangement can be used to present a slide to the right or left visual field. Since the projectors have tachistoscopic shutters, the subjects will receive the stimulus for only a brief period and will not be able to move their eyes to focus on the stimulus. The mirror is under computer control so that the presentations can be randomized, preventing any anticipations by the subjects.

Standard slide projectors, TV scopes, oscilloscopes, and simple light displays (e.g., inline displays) are the most common visual displays used today. However, other useful devices are being introduced. One such device is video records (Broadbent, 1976; Jerome, 1976; RCA, 1976). These records are like ordinary phonograph records, except they also contain visual information for display on a TV screen. Some of the records are read by laser beams that can easily be focused over a single track. By fixing the beam on one track, the same image remains on the TV screen; by moving the beam, successive tracks are scanned. A 12-inch record can hold about 30 min of TV, or over 100,000 TV images. When TV images are stored on tape, the tape must be scanned serially to find a given image. With the records, one can select images very rapidly, probably within 50 msec. (The analogy here between magnetic tape and magnetic disk is close.) This device offers the potential for experiments using complex images in random sequence. Computers can now generate dot and line patterns using an oscilloscope, but TV images can be far more natural and can even include color. Such a device could be important for computer-assisted instruction. Instead of sending out 1600 characters, one by one, to present text to subjects, the computer would only have to select the right track of the TV record. Since one record contains 100,000 full-screen images, a whole library of books would be readily available under computer control.

Our second important sense is hearing. The techniques for the generation of auditory stimuli parallel those for visual stimuli. Standard electronic devices, such as tone generators, filters, tape recorders, and simple switch closures, can be controlled by a computer. A signal is produced by the device and the computer turns it on or off or modulates the volume. The advantage of such control is that, as with slides in the visual mode, the signal can be as complicated and as natural as desired. The disadvantage is that the stimuli must be made before the experiment and so are not truly "generated," thus limiting their number and the control of their presentation.

A more "generative" technique for producing auditory stimuli is to use a digital-to-analog converter (D/A converter). Here a number within some range determined by the accuracy of the converter is used to specify the voltage output of a signal. Since a D/A converter can produce an output as often as every 10 μsec, signals of up to 100 kHz are potentially possible. A more reasonable upper limit for signals of any length is about 25 kHz. There are some important limitations, however, on the sampling and production of analog signals. Without going into details here, the most important limitation is that the conversion frequency (Nyquist rate) should be at least twice the frequency of the signal to be generated (Nyquist frequency). Since human hearing can extend to above 15 kHz, a conversion rate of 30 kHz is necessary for work with very high frequencies. Fortunately, the maximum frequencies in speech that are critical for understanding are less than 5 kHz, and so a production rate of 10 kHz is considered adequate (Rabiner & Schafer, 1976).

The computer can change the voltage level rapidly enough to produce sounds of sufficiently high frequency for speech, but it cannot do this for very long. For example, to produce 1 sec of speech at a D/A conversion rate of 20 kHz requires 10,000 stored values. These values must be stored somewhere before their conversion because the time to generate them would interfere with their transmission to the D/A device and because, if they are speech sounds, there is no known way to generate them in real time.

There are alternative solutions for the problem of storage. The simplest is to generate the sounds one by one and store them on magnetic tape to be played to the subjects later during the experiment. If two channels are used (or three for dichotic presentations), the extra channel can be time-marked so that warning signals and subjects' responses can be synchronized with the off-line speech presentation. The amount of storage required is determined by the length of the longest stimulus (Poltrock & Mathews, 1976).

The second technique is to have a large amount of fast-access storage, for example, magnetic tape or disk. Magnetic tape is easier to use than off-line audio-tape but has the same problem: It does not allow random access to the signals. A disk solves the problem of selecting the digitalized signal randomly but has a problem of its own: Usually, the data are transferred off disk in blocks, and each transfer requires some computing time to set up the parameters of the transfer. Core is rarely large enough to store a whole signal (although it may be large enough for short speech sequences). Careful programming can overcome the transfer problem, but usually at some cost to the generality of the program.

The third technique uses models of the vocal tract. These have evolved over the years from the early pattern-playback devices that reversed the speech spectrograph so that drawings of formants could be used to produce speech sounds, down to recent synthesizers in which a number of special sound sources are modulated and mixed to produce natural-sounding speech (Allen, 1976; Cohen & Massaro, 1976; McIlroy, 1974). These later devices are easy to use because they require that only a few parameters, at most 15, be changed every 5 to 10 msec. The storage requirements for such generative systems is trivially small compared to the D/A technique, and, moreover, the speech is truly generated. For that very reason, it is, of course, not as natural either, and the prosodic features of speech are poorly reproduced.

The resonance synthesizer is actually a theory of speech generation and, as such, allows experimentation and relatively simple programming control. In fact, the technique is so successful that fairly inexpensive devices are available (e.g., Votrax), and it is being used by telephone companies to generate telephone numbers. The more recent steps have been to include more and more special rules and to put them into an LSI chip. There is no doubt that we are within a few years of having a reasonable talking computer.

In summary, computers can be used as signal generators to present letters, slides, and simple graphics in the visual mode and to control tape recorders, limited segments of speech, and repetitive sounds of some complexity in the auditory mode. Although higher-level languages can be used to produce many stimuli, more refined software is frequently required to generate more sophisticated signals. In the not too distant future, we can expect to have elaborate TV picture control, color, and much more flexible graphics capability, very good speech synthesizers, and much more control over auditory signals.

Response Measurement

Regardless of how elaborate stimuli become, if responses are severely constrained, the ability to model internal mechanisms will be limited. There is certainly more information in reproduction—responses that allow the subjects to draw what they have seen or to discourse at length on what they remember—than there is in a simple choice response. Ideally, we should always use unrestricted responses. The problem is that such responses contain *too much* information, and relating them to our relatively simple and narrow theoretical structures is difficult. Some of the theoretical constraints, however, have been due to limitations in response recording. The computer will help us overcome some of these limitations, although not immediately and not without a concomitant growth in our conceptual models of behavior.

Little needs to be said about the typical responses recorded by computers in cognitive research today. Push buttons and keyboards are easily interfaced to computers and are widely used. Latency is measured with high accuracy, although some cautionary remarks are necessary here. Many researchers are using older keyboards in which the code for a character is sent serially to the interface buffer. At low baud rates (110 or 300), there is a substantial delay between the time the key is struck and the time that the interface buffer receives the character and sets the flag. Since this is usually a constant, it is not a serious problem unless the software uses a polling algorithm with substantial delays between successive checks of a keyboard. In such a case, there can be a uniformly distributed random error. For this reason, terminals cannot be used on large time-shared computers.

An easy solution to this problem is already available in rudimentary form (Potts, 1976). A timer is connected to the terminal so that the first response made after a special character is sent is timed exactly, and the time is sent back to the main computer. Of course, only single responses can be measured, and there is still little control over intertrial intervals. The next step will be to build a microprocessor into a terminal and program it from the large time-shared machine. The microprocessor can have a large enough buffer to store all the events constituting a trial or a block of trials and then asynchronously send the data back to the large machine as a background task. Psychological experiments usually have a sufficiently small amount of data for data to be sent back to the central computer while the experiment is still in progress. By using microprocessors, any researcher could have a "minilaboratory" for cognition for less than $3000.

As we try to follow the course of information transformation through the cognitive system, micromodels of response-production subsystems will be necessary. Three relatively elaborate response-recording systems are of particular interest to cognitive scientists: measurement of motor responses, measurement of eye movements, and natural-language processing.

Measurement of Motor Responses.   The ability to record continuous changes of a motor response is important because humans seem to be able to relate sensations from different modalities and to make scaled judgments relatively easily. Light pens provide a "pointing" response that is natural and particularly easy for children to use. Light pens, however, require a high overhead in computer-processing since the CPU must constantly look for the location of the pen. (A microprocessor dedicated to tracking the pen is an ideal solution here.) Response tablets are somewhat easier to use since the position of the pen is registered as an analog signal and the x and y axes are simply converted by an A/D converter and read into the machine at appropriate intervals.

An example of some interest to cognitive psychologists is Bartlett's (1932/1967) work on the reproduction from memory of visual stimuli as a function of time and previous description. One might imagine that a "writing tablet" connected to a computer would be ideal for such research. The difficulty lies not in the availability of the equipment to record continuous line drawings but in a reasonable model to guide the analysis and measurement of such drawings. Although Lashley (1917) very early gave us the idea of stored motor programs, specific theories involving that idea have been rare. Schmidt (1975) has recently done some interesting work in this area, and, with a more thoroughly developed "schema" theory, computer recording of complex responses might become fairly common. Work on the development of motor behavior by ethologists (Connolly, 1973) also supports an information-processing point of view, one that could make continuous recording of motor responses necessary.

Both these examples, however, really emphasize the role of computers as models for theory development more than they do the use of computers as on-line recording devices. Before we make elaborate measurements of responses, we should have a theory telling us what to do with them. In robotology work, for example, researchers in artificial intelligence are trying to make robots act reasonably (e.g., to recognize and pick up objects or to move around rooms). The difficulties in achieving success in these areas help explain the slow progress being made in analyzing human behavior. The work in artificial intelligence does, however, provide useful theoretical models that can be used to direct the recording of responses. If we had good models of how to control responses, the robot problem would be simply an engineering problem. It is not. The engineers are trying to solve some of the same problems faced by the cognitive scientist.

Measurement of Eye Movements.   The second area of interest to cognitive scientists is the recording of eye movements. Early investigators of eye movements were influenced by strict behaviorism and naively assumed that the only selective attention possible by an organism was some controlling response, such as focusing the eye on a particular part of the stimulus. Then internal selective attention was demonstrated as important, and external attention via motor control was discounted as unimportant. But obviously the location of the eye determines what is seen and, if that information is available, there is less noise in the system.

At the 1974 meeting of the National Conference on the Use of On-Line Computers in Psychology, a symposium was held to discuss the various techniques for recording eye movement (Symposium: On-line eye movement recording, 1975; Young & Sheena, 1975). At the 1975 meeting, Just and Carpenter (1976) discussed the hypothesis that the eye fixates the referent of the symbol currently being processed mentally. A sentence-verification study supported the hypothesis. A second study involving the mental rotation of geometric shapes showed eye movements that correlated with the rotation times (Carpenter & Just, 1977).

Another striking example of how eye movements can help analyze cognitive processes involves chess playing. Here the kind of hypothesis a subject has can be determined more easily if his eyes are followed (Chase & Simon, 1973). Finally, studies of recognition memory for pictures (Loftus, 1972) and eye movements during reading have made important contributions to cognition. The latter is particularly interesting because there is a long history of recording eye movement during reading. The latest technique clearly demonstrates the advantages of the computer. McConkie and Rayner (1975) and Rayner and McConkie (1977) used the position of the eye as a way of controlling the "window" of text present to the subject. A CRT display was used to present text in a jumbled form (e.g., all Xs, no spaces or punctuation, correct word length but random letters), except at the point where the eye was focused. The number of letters presented on a line to the left and right of the point of fixation was varied. The central question was the extent to which information in the periphery was encoded by the subject. For example, did the length of a word in peripheral vision provide information to the subject? There seemed to be some evidence that it did, at least to guide the length of the saccades.

It is hard to separate the increased ability to measure a process from the increased sophistication of the theories being studied. The literature on eye movement is a good example of this. The models of information processing underlying much of the research are heavily influenced by the computer.

Natural-Language Processing.   In natural-language processing, there are two major response modes of interest, speech and typed input. (Handwriting can be considered a variant of typed input with the added complication of pattern recognition. The pattern-recognition problem is not trivial and makes handwriting almost as difficult to understand as speech.) Chapanis (1975) studied problem-solving behavior in an interactive communications experiment. One of the subjects had to solve a problem and the other subject had information about how to do it. They could communicate by voice, video, handwritten notes, typewriter, or a combination of these modes. There was a large difference in the speed of problem solving under the different modes: Voice was superior to all the other modes. However, there were many more communication acts with speech than with the other means of communication because more words can be spoken per min than can be typed. Anyone who has tried to communicate over a terminal will understand these results. (A common response of our consultants to a difficult question is "Call me at 2221.")

Speech is a form of human behavior so natural and so familiar that even sophisticated scientists not versed in the technicalities of its analysis sometimes naively wonder why machines do not exist to understand it. All business executives know that it costs more to train personnel to use a computer than the computer itself costs. They wonder why engineers do not make machines that understand simple English. The Chapanis study indicates how important and efficient speech is—about four words/sec compared to one word/sec for typing and four-tenths words/sec for handwriting. There are also qualitative differences, including the facts that speech leaves the hands free and that handwriting and typing require special training. So naturally there is a great deal of work going into producing a machine that understands speech.

To date, most of this work has been done by engineers, not by psychologists and linguists. Yet many people believe that a total systems approach must be taken. Such an approach will have to model human cognition as well as the pragmatics of the situation, and the semantics, syntax, and phonetics of language itself. Simple mathematical analyses by themselves are not enough. Hence, the role of the psychologist and linguist will necessarily be of increasing importance as these projects develop (see Aaronson & Scarborough, 1976).

It might seem obvious that an adequate understanding of human cognition would provide us with a working model of speech comprehension. In fact, the converse is more likely to be true: Only a working speech-comprehension system will provide us with an understanding of human cognition. We can record the time to say a word; word-recognition devices calibrated for a particular speaker can achieve recognition rates over 99 percent for vocabularies of 30 words, and a few large expensive experimental systems can comprehend spoken sentences. But at present it is impossible to use normal speech to measure cognitive processes.

In 1971, the Advanced Research Projects Agency (ARPA) initiated support of the development of speech-comprehension systems (Newell, Barnett, Forgie, Green, Klatt, Licklider, Munson, Reddy, & Woods, 1971). Three major groups were supported for a 5-year "experiment" to investigate the extent to which present-day ideas and technology could be used to understand speech. Reddy (1976) has an excellent review article on speech-comprehension systems that should be consulted for details as well as for an overview. Only a few brief comments will be made here about two of these systems, HEARSAY and WHIM.

HEARSAY was developed at Carnegie-Mellon University to understand chess moves spoken to a computer that was playing chess. [Rumelhart (1977) has a good elementary exposition of the HEARSAY system.] The HEARSAY system was limited to this highly restricted conversational domain because the inherent constraints of the domain allowed a reasonable specification of the vocabulary, syntax, semantics, and pragmatics of the system. The researchers at Carnegie-Mellon believed, as do almost all researchers concerned with speech understanding, that a system will be successful only if it incorporates all levels of language processing. Because a simple game of chess has explicit rules concerning legal and sensible moves, the system could begin with a ranking of plausible hypotheses (i.e., possible moves). These hypotheses could be translated into lexical representations (or, roughly, words) and their syntactic arrangements. Words in turn have phonemes that are used to predict certain features in the speech chain. Of course, the system is not as "top-down" as this description implies, since each level of analysis has its own information that leads to its own hypotheses. The main part of the program is a set of decision processes used to choose among alternative hypotheses and to update continuously the measures associated with goodness ratings of each hypothesis. An important point to note is that minimal use is made of the acoustic signal itself.

Another system, developed at Bolt, Beranek, and Newman under Woods' direction, was dubbed "Hear what I mean" (WHIM). It is similar in a general way to HEARSAY, although it deals with a more natural speech environment — trips and travel budgets. For example, such sentences as "When did Bill go to Mexico?" might be presented. Rather than try even to summarize this highly complex system, I will make a few remarks about its success. A number of goals were set up for the project, and many were satisfactorily accomplished. To give some idea of the nature of the system, as well as its limitations, in the next sentence I have put the goals in parentheses when they differed from the accomplishments and have italicized the additional features not originally specified as goals.

The system accepted connected (continuous) speech from three (many) *male* speakers in a *somewhat* quiet computer room, over an ordinary (good) microphone, with *no* tuning of the system for individual speakers on a 1000-word vocabulary in a (highly constrained) well-defined task.

The performance itself was perhaps less than exciting from an absolute point of view, although not when one considers how little was known before the project began. The semantic error (i.e., failure to interpret the utterance correctly) was 56 percent. It took a PDP-10 computer, on the average, 1350 times real time to process a sentence. The authors of the summary report (Woods, Bates, Brown, Bruce, Cook, Klovstad, Makhoul, Nash-Webber, Schwartz, Wolf, and Zue, 1976) noted that the system improved substantially after test runs were made and that misinterpretation of an entire utterance concealed the very high level of word comprehension.

We are still a long way from using speech to evaluate cognitive processes in psychological experiments. On the other hand, programming computers to understand natural speech is perhaps one of the most meaningful of psychological experiments since it entails almost all aspects of human cognition. Although so complex a problem cannot be solved all at once, some overview is needed to identify and focus on appropriate subproblems; the speech-comprehension systems have provided a good preliminary model with which to work.

The second kind of language processing, typed input, is a little more promising simply because the problem of segmenting the continuous flow of speech into words has already been solved. The goals, however, usually become more ambitious because a more complete level of comprehension is desired. Also, although words are separated, they are not always spelled correctly and, just because a sentence is typed, does not mean it is grammatical. Syntax, semantics, and pragmatics still interact in complex ways.

A number of working systems comprehend sentences typed into the computer, and all of them work within limited domains, fairly general syntax, and "comprehend" in special ways. One of the first programs was ELIZA, written to simulate a psychiatrist's interaction with a patient. This program contained no model of the patient, of semantics, or even of the meaning of the words used. It accomplished its goal of sounding like a psychiatrist simply by matching sentence patterns; it relied heavily on the implicit knowledge people have of the psychiatric interview situation. These results make it clear that the evaluation of a program cannot be based solely on its performance. A good program for comprehension includes a theory of comprehension and knowledge, and the elements of the program must be scrutinized for principles of psychological importance.

The most widely known system to date is Winograd's (1972) Blocks World. Colored cubes and pyramids are placed on a table, and the computer moves them around (symbolically, not physically) under command of the user of the program. To do this, the system must understand the pragmatic rules of blocks (e.g., cubes cannot be placed on pyramids or on another cube if that cube already has a block on it). It must understand English well enough to parse sentences and carry out the commands made. As an added level of understanding, Winograd included a memory for reasons why certain tasks were done. For example, if, after removing a red pyramid from a green cube in order to put the green cube on another red cube, the system is asked why the pyramid is on the table, the system will reconstruct the sequence of actions that led to that state of the pyramid. "Because it was on the green cube which had to be moved." Why was the green cube moved? "Because you asked me to move it." Other comprehension systems less directly concerned with understanding language will be discussed later. For an especially practical system, see Woods, Kaplan, and Nash-Webber (1972).

Many psychologists and linguists wonder why these computer systems should be important to them. Psycholinguists usually work within a relatively narrow area and with their own set of theoretical hypotheses. Their experiments are rarely definitive, but only provide evidence for or against an hypothesis. Generally, the hypotheses are stated verbally and, even if fairly specific, fit into a broader theoretical rubric that is rather vague. One example will illustrate this point.

A number of experiments have been conducted to see how people perceive the subunits of a sentence. Garrett, Bever, and Fodor (1966) looked at this question by presenting a sentence to one ear and a click to the other ear at some point during the sentence presentation. The subjects were required to judge at what point in the sentence the click occurred. Garrett et al. found that subjects tended to place the click close to a break between grammatically organized units. If one accepts the logic of the experimental method, then the results support certain theories of sentence organization. But this experiment does not provide very much information about *how* such segmentation is accomplished. For one thing, the theory that gave rise to the experiment ignores the integration of phonological, syntactic, and semantic information.

The attempts to make computers understand speech may lack realism by not trying to simulate human behavior, but they certainly deal more directly with the whole problem. One might even argue that the constraints on understanding speech are so great as to preclude there being several different solutions to the problem. If such is the case, a computer solution will be close to a human model of speech perception.

THE COMPUTER AS A MODEL FOR COGNITIVE THEORY

The third influence of computers on cognitive science is based on analogies between humans and computers. These analogies have been so pervasive that it is hard to remember what it was like to study cognition without them. Although many scientists have severe reservations about the analogies between computers and human cognition (e.g., Weizenbaum, 1976), numerous mechanisms deriving directly from computer technology have been introduced as solutions to cognitive problems. It is of course quite possible that these ideas were first introduced as solutions to computer problems because the designers of computers were humans. In other words, it may be that computers suggest human processes because people build computers and, in so doing, introduce human cognitive processes into the machines.

Although, to many people, the influence of the computer on cognitive theory is obvious, it is worth stating again. For example, consider some recent thoughts by one of the fathers of cognitive psychology, Urlic Neisser (1976). After discussing why introspection failed and why behaviorism and Freudian psychology succeeded, he mentioned the recent paradigm shift in psychology; Neisser (1976) then went on to say:

> There are several reasons for this turn of events, but the most important was probably the advent of the computer. This was not just because computers allow one to conduct experiments more easily or analyze data more thoroughly, though they do. Rather, it was because the activities of the computer itself seemed in some ways akin to cognitive processes. Computers accept information, manipulate symbols, store items in "memory" and retrieve them again, classify inputs, recognize patterns, and so on. Whether they do these things just like people was less important than that they do them at all. The coming of the computer provided a much-needed reassurance that cognitive processes were real; that they could be studied and perhaps understood. It also provided a new vocabulary and a new set of concepts for dealing with cognition; terms like *information, input, processing, coding,* and *subroutine* soon became commonplace. Some theorists even maintained that all psychological theories should be explicitly written in the form of computer programs. Others differed, and continue to differ, but no one doubts the importance of the computer metaphor for contemporary psychology [pp. 5–6].

An exhaustive listing of the variety of ways in which computers have influenced psychological theory would be impossible; there are simply too many ways, and they interact at too many levels. This influence – or better, interaction, since there are reciprocal effects on computer science as well – is only just beginning. The reason for this interaction is obvious: Both people and computers are information-processing machines, and, hence, theories about information-processing potentially apply to both. Eventually, of course, certain facts about information-processing will be restricted to machines and other facts will be restricted to people, but all the facts will concern information storage, transformation, and transmission. Because of these complex interrelationships, future cognitive scientists will need to study computer science, psychology, and linguistics, and not just one of these three sciences.

Historical Review

One of the first signs of the influence of computers on psychology was Hebb's (1949) cell assemblies and McCulloch and Pitts' (1943) neuron circuit that could represent symbolic logic. Farley and Clark (1954) actually tried to simulate a "self-organizing" system designed to recognize patterns. This was followed by Rosenblatt's (1958) Perceptron and Selfridge's (1959) Pandemonium. These early efforts emphasized, naturally enough, the relationship between the brain and the logical circuits in a computer. These first attempts were not especially successful, at least partly because the relationship between a computer and a brain is not as direct and concrete as the relationship between neural circuits and logical circuits. Instead, the relationship is more like a multilevel analogy.

Other researchers, such as Newell and Simon (1961), tried to make computers discover theorems in logic and solve problems. Although these efforts were not strictly aimed at simulation of human behavior, they were attempts to make the computer perform human functions. The steps in the programs were considered to be analogous to steps in the human mental program, although obviously performed with a different type of hardware.

A more empirically oriented theory was Feigenbaum's (1963) Elementary Perceiver And Memorizer (EPAM), which had many of the characteristics with which psychologists today are concerned, such as a short-term memory, a long-term memory, a discrimination net, attentional mechanisms, rehearsal processes. Furthermore, EPAM could be made to simulate human behavior in rote-learning tasks familiar to psychologists (paired-associate learning, serial learning, and probability learning). In 1960, Hunt and Hovland, borrowing ideas from Bruner, Goodnow, and Austin (1956), introduced an "information-processing analysis" of concept learning. These approaches have since become an integral part of psychology. A good introduction to this early work can be found in Newell and Simon (1963), in Feigenbaum and Feldman (1963), and Miller, Galanter, and Pribram (1960).

Information theory (Shannon & Weaver, 1949) and its application to communication (Cherry, 1957) represent a different approach. Miller (1953) introduced psychologists to information theory with the expectation that the ability to measure information would have profound effects on the study of psychology. Actually, the measurement of information has turned out to be less important than Miller anticipated, but many of the related concepts, when imaginatively applied to psychological questions, have had important effects. Perhaps the most perceptive was Miller's (1956) own discovery of the ubiquity of the number seven in art, history, folklore, and psychology. This "magic" number showed up in subitizing, the span of immediate memory, and in absolute judgment. Information theory also made clear the importance of "chunking" and introduced concepts like channel capacity, encoding and decoding, and the role of noise in communication. Research on attention (Broadbent, 1958) added a new dimension to cognitive processes.

There is a natural affinity between engineers and linguists because they both study communication, the transmission of a coded message across a noisy channel. The development of computers requires an understanding of language since programming a machine requires communicating with it. The investigation of higher-level languages produced further interaction between computer science and linguistics. Chomsky (1963) in "Formal Properties of Grammars" and Chomsky and Miller (1963) in "Formal Analysis of Natural Language" made explicit the relationship between automata and different types of grammars. As a result, the theory of types of computers and the theory of types of syntactic structures became intertwined. Since language is a primary source of information for people, and since both machines and people must deal with language codes, it has become obvious that psychologists have much to learn from both linguistics (psycholinguistics) and computer science.

Another development has been the strong, although sometimes controversial, influence of artificial intelligence on both psychology and linguistics. It began with the seminal work by Turing (1950), "Computing Machinery and Intelligence," in which he seriously considered the possibility that machines could be made to think. The initial goal of artificial intelligence was to make computers do intelligent things. But before this could be accomplished, a theory of intelligence was necessary (Minsky, 1963). At first, the emphasis was on games like chess (Newell, Shaw, & Simon, 1963), theorem proving (Gelernter, Hansen, & Loveland, 1960), and question answering (Green, Wolf, Chomsky, & Laughery, 1961). (I distinguish here between artificial intelligence and the attempts by Newell and Simon and by Feigenbaum to simulate human behavior. To be sure, the dichotomy is not always clear.) Later work emphasized semantic information-processing (Minsky, 1968), which will be discussed more thoroughly later.

An important development in artificial intelligence was the invention of special languages for dealing with symbolic objects. At Carnegie-Mellon, Newell and his coworkers (Newell, 1961) created Information Processing Language (IPL), which had as its basis an associative memory. Within linguistics, the string-processing language COMIT (Yngve, 1961) was developed, later to be superseded by SNOBOL (Farber, Griswold, & Polonsky, 1964). McCarthy, Abrahams, Edwards, Hart, and Levin (1962) wrote LISP, based in part on Church's lambda calculus. LISP has been by far the most influential language in the development of artificial intelligence. Today there are many special languages for programming symbolic structures. Most of them are either extensions of LISP or are other languages with LISP-like additions. Future work in cognition will require new and more specialized languages because such languages are among the most important analytical tools of the science.

Empirical studies of psychological processes also contributed to the shift from behaviorism to cognitive psychology. Among these were the discovery of the icon (Sperling, 1963), studies of the function of short-term memory (e.g., Atkinson & Shiffrin, 1968; Sternberg, 1969; Waugh & Norman, 1968; Wickelgren, 1970), of encoding processes (Bower, 1972), of organization processes (Mandler, 1967), of feature analysis (Craik & Lockhart, 1972), and of concepts (Posner, 1969).

The above summary of major influences from computer science and information processing illustrates the extent to which these fields have come to dominate psychological theory. Almost all facets of psychology show some changes attributable to the computer revolution. Even personality theory has been influenced (Colby, 1967). Of course, this influence is not unique to psychology. Linguistics has been profoundly affected, as have the biological, physical, and social sciences. But perhaps psychology and linguistics have been particularly receptive because an essential component of human activity is information processing, and the ideas derived from the development of computers are necessary ideas for psychology and linguistics. Even without the invention of computers, the cognitive sciences would eventually have developed information-processing concepts. Conversely, many computer ideas are no doubt due to human introspection (Winograd, 1975a). This "cross-talk" among the fields of psychology, linguistics, computer science, anthropology, engineering (and certain areas of education and philosophy) has led to the term *cognitive science*, a classification parallel in abstraction to the terms *physical science* and *social science*.

Recent Developments

The last 7 years have seen a sharp shift in the focus of theoretical work in cognitive science. Within psychology there has been a spate of theories about the nature of long-term memory along with mechanisms for inference, storage, and retrieval. Most of these theories are realized in computer programs written in LISP-like languages. Three theories are particularly dependent on the computer: Anderson and Bower's (1973) Human Associative Memory (HAM), Norman and Rumelhart's (1975) LNR (or ELINOR), and Schank's (1975) theory of Conceptual Dependencies (CD). All three of these approaches are language-analysis programs. All take a natural English sentence as input and produce as output an internal representation encoding its meaning. Unlike earlier theories of memory such as Katz and Fodor's (1963) feature theory and Quillian's (1968) network theory of semantic memory, these theories are not static; they allow the addition of new information to existing memory, search memory in response to questions, and produce various kinds of responses. All consist of a network of linked nodes representing concepts and their relationships.

The formalism used for memory representation, however, differs greatly among the three models. HAM uses binary tree structures that directly reflect the surface structure of the sentence. For example, his major binary divisions are context–time, subject–predicate, and relation–object. ELINOR uses an *n*-ary relational structure as a proposition with concepts and/or other propositions as arguments. In ELINOR, nouns and adjectives as well as verbal concepts are represented as propositions. CD is a kind of case grammar based on a "primitive" set of conceptual categories. These conceptual categories combine according to a conceptual syntax. The categories are nominals, actions, locations, time adverbials, and attributes. The method of parsing sentences also differs among the three approaches. HAM takes a simple subset of English requiring only a "surface grammar" or phrase-structure grammar. ELINOR uses an Augmented Transition Network (ATN) developed by Woods (1970). CD minimizes the syntax used by incorporating syntax, insofar as possible, into the semantic component; semantics is considered first, and, if the results are interpretable, syntactic analysis is ignored.

Each approach has some unique characteristics, of which we can mention only the most salient. HAM was structured to account for experimental data arising from memory paradigms (e.g., memory for lists of words and for propositions presented in sentence form). It was not designed as a complete understanding system, although by incorporating details of how information is processed, it is in some ways more complete than the other two models. ELINOR was designed to be complete and psychologically plausible, and little or no attempt was made to relate it to experimental data. The general idea was that it should "act" as people act when it solves a problem or answers a question. CD is a more abstract theory in that the conceptual system is uniquely structured and relatively independent of the language input. In fact, its forte is translating the language input into various levels of paraphrase or into another language. Schank (1975) thinks of his CD network as a model of human memory, although the total system is limited in that it does not make inferences about some real-world domain, and its information-processing component is not intended as a theory of human information processing.

Brief as this description of the three theories has been, it perhaps can serve to illustrate the point that future psychological theories will necessarily evolve from such approaches. These models depend on computer programs written in special languages. It is obvious that cognitive scientists in the future will have to be familiar with the programming languages relevant to their theoretical work. Also, these theoretical developments are not without their more practical side effects. For example, the latest theories of instruction utilize network structures in representing knowledge. Greeno (1976) provides an excellent example of work in this area.

A number of aspects of these systems point to more general theoretical issues. One of the most important of these is a distinction between two ways to store knowledge: declarative and procedural. Although the declarative–procedural issue was initially rather vague, Winograd (1975b) has recently clarified it. Fundamentally, it involves the question of how knowledge is stored. Declarative knowledge is stored as data that are acted upon by a number of general procedures. The "data" can be represented in a number of different ways but they are always static. Procedural knowledge is knowing "how" as opposed to knowing "what." It is the program rather than the data. Of course, as any programmer knows, the distinction between data and program is somewhat arbitrary, and so, in modeling human cognition, it is difficult to decide whether knowledge should be stored procedurally or declaratively. "Knowledge" such as knowing how to ride a bike is, according to my intuition, highly procedural. Knowing my wife's birthday, on the other hand, is declarative knowledge.

Anderson (1976), taking an idea from Ryle (1949), has three criteria for distinguishing these two types of knowledge. First, declarative knowledge is either completely known or is not known at all, whereas procedural knowledge can be partially known. Second, declarative knowledge is learned suddenly in an all-or-none fashion, whereas procedural knowledge can be gradually acquired. Third, declarative knowledge can be verbally communicated but procedural knowledge cannot. These criteria certainly seem to distinguish knowing how to ride a bike and knowing that my wife's birthday is July 27. Nonetheless, one can imagine a procedural subroutine that took as its parameters the name of the person and returned his birth date or a declarative interpretation according to which knowing how to ride a bike requires a collection of schema, each of which declaratively stores the parameters of the motor responses required to ride a bike.

Anderson (1976) used the distinction between declarative and procedural knowledge to develop what appears to be a powerful mix of two techniques standardly used in computer programs to code knowledge: networks of concepts (Quillian, 1968) and production systems (Newell, 1972). The idea of a network of concepts connected by links representing relations is fundamental to the three semantic theories being discussed, so all can be classified as declarative in this respect. Such networks represent situations, episodes, events, etc., but do not produce any actions. Procedures are needed to change the network structure or to produce an action external to the system.

Newell's Production Systems model (PS) assumes a short-term memory (STM) of fixed size and a set of productions that act upon STM and perform input—output operations. Each production is essentially an operator or function using the items in STM as parameters and rewriting STM as output. Productions can also request an input from outside the system or produce an output. Productions presumably are stored in long-term memory (LTM). Early versions of the theory did not consider where the productions came from, but more recent versions (e.g., Klahr & Wallace, 1976) are trying to build learning into the systems. The system works by setting up an STM structure and then letting the sequence of productions "run off." The order of "firing" is determined by the order of productions on a list and by the current state of STM. The first production on the list is matched against STM. If it matches, it is fired; if it does not match, the production next in order is tested. If no production matches, the system simply stops. This system can be used to construct models of STM scanning as in the Sternberg (1969) task, cryptarithmetic (Newell & Simon, 1972), and seriation by young children (Young, 1973). Klahr and Wallace (1976) and Farnham-Diggory (1972) presented several examples of the use of production systems.

PS has a number of problems. Because it is entirely procedural, simple facts must be stored as procedures. This means that if a fact is to be used in two or more ways, it must be stored in two or more different procedures. Also, all computation takes place in STM, with LTM serving simply as a storehouse of productions. Input and output are under the control of the system, and there is no way to "interrupt" the system. That is, unless an input is programmed by a production, it cannot be accepted. Although modifying PS to accept interrupts is easy, the role of STM still seems overly large.

Recently, Anderson (1976) has developed a revised and expanded version of HAM that he calls ACT. ACT is unique in that it represents declarative knowledge by networks simultaneously as it represents actions by productions. Intuitively, it seems that ACT explains a number of phenomenological experiences and resolves many of the major complaints recently made by Neisser (1976). We lack the understanding to model many experimental situations adequately. One of the difficulties lies in determining the tradeoff between declarative and procedural aspects of a situation. In ACT, a balance can be worked out between these two aspects and various combinations can be experimented with. Similarly, ACT apparently can handle two aspects of learning, the simple acquisition of new facts and the learning of new acts.

As in HAM, declarative knowledge in ACT is represented in memory by a propositional network. Each node and link is either active or inactive. Links are also assumed to have different strengths. The strength of any given link is incremented whenever it is matched in a production. During a cycle of the system, an active node spreads its activity to adjacent links and nodes with a probability that depends on the number of links connected to a node. A dampening effect halts the "spreading excitation" (Quillian, 1968) so that the activity does not eventually spread to all the memory nodes. Finally, a special set of active nodes, to which productions are matched, is not dampened and is treated much as an STM buffer. This "working memory" is of limited size, and items in it are lost only by being pushed off by newly activated nodes.

Procedural knowledge in ACT is represented as productions, as in the Newell PS model. (As noted above, a production consists of a condition followed by an action.) However, a number of new features have been added in ACT. First, productions have strengths that, along with the number of productions on the APPLYLIST, determine the probability that a production will be activated. Whether activated or not, a production is removed from the APPLYLIST after the time allowed for its application has elapsed. A production is selected if its condition matches the set of active nodes. First, all productions are tested for a partial match with the list of active nodes. If a partial match is found, the production is placed on the APPLYLIST. Productions on the APPLYLIST are then checked more thoroughly and, if they meet the test of a perfect match, they are executed. Note that a number of productions can be executed at one time. The actions of a production serve to activate portions of memory, cause new memory structures to be built, and initiate input and output processing. It should be clear that these added assumptions make ACT work in a very different way from PS, and that the use of productions in ACT is not simply a matter of adding PS to a network theory.

Production systems are also common in applied programs. Three recent papers illustrate the increasing realization that production systems provide a degree of freedom not available in more structured systems. Bobrow and Winograd (1977) describe a general "Knowledge Representation Language"

(KRL) designed for use in understanding systems. KRL uses both declarative and procedural knowledge represented in networks and procedural attachments. It seems to be an extension of the ELINOR system much as ACT was an extension of HAM.

Another development is the construction of systems that learn new productions as they are needed to solve problems. Hedrick (1976) has discussed one such system. The implications for psychological theories of learning should be fairly obvious. Another, more practical, application of productions is the MYCIN system that selects antibiotic therapy for bacteremia. Here, the "domain-specific knowledge" is represented as a set of over 200 production rules. Details can be found in Davis, Buchanan, and Shortliffe (1977).

This example concerning the declarative–procedural dichotomy illustrates how theoretical models can raise fundamental questions. The computer is not used merely to simulate a particular cognitive theory, but cognitive theory is often directly affected by theories from computer science. Interactions between computer science and cognitive science occur at many levels: language processing, memory structures, information storage and retrieval, and data representations.

COMPUTERIZED COGNITIVE LABORATORIES

Historical Review

The availability of relatively inexpensive computers in the mid 1960s allowed the establishment of a number of psychology laboratories to study learning, decision-making, perception, and thinking. Miller, Bregman, and Norman (1965) in a very early report discuss using the computer for psychological research. They mention a number of research efforts using computers and provide a summary of developments prior to 1965.

Soon after 1965, minicomputers became accessible to an even larger number of researchers. Some of the smaller systems using minicomputers were described in a book published by the Digital Equipment Corporation (e.g., Link, 1972; Millward et al., 1972). These laboratories were usually designed for specific kinds of research, such as perception, animal control, or learning experiments. Nevertheless, they were generally much more flexible than previous laboratories that had depended on relay control.

Software was, however, a serious problem for these stand-alone minicomputers. Compiling assembly-language programs was cumbersome because paper tape was generally the input–output medium, and core storage was so small that programs and compilers could not be simultaneously resident. At Brown University, two solutions were found to these problems. The first was to build a general real-time system, GASPS (Wickens, Howard, Rice, & Millward, 1972), very similar to the present RT-8 system distributed by Digital Equipment

Corporation. It required programming in assembly language but only short routines, called *tasks*, had to be written. Since these were one-page codes, the programming problems were not serious.

Nevertheless, programming, editing, and debugging still took a great deal of computer time, and multiple uses and users were limited by the available software. Therefore, a cross-compiler was programmed on the IBM/360 (Hoadley & Getty, 1975). With it, many students could write programs without tying up the small machine. Such a division of labor is obviously sensible and no doubt will become standard practice in the future.

Of course, larger systems continued to develop, and by the early 1970s, there were many department-size computers interfaced to a number of different laboratories. One of the earliest of these all-purpose systems was designed for Computer Assisted Instruction at the Learning, Research & Development Center (LRDC) in Pittsburgh. This system has a 16K-PDP-7 computer with 16 levels of interrupt, a RAND tablet, a scope with a light pen, taped audio, a touch-sensitive display, and slide projectors. It controls eight laboratories (Ragsdale, 1969). Other large systems include the Colorado CLIPR system (Bailey, 1972), the system at NIMH (Knight, Colburn, Owens, Freeman, Syed, & Rasband, 1974), the system at UCLA (Carterette, Barnebey, Lovell, Nagel, & Friedman, 1972), the IBM 1800 systems at Indiana and at Michigan directed by Restle and Greeno, respectively, and the Carnegie-Mellon laboratory by Gregg.

Software development for these systems was extremely diverse. This diversity is easily explained: The systems involved different computers, different peripheral equipment, and were developed at different times. Programming concepts like time-sharing and real-time systems were limited to large machines, and their development was too expensive for small laboratories. Polson (1973) at Colorado developed a "state change algorithm translator" (SCAT) because it allowed the easy translation of experimental procedures into programs. On the other hand, McLean (1969) at Carnegie-Mellon opted for PSYCHOL, a higher-level language, because it was similar to standard languages such as ALGOL. Finding FORTRAN inadequate as a control language, Scholz (1973) developed PROSS at Indiana, and Kieras (1973) designed GEPS for the Michigan IBM 1800. These developments illustrate that the know-how for better language systems was available, but complete systems were not being offered by the computer vendors. A great deal of labor was spent on these systems even though future developments will surely make these particular languages obsolete.

Other tricks were being developed to help the researcher perform complex experiments with the aid of computers. For example, connecting a minicomputer to a large time-shared machine allowed for data backup, analysis using high-level languages, and, with cross-compilers, the opportunity for multiple users. All of these benefits freed the minicomputer so that it could be dedicated to experiments (Aikin & Millward, 1972; Sedelow, 1976).

For a time in the 1960s, the general philosophy of computer scientists was "the bigger the better." At one time the idea was bandied about that the ultimate solution to all computing problems was to put a super computer in Denver and have everyone tie into it. This philosophy arose because larger machines were more efficient, and peripheral equipment had not yet been developed for smaller machines. The success of time-sharing software and hardware also reinforced this idea. On the other hand, some researchers who needed fast real-time computing argued that each researcher should have his own minicomputer, and any attempt to share a computer would inevitably interfere with good research. Although these may seem like exaggerated examples, both these ideas had their impact and are to some extent still with us. Most universities have chosen to introduce a large central computer at the expense of minicomputers and have even put their administrative data-processing and student instruction on the same machine. Unfortunately, there are incompatibilities among the users, and trying to have them all use one machine has usually meant that someone suffers. Conversely, there are departments with many small machines that are not being used efficiently because each laboratory is too small to support the development necessary for efficient use.

The last few years have seen a new trend in computer laboratories. This trend is toward more flexible laboratories designed to utilize the power and efficiency of the systems involved as well as meet the needs of the various users. Gilman, Lapin, and Buckley (1974) described a hierarchical system that sounds very reasonable. Further work at the LRDC in Pittsburgh (Lesgold & Fitzhugh, 1977) has provided a software system that makes more efficient use of the full power of their midicomputer. Scholz and Halff (1974) described a system that uses their IBM 1800 to "supervise" minicomputers in multiple laboratories. They have developed software along the lines of GEPS at Michigan (Halff, Scholz, & Walker, 1975).

At the hardware level, there are computer systems that support time sharing even though they are relatively small and cost less than $20,000. The vendors are providing monitors that make programming in higher level languages relatively easy. Peripheral devices being built with microprocessors need less control from the laboratory computer itself. That is, polling these devices is acceptable since they have their own controllers to handle the necessary fast responses. With the newer disk systems, storage on the small computers has become large and inexpensive. Interconnecting computers, although still troublesome because of inadequate software, is becoming easier. All these developments mean that some new models are needed for future cognitive-science laboratories.

A Cognitive Laboratory for the Future

Earlier, I reviewed three influences of computers on cognitive science. The future cognitive scientist will use high-powered statistical procedures, sophisticated on-line control computers, and ideas derived from information-processing theory. The future cognitive-science laboratory must be flexible and hierarchically structured. Although the larger existing laboratories were not designed according

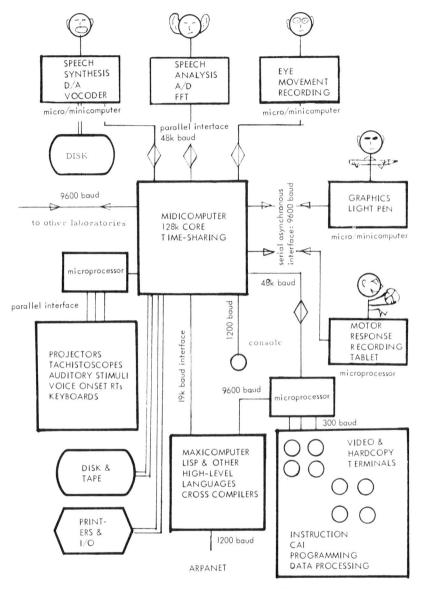

FIG. 8.1.   A computer laboratory for cognitive science.

to an overall plan, many have most of the requirements needed to meet the developments in cognitive science. Now that hardware costs are lower and good software systems more widely distributed, newer laboratories can be designed that will be more than adequate for a number of years.

The ideal laboratory would have many users and many subsystems. This implies not simply time sharing, but a hierarchical arrangement of hardware and software components (Korn, 1977). There would be a number of independent smaller systems using a midicomputer as a time-shared host. More important, the total system would be integrated to allow for highly flexible communication between components and to allow users to move easily from one subsystem to another. Students and researchers could begin by learning the higher-level languages, then one of the laboratory subsystems, and then move to the other subsystems as required for their research. (At present, as the above description of existing laboratories should make clear, moving to another laboratory often requires months of relearning.) This homogeneity would not be forced on the system by making every subsystem conform to a limited language but would be attained by simple conventions and powerful software utility programs (Ritchie & Thompson, 1974). Subsystems must be designed for relatively easy combination and recombination. For example, studies of reading might demand both eye-movement recording and speech recording. (The reader can easily imagine other combinations.)

Figure 8.1 presents a schematic diagram of an ideal laboratory. The purpose of the diagram is not to illustrate the specifics of the system but rather the general versatility and modularity of the components. Each research unit would implement its own version of the diagram. On the other hand, certain common solutions to interfacing problems and to design considerations would provide a degree of standardization not previously possible.

Figure 8.1 shows a number of different types of connections. There are 300 baud serial asynchronous lines connecting simple video terminals and 9600-19k baud serial asynchronous lines connecting microprocessors and the laboratory midicomputer. These serial interfaces are easy to install, reliable, not too expensive, and good for longer distances. They would be supported by software now being designed for networks (e.g., DECnet). Parallel interfaces connect microprocessors and the midicomputer to provide higher rates of data transfer under program control. The distances here are more restricted, and the required software would probably have to be written. Not shown in Fig. 8.1 are intercomputer connections using high-speed core-to-core channels. Such connections require little program intervention but are expensive. They are rarely needed for work in cognitive science, but could be justified in speech-recognition systems.

The subsystems pictured in Fig. 8.1 need little explanation because they have been mentioned earlier in this review. Three major laboratories using microprocessors would be the speech-synthesis, speech-analysis, and eye-movement systems. Each of these would be rather elaborate and, although I have specified a microprocessor, a minicomputer might serve them better. The midicomputer would back up these systems with data storage, analysis, stimulus generation, and input—output. A maxicomputer would be available for the extensive processing often associated with such systems. The graphics system is open-ended in the sense that one could put a simple storage scope (e.g., Tektronix) or an elaborate real-time 3-dimensional color scope on the system. The motor-response laboratory would be designed specifically for the experiments being run.

Another subsystem in Fig. 8.1 is the standard slide projector, video scope, keyboard, and limited audio, a subsystem commonly used today. With microprocessors, a number of booths could be installed if necessary. The video and hardcopy terminals would be used for program preparation, CAI, data-analysis sessions, and so on. These terminals would allow the user to transfer programs from the midicomputer to the maxicomputer and to write programs for computers at any level. The midicomputer would serve as a backup for the microsystems so that they would not require multiple disks, printers, scopes, and the like. The midicomputer would have to be a time-shared system but not necessarily a real-time system. On occasion it could be dedicated to one of the microprocessors so that it would act in real time, but polling techniques usually would be fast enough to collect the data from the laboratory systems. In any case, simple background tasks responding to interrupts could be introduced for highly demanding subsystems.

The maxicomputer would be used for larger data-processing jobs, running simulation programs in higher level languages such as LISP, teaching programming to students, running cross-compilers, and so forth. It could also be connected to outside networks such as ARPA. Certainly, much of the theoretical work would be done with languages like LISP and INTERLISP that require large systems. Although attempts are being made to build a smaller machine for LISP, it is not yet certain that it will be large enough for the kind of understanding systems now being developed. Larger analysis programs like MDS are also easier to use on large computers. Hence, even though microprocessors are becoming impressively powerful, the day of the large central computer is not yet over.

ACKNOWLEDGMENT

This work was supported in part by National Science Foundation Grant No. BMS75-08439 to the author.

REFERENCES

Aaronson, D., Grupsmith, E., & Aaronson, M. The impact of computers on cognitive psychology. *Behavior Research Methods & Instrumentation,* 1976, *8,* 129–138.

Aaronson, D., & Scarborough, H. S. Performance theories for sentence coding: Some quantitative evidence. *Journal of Experimental Psychology: Human Perception and Performance,* 1976, *2,* 56–70.

Aikin, J. O., & Millward, R. B. Some comments on connecting a small on-line computer to a large data processing machine. *Behavior Research Methods & Instrumentation,* 1972, *4,* 99–100.

Allen, J. Synthesis of speech from unrestricted text. *Proceedings of the IEEE,* 1976, *64,* 433–442.

Anderson, J. R. *Language, memory, and thought.* Hillsdale, N. J.: Lawrence Erlbaum Associates, 1976.

Anderson, J. R., & Bower, G. H. *Human associative memory*. Washington, D.C.: V. H. Winston & Sons, 1973.
Atkinson, R. C., & Shiffrin, R. M. Human memory: A proposed system and its control processes. In K.W. Spence & J.T. Spence (Eds.), *The psychology of learning and motivation* (Vol. 2). New York: Academic Press, 1968.
Bailey, D. E. The computer laboratory for instruction in psychological research. *Behavior Research Methods & Instrumentation, 1972, 4,* 95–96.
Bartlett, F. C. *Remembering*. Cambridge: Cambridge University Press, 1967. (Originally published, 1932.)
Bobrow, D. G., & Winograd, T. An overview of KRL, a knowledge representation language. *Cognitive Science, 1977, 1,* 3–46.
Bower, G. H. Stimulus-sampling theory of encoding variability. In A. W. Melton & E. Martin (Eds.), *Coding processes in human memory*. New York: V. H. Winston & Sons, 1972.
Broadbent, D. E. *Perception and communication*. Oxford: Pergamon Press, 1958.
Broadbent, K. D. A review of the MCA disco-vision system. *Information Display, 1976, 12,* 12–19.
Bruner, J. S., Goodnow, J., & Austin, G. A. *A study of thinking*. New York: John Wiley & Sons, 1956.
Carpenter, P. A., & Just, M. A. Reading comprehension as eyes see it. In M. Just & P. Carpenter (Eds.), *Cognitive processes in comprehension*. Hillsdale, N.J.: Lawrence Erlbaum Associates, 1977.
Carroll, J. D. Individual differences and multidimensional scaling. In R. N. Shepard, A. K. Romney, & S. B. Nerlove (Eds.), *Multidimensional scaling* (Vol. 1). New York: Seminar Press, 1972.
Carterette, E. C., Barnebey, A., Lovell, J. D., Nagel, D. C., & Friedman, M. P. On-line computing with the Hewlett-Packard 2116B moving-head disk operating system. *Behavior Research Methods & Instrumentation, 1972, 4,* 89–94.
Chang, J. J. On-line multidimensional scaling programs with interactive graphical display. *Behavior Research Methods & Instrumentation, 1973, 5,* 99–103.
Chapanis, A. Interactive human communication. *Scientific American, 1975, 232,* 36–49.
Chase, W. G., & Simon, H. A. The mind's eye in chess. In W. G. Chase (Ed.), *Visual Information processing*. New York: Academic Press, 1973.
Cherry, C. *On human communication*. Cambridge, Mass.: MIT Press, 1957.
Chomsky, N. Formal properties of grammars. In R. D. Luce, R. R. Bush, & E. Galanter (Eds.), *Handbook of mathematical psychology* (Vol. II). New York: John Wiley & Sons, 1963.
Chomsky, N., & Miller, G. A. Introduction to the formal analysis of natural language. In R. D. Luce, R. R. Bush, & E. Galanter (Eds.), *Handbook of mathematical psychology* (Vol. II). New York: John Wiley & Sons, 1963.
Christian, T. W., & Polson, P. G. The precision of latency measures on real-time computing systems. *Behavior Research Methods & Instrumentation, 1975, 7,* 173–178.
Cohen, M. M., & Massaro, D. W. Real-time speech synthesis. *Behavior Research Methods & Instrumentation, 1976, 8,* 189–196.
Colby, K. M. Computer simulation of change in personal belief systems. *Behavioral Science, 1967, 12,* 248–253.
Connolly, K. Factors influencing the learning of manual skills by young children. In R. A. Hinde & J. Stevenson-Hinde (Eds.), *Constraints on learning: Limitations & predispositions*. New York: Academic Press, 1973.
Craik, F. I. M., & Lockhart, R. S. Levels of processing: A framework for memory research. *Journal of Verbal Learning and Verbal Behavior, 1972, 11,* 671–684.

224   MILLWARD

Davis, R., Buchanan, B., & Shortliffe, E. Production rules as a representation for a knowledge-based consultation program. *Artificial Intelligence,* 1977, *8,* 15–46.
Degerman, R. Multidimensional analysis of complex structures: Mixtures of class and quantitative variation. *Psychometrika,* 1970, *35,* 475–491.
Farber, D. J., Griswold, R. E., & Polonsky, I. P. SNOBOL, A string manipulation language. *Journal of the Association for Computing Machinery,* 1964, *11,* 21–30.
Farley, B. B., & Clark, W. A. Simulation of self-organizing systems by a digital computer. *IRE Transactions on Information Theory,* 1954, *IT-4,* 76–84.
Farnham-Diggory, S. (Ed.). *Information processing in children.* New York: Academic Press, 1972.
Feigenbaum, E. A. The simulation of verbal learning behavior. In E. A. Feigenbaum & J. Feldman (Eds.), *Computers and thought.* New York: McGraw-Hill, 1963.
Feigenbaum, E. A., & Feldman, J. (Eds.). *Computers and thought.* New York: McGraw-Hill, 1963.
Garrett, M., Bever, T. G., & Fodor, J. The active use of grammar in speech perception. *Perception & Psychophysics,* 1966, *1,* 30–32.
Gelernter, H., Hansen, J. R., & Loveland, D. W. Empirical explorations of the geometry-theorem proving machine. *Proceedings of the Western Joint Computer Conference,* 1960, *17,* 143–147.
Gilman, C. B., Lapin, D. J., & Buckley, P. B. Hierarchically distributed processing for psychology. *Behavior Research Methods & Instrumentation,* 1974, *6,* 149–154.
Green, B. F., Wolf, A. K., Chomsky, C., & Laughery, K. Baseball: An automatic question answerer. *Proceedings of the Western Joint Computer Conference,* 1961, *19,* 219–224.
Greeno, J. G. Cognitive objectives of instruction: Theory of knowledge for solving problems and answering questions. In D. Klahr (Ed.), *Cognition and instruction.* Hillsdale, N.J.: Lawrence Erlbaum Associates, 1976.
Halff, H., Scholz, K. W., & Walker, J. H. An extension of Kieras' general experimental programming system. *Behavior Research Methods & Instrumentation,* 1975, *7,* 464–470.
Hebb, D. O. *Organization of behavior.* New York: John Wiley & Sons, 1949.
Hedrick, C. L. Learning production systems from examples. *Artificial Intelligence,* 1976, *7,* 21–50.
Hoadley, K. W., & Getty, D. J. A remote assembler for PDP-8 programs. *Behavior Research Methods & Instrumentation,* 1975, *7,* 143–144.
Hunt, E. B., & Hovland, C. I. Orders of considerations of different types of concepts. *Journal of Experimental Psychology,* 1960, *59,* 220–225.
Jerome, J. A. Systems application of film-based optical video discs. *Information Display,* 1976, *12,* 6–11.
Just, M. A., & Carpenter, P. A. The role of eye-fixation research in cognitive psychology. *Behavior Research Methods & Instrumentation,* 1976, *8,* 139–143.
Katz, J. J., & Fodor, J. A. The structure of semantic theory. *Language,* 1963, *39,* 170–210.
Kieras, D. A general experimental programming system for the IBM 1800. *Behavior Research Methods & Instrumentation,* 1973, *5,* 235–239.
Klahr, D., & Wallace, J. G. *Cognitive development: An information processing view.* Hillsdale, N.J.: Lawrence Erlbaum Associates, 1976.
Knight, J., Colburn, V., Owens, D., Freeman, L., Syed, D., & Rasband, W. An experimental control computer system time shared by several laboratories. *Behavior Research Methods & Instrumentation,* 1974, *6,* 143–146.
Korn, G. A. A distributed computer system for laboratory automation. *Computer Design,* 1977, *16,* 177–183.
Kruskal, J. B. Multidimensional scaling by optimizing goodness of fit to a nonmetric hypothesis. *Psychometrika,* 1964, *29,* 1–27.

Lashley, K. S. The accuracy of movement in the absence of excitation from the moving organ. *American Journal of Physiology,* 1917, *43,* 169–194.

Lesgold, A. M., & Fitzhugh, R. J. An on-line psychology laboratory for teaching and research. *Behavior Research Methods & Instrumentation,* 1977, *9,* 184–188.

Link, S. W. An on-line laboratory for visual perception and human learning. In *Computers in the psychology laboratory* (Vol. 2). Maynard, Mass.: Digital Equipment Corporation, 1972.

Loftus, G. R. Eye fixations and recognition memory for pictures. *Cognitive Psychology,* 1972, *3,* 525–551.

Mandler, G. Organization and memory. In K.W. Spence & J. T. Spence (Eds.), *Psychology of learning and motivation* (Vol. 1). New York: Academic Press, 1967.

McCarthy, J., Abrahams, P. W., Edwards, D. J., Hart, T. P., & Levin, M. I. *LISP 1.5 Programmer's manual.* Cambridge, Mass.: MIT Press, 1962.

McConkie, G. W., & Rayner, K. The span of the effective stimulus during a fixation in reading. *Perception & Psychophysics,* 1975, *17,* 578–586.

McCulloch, W. S., & Pitts, W. A logical calculus of the ideas immanent in nervous activity. *Bulletin of Mathematical Biophysics,* 1943, *5,* 115–137.

McIlroy, M. D. *Synthetic English speech by rule* (Computing Science & Technical Report No. 14), Murray Hill, N.J.: Bell Laboratories, 1974.

McLean, R. S. PSYCHOL: A computer language for experimentation. *Behavior Research Methods & Instrumentation,* 1969, *1,* 323–328.

Miller, G. A. What is information measurement? *American Psychologist,* 1953, *8,* 3–11.

Miller, G. A. The magic number seven, plus or minus two: Some limits on our capacity for processing information. *Psychological Review,* 1956, *63,* 81–96.

Miller, G. A., Bregman, A. S., & Norman, D. A. The computer as a general purpose device for the control of psychological experiments. In R. W. Stacey & B. Waxman (Eds.), *Computers in biomedical research.* New York: Academic Press, 1965.

Miller, G. A., Galanter, E., & Pribram, K. H. *Plans and the structure of behavior.* New York: Holt, Rinehart & Winston, 1960.

Millward, R. B., Aikin, J., & Wickens, T. The human learning laboratory at Brown University. In *Computers in the psychology laboratory* (Vol. 2). Maynard, Mass.: Digital Equipment Corporation, 1972.

Millward, R. B., & Spoehr, K. The direct measurement of hypothesis-sampling strategies. *Cognitive Psychology,* 1973, *4,* 1–38.

Millward, R. B., & Wickens, T. D. Concept-identification models. In D. H. Krantz, R. D. Luce, R. C. Atkinson, & P. Suppes (Eds.), *Learning, memory, and thinking.* San Francisco: W. H. Freeman, 1974.

Minsky, M. Steps toward artificial intelligence. Reprinted in E. A. Feigenbaum & J. Feldman (Eds.), *Computers and thought.* New York: McGraw-Hill, 1963.

Minsky, M. (Ed.). *Semantic information processing.* Cambridge, Mass.: MIT Press, 1968.

Neisser, U. *Cognition and reality.* San Francisco: W. H. Freeman, 1976.

Newell, A. (Ed.). *Information processing language-V manual.* Englewood Cliffs, N.J.: Prentice-Hall, 1961.

Newell, A., Barnett, J., Forgie, J., Green, C., Klatt, D., Licklider, J. C. R., Munson, J., Reddy, R., & Woods, W. *Speech-understanding systems: Final report of a study group.* Unpublished manuscript, Carnegie-Mellon, 1971. (Reprinted by North-Holland/American Elsevier, Amsterdam.)

Newell, A. A theoretical exploration of mechanisms for coding the stimulus. In A. W. Melton & E. Martin (Eds.), *Coding processes in human memory.* Washington, D.C.: V. H. Winston & Sons, 1972.

Newell, A., Shaw, J. C., & Simon, H. A. Chess-playing programs and the problem of complexity. In E. A. Feigenbaum & J. Feldman (Eds.), *Computers and thought.* New York: McGraw-Hill, 1963.

Newell, A., & Simon, H. A. Computer simulation of human thinking. *Science,* 1961, *134,* 2011–2017.

Newell, A., & Simon, H. A. Computers in psychology. In R. D. Luce, R. R. Bush, & E. Galanter (Eds.), *Handbook of mathematical psychology* (Vol. I). New York: John Wiley & Sons, 1963.

Newell, A., & Simon, H. A. *Human problem solving.* Englewood Cliffs, N.J.: Prentice-Hall, 1972.

Norman, D. A., Rumelhart, D. E., & the LNR Research Group. *Explorations in cognition.* San Francisco: W. H. Freeman, 1975.

Polson, P. G. SCAT: Design criteria and software. *Behavior Research Methods & Instrumentation,* 1973, *5,* 241–244.

Poltrock, S. E., & Mathews, N. N. A system for computer control of auditory stimuli. *Behavior Research Methods & Instrumentation,* 1976, *8,* 197–199.

Posner, M. I. Abstraction and the process of recognition. In G. H. Bower & J. T. Spence (Eds.), *Psychology of learning and motivation* (Vol. 3). New York: Academic Press, 1969.

Potts, G. R. Use of a campus-wide time-sharing computer to run reaction time experiments. *Behavior Research Methods & Instrumentation,* 1976, *8,* 179–184.

Quillian, M. R. Semantic memory. In M. L. Minsky (Ed.), *Semantic information processing.* Cambridge, Mass.: MIT Press, 1968.

Rabiner, L. R., & Schafer, R. W. Digital techniques for computer voice response: Implementation and applications. *Proceedings of the IEEE,* 1976, *64,* 416–433.

Ragsdale, R. G. The learning research and development center's computer assisted laboratory. In *Computers in the psychology laboratory* (Vol. 1). Maynard, Mass.: Digital Equipment Corporation, 1969.

Rayner, K., & McConkie, G. W. Perceptual processes in reading: The perceptual spans. In A. S. Reber & D. L. Scarborough (Eds.), *Toward a psychology of reading.* Hillsdale, N.J.: Lawrence Erlbaum Associates, 1977.

RCA "SelectaVision" video Disc system. *Information Display,* 1976, *12,* 21–24.

Reddy, D. R. Speech recognition by machine: A review. *Proceedings of the IEEE,* 1976, *64,* 501–531.

Ritchie, D. M. & Thompson, K. The UNIX time-sharing system. *Association for Computing Machinery,* 1974, *17,* 365–375.

Rosenblatt, F. The perceptron: A probabilistic model for information storage and organization in the brain. *Psychological Review,* 1958, *65,* 386–407.

Rumelhart, D. E. *Introduction to human information processing.* New York: John Wiley & Sons, 1977.

Ryle, G. *The concept of mind.* London: Hitchinson, 1949.

Schank, R. C. *Conceptual information processing.* Amsterdam: North-Holland Publishing Company, 1975.

Schmidt, R. A. A schema theory of discrete motor skill learning. *Psychological Review,* 1975, *82,* 225–260.

Scholz, K. W. PROSS: A process control programming language. *Behavior Research Methods & Instrumentation,* 1973, *5,* 245–247.

Scholz, K. W., & Halff, H. A decentralized computer network for supervision of multiple psychological laboratories. *Behavior Research Methods & Instrumentation,* 1974, *6,* 139–143.

Sedelow, W. A., Jr. Some implications of computer networks for psychology. *Behavior Research Methods & Instrumentation,* 1976, *8,* 218–222.

Selfridge, O. G. Pandemonium. In D. V. Blake & A. M. Uttley (Eds.), *Proceedings of the London symposium on the mechanization of thought processes* (National Physics Laboratory, Teddington, England). London: H. M. Stationary office, 1959.

Shannon, C. E., & Weaver, W. *The mathematical theory of communication.* Urbana: University of Illinois Press, 1949.

Shepard, R. N. The analysis of proximities: Multidimensional scaling with an unknown distance function. *Psychometrika,* 1962, *27,* 125–140.

Sperling, G. A. A model for visual memory tasks. *Human Factors,* 1963, *5,* 19–31.

Sternberg, S. Memory scanning: Mental processes revealed by reaction-time experiments. *American Scientist,* 1969, *57,* 421–457.

Symposium: On-line eye movement recording systems. *Behavior Research Methods & Instrumentation,* 1975, *7,* 201–215.

Turing, A. M. Computing machinery and intelligence. *Mind,* 1950, *59,* 433–460.

Votrax. Vocal Interface Division. Federal Screw Works. 500 Stephenson Highway, Troy, Michigan, 48084.

Waugh, N. C., & Norman, D. A. Primary memory. *Psychological Review,* 1968, *72,* 89–104.

Weizenbaum, J. *Computer power and human reason: From judgment to calculation.* San Francisco: W. H. Freeman, 1976.

Wickelgren, W. A. Multitrace strength theory. In D. A. Norman (Ed.), *Models of human memory.* New York: Academic Press, 1970.

Wickens, T. D., Howard, J., Rice, G. & Millward, R. B. GASPS: A general asynchronous processing system for the PDP-8. *Behavior Research Methods & Instrumentation,* 1972, *4,* 108–109.

Winograd, T. A. A program for understanding natural language. *Cognitive Psychology,* 1972, *3,* 1–191.

Winograd, T. Computer memories: A metaphor for memory organization. In C. N. Cofer (Ed.), *The structure of human memory.* San Francisco: W. H. Freeman, 1975.(a)

Winograd, T. Frame representations and the declarative–procedural controversy. In D. G. Bobrow & A. Collins (Eds.), *Representation and understanding:Studies in cognitive science.* New York: Academic Press, 1975. (b)

Woods, W. Transition network grammars for natural language analysis. *Communications of the ACM,* 1970, *13,* 591–606.

Woods, W., Bates, M., Brown, G., Bruce, B., Cook, C., Klovstad, J., Makhoul, J., Nash-Webber, B., Schwartz, R., Wolf, J., & Zue, V. *Speech understanding systems* (BBN Report No. 3438). Cambridge, Mass.: Bolt, Beranek, & Newman Inc., 1976.

Woods, W. A., Kaplan, R. M., & Nash-Webber, B. *The lunar sciences natural language information system* (BBN Report No. 2378). Cambridge, Mass.: Bolt, Beranek, & Newman, Inc., 1972. (Also NTIS N72-28984.)

Yngve, V. H. *COMIT Programmer's reference manual.* Cambridge, Mass.: MIT Press, 1961.

Young, L. R., & Sheena, D. Survey of eye movement recording methods. *Behavior Research Methods & Instrumentation,* 1975, *7,* 397–429.

Young, R. M. *Children's seriation behavior: A production-system analysis.* Unpublished doctoral dissertation, Carnegie-Mellon University, 1973.

9 The Minicomputer and Neurophysiological Techniques

W. S. Rhode
University of Wisconsin

INTRODUCTION

The relatively recent development of recording electrodes, either surface, gross, or microelectrodes, along with the necessary electronics to amplify and filter the signals, resulted in a vast increase in the amount of data that could be collected in a neurophysiological study. One early analysis technique, which readily points up the need for automation, was the analysis of neural spikes or discharges, recorded from neurons. This involved illuminating a point on an oscilloscope with the time of the neural discharge encoded as the distance from a left-hand marker and taking photographs of the screen. The time of occurrence of the discharge could then be measured using a ruler, and any of a number of simple statistical computations could be performed. This was extremely tedious and severely limited the productivity of the neural scientist. The inability to deal with the vast amounts of data and a need to quantify observations led to a quick acceptance and use of computers in neurophysiology.

An important milestone was achieved in the early 1960s with the development of a small computer that was designed for use by biologists as a laboratory system. It was intended to be connected to equipment that was either already present in the lab or special purpose devices that would be designed and "interfaced" to the computer. A computer, the "LINC" or Laboratory Instrument Computer (Clark & Molnar, 1965) included many architectural innovations that were to become standard in the minicomputer industry in the years to follow. The prototype was built and demonstrated in 1962 at MIT's Lincoln Laboratory. It was promoted by NIH through its Biotechnology Resource Branch in an evaluation program that gave 11 LINCs to various groups, including the University of Wisconsin's Laboratory of Neurophysiology in 1963.

The goals of the LINC development (listed because they are still very much applicable to the neural sciences) are to build a machine that: (1) is *small* enough in scale so that the individual research worker or small laboratory group can assume complete responsibility for all aspects of administration, operation, programming, and maintenance; (2) provides direct, simple, effective means whereby the experimenter can *control* the machine from its console, with immediate displays of data and results for viewing or photographing; (3) is *fast* enough for simple data processing "on-line" while the experiment is in progress and logically powerful enough to permit more complex calculations later if required; (4) is *flexible* enough in physical arrangement and electrical characteristics to permit convenient interconnection with a variety of other laboratory apparatus, both analog and digital, such as amplifiers, timers, transducers, plotters, special digital equipment, while minimizing the need for complex intermediating devices; and (5) includes features of design that facilitate the *training* of persons unfamiliar with the use of digital computers.

Fifteen years have passed since the LINC development, and a great deal of progress has been made in computer technology both in hardware and software. CPUs more powerful than the LINC are available in a single itegrated circuit for less than $100, and the continual decline in the price of memory, a factor of 100 in the last 15 years, argues that larger computers will be the norm of the future. As large-scale integration of logic circuits permits more functionality in the hardware, perhaps we will soon see computers that again embrace the original goals of the LINC program.

Speed and memory size are important features for any computer since they can limit the applications that can be handled. For example, a microprocessor may be sufficient to control and record responses in a behavioral laboratory but it very likely will be inadequate for digitizing (converting an analog signal to digital number) and analyzing 16 channels of EEG. Another example is picture-processing operations requiring the graphical manipulation of images (e.g., neural structures such as a impregnated neuron). These structures can be rotated on a graphical display to create an illusion of depth or the image of a 3-dimensional object. This requires a reasonably powerful system to perform the necessary transformation computations and manipulations.

There are a wide variety of systems available for use in laboratories today. While the choice of systems is usually dictated by the number of dollars available, many considerations do come into play: (1) the data rates of the experiment; (2) the knowledge of the users about digital technology (e.g., can they interface their laboratory apparatus to the computer? What programming languages do they know?; (3) the size of programs used to analyze data; (4) past experience and availability of computers; (5) local support for maintenance, programming, spare parts, peripherals, etc.; and (6) what kind of computer do their friends use for related research?

But before considering the role of computers, let us ask, what are the goals of the neural sciences? In studying the central nervous system, we would like to elucidate its operation at an electrochemical, anatomical, or physiological level. The explanation of the action of the brain or nervous system must be guided by some general principles (Szentágothai & Arbib, 1975); (1) the theory must be action oriented, that is one seeks to explain the interactions with the environment that the animal engages in; (2) perception is not only of "what" but is related to the environment in which interaction occurs, that is "where"; (3) an adaptive system, such as the brain, must be able to correlate sensory data in a manner that facilitates the evolution of an internal model of the experience; (4) the organization must be hierarchical with adequate feedback loops to coordinate the many subsystems; and (5) the brain can be thought of as a layered (cortical layers) somatotopically organized computer.

These principles cover simple animal reactions, perception, memory, and the adaptive nature of the organism. The investigative strategy for these principles varies with a multidisciplinary approach often required. There is no one best way to investigate and explain these basic principles.

One area that is being intensively pursued is the investigation of sensory processes. For example, electrophysiology, biochemistry, neuroanatomy, psychoacoustics, etc., have all been employed in pursuit of the explanation of how sound is encoded within the inner ear. In the course of the last few years, many techniques have been used to determine the motion of the basilar membrane that in large part determines the excitation of the hair cells in the cochlea or inner ear. Direct observation techniques have included the use of the light microscope, the Mössbauer effect, the capacitance probe and the laser interferometer. Indirect observations of the motion of the basilar membrane have used auditory nerve recording, spiral ganglion recording, cochlear potentials, psychoacoustics, and mathematical models to infer the form of vibration. This is typical of any contemporary investigative area. Multidisciplinary approaches often using a computer to assist in handling the large amounts of data are commonplace.

Since much of my own experience is in hearing research, most of the following discussion of the use of computers in neurophysiology will involve hearing, although many of the hardware and software items I discuss are common to visual and somatosensory areas. In addition, the use of some of these techniques and devices is not limited to sensory research but have been applied in other areas of neuroscience.

DEVICES FOR NEUROPHYSIOLOGICAL RESEARCH

Those physical devices that are used for stimulus generation and control, data collection, and data analysis are called *hardware*. Experience has unequivocally shown that any device that can be bought should not be built. Considerations of time, personnel, documentation, and maintenance all point to purchasing well-worn devices. Nevertheless, there are many instances when a particular experiment requires something not available off the shelf, and devices must be designed and built. Timing subsystems, event digitizers, analog-to-digital (A/D) converters, and displays are the devices most commonly constructed.

The form of these devices varies depending on the use. The sensory system to be studied (e.g., vision, audition, somato-sensory system) will affect the selection of stimulus generating and/or delivering equipment. If it is a behavioral experiment, then devices for detecting and recording the responses may involve levers, lights, buzzers, buttons, etc. If a mapping of part of the cortex or other part of the nervous system is planned, then one has to decide on whether the evoked response is to be recorded with gross electrodes, microelectrodes that permit multiple-unit recording, or microelectrodes that permit only single unit recording. A multiple-electrode configuration could also be used with any of these techniques and would require additional equipment and possibly increased computer capability. EEG recording with 16 or more channels at sampling rates of up to several hundred samples per second could require special handling of the A/D system since programmed input/output (I/O) rates greater than 1000/sec are usually infeasible.

In order to provide a better idea of the range of equipment that has been used in neurophysiology, I use an auditory lab as an example. Other examples can be found in Brown (1976).

Stimulus Generation and Control

Timers. One would think that a device as simple and basic as a digital timer would be commercially available, and some colors and flavors are. But in any particular implementation of an experimental setup, individual requirements (such as the number of timers, logic interconnections, logic level outputs, displays of current or preset time, the ability to use recurrently without resetting, the ability to set manually or via computer, timer resolution, and range) may prevent a simple-purchase solution. Any of these may not be compatible with readily available solutions. Available off-the-shelf integrated circuits have made simple timers a piece-of-cake. Nevertheless, individual requirements or preferences usually complicate things and increase the cost, often to the point of being exorbitant.

One system implementation we have used consists of three of the basic timers shown in Fig. 9.1. Each has a four-decade range and a time base that can be adjustable from 1 μsec to 1 sec. A set of three of these timers can be interconnected (Fig. 9.2) to provide timing sequences, such as those illustrated in Fig. 9.3, where a second timing chain may control a second event.

The basic timing system has proven to be sufficient for our use. It is by no means the only approach to the problem. For example, it is possible to implement timing schemes with microprocessors. The microprocessor can count clock pulses or utilize timing integrated circuits (ICs) to implement arbitrarily complex timing sequences and multiple timers. The programmability and standard output register of this microprocessor offers a great deal of power in implementation,

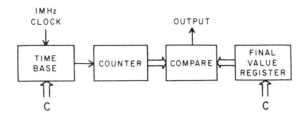

FIG. 9.1. An illustration of the basic timer unit. The counter register and the set value register are 4-decades long, and each can be selected for viewing with a Light Emitting Diode (LED) display. The device can be used manually or under computer control. C is the computer input to timer.

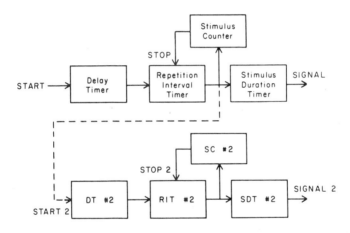

FIG. 9.2. A block diagram of a complete timing subsystem. Following the initial delay time (DT), the repetition interval timer (RIT) and stimulus duration timer (SDT) are triggered repeatedly until the number of repetitions specified in the stimulus counter has been satisfied.

FIG. 9.3. An illustration of a possible timing sequence when two timing subsystems are used. The stimulus duration timers determine when the stimuli are presented. A raised level, upward deflection of the line, implies the logic level is true and the unit is on. The repetition interval timers only put out a pulse.

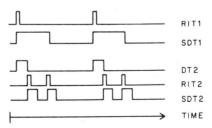

but caution should be exercised so that the microprocessor does not trap one in a project with an uncontrolled cost and time overrun.

Stimulus Generation Equipment.   Depending on the sensory system being investigated, the form and content of the stimulus can vary considerably. While the investigation of temperature, taste, or smell may require only simple stimulus control, touch, vision, and audition often require special devices to fit the experimental paradigm (although this is only a generalization).

In auditory neurophysiology a basic exercise is the determination of the response to a set of tones over a range of varying intensity and frequency, though it need not be limited to these parameters. A method of controlling the signal that is usually a sinusoid, is to use an oscillator that has digital stepper motor (one that rotates a fixed number of degrees when given a pulse) to the frequency selector knob. The limiting features of this approach are the accuracy, speed, and repeatability of frequency setting. It can take several sec to set a frequency with a 0.1% accuracy that may be inadequate in many instances. An all-digital waveform synthesizer was designed and built that overcomes the drawbacks of the stepper motor system.

A simplified example of the technique for digitally synthesizing a sinewave using a table look-up procedure is shown in Fig. 9.4. The contents, F, of a 4-bit frequency register are added to θ, the contents of the sine address register, which at time T equals $F \cdot T$ modulo (2^6) where $T = 0,1,\ldots,\infty$, and $2^6 =$ the clock frequency. A table of 64 values of the sine function is stored in a memory for each of the 64 possible values of θ. The value of F (1 to 15) determines the size of the step through the sine table. If $F = 1$, then each of the 64 values of the sine (θ) are read out each sec, whereas if $F = 2$ then every second value of the sine function is read out twice a sec. It should be obvious that the value of F is the frequency of the synthesized sinewave. The results of synthesizing 4 and 8 Hz sinewaves are shown in Fig. 9.5. The effect of quantizing a signal both in time

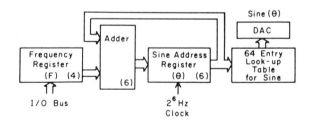

FIG. 9.4.   Simplified diagram of a digital sinewave generator. The contents of the sine address register at the Nth clock interval are $\theta(N\Delta t) = \theta((N-1)\Delta t)+F$, where $\Delta t = 1/$clock rate. The clock rate is $2^L = 2^6$, where L is the bit-length of the sine address register, SAR. The number of bits of the key devices are indicated in parenthesis. The output of the digital-to-analog converter, or DAC, is shown in Fig. 9.5.

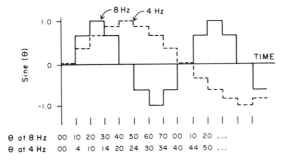

FIG. 9.5.   An illustration of the output of the sinewave generator for a frequency of 8 Hz (solid line) and for a 4 Hz (dashed line) frequency. It is obvious that larger changes in output occur for higher frequencies. The values listed for the sine address are octal numbers.

and amplitude is obvious and can be reduced by shortening the sample time (higher clock rate) and using more bits to represent the signal.

The actual waveform generator is part of a Digital Stimulus System (DSS) and has a 16-bit frequency register and a 19-bit sine address register; therefore, it has a frequency range of 64,000 Hz and a clock rate of 2^{19} or 524,000 Hz. If the sine (θ) was stored for each of the 2^{19} values of the sine address register at an accuracy of 16 bits, and 8,000,000 bit memory would be necessary. But only one-quarter of the sine function needs to be stored, and trigonometric identities can be used to reduce further the size of the Read Only Memory (ROM) to 16,000 bits (Rhode & Olson, 1975). A small sacrifice in accuracy is made to accomplish this savings in memory size; the table is accurate to 1 part in 2^{15} for 2^{17} arguments of θ. The distortion of the waveform had been determined to be less than 0.02% for frequencies below 10 kHz; this distortion is due to the digital-to-analog (D/A) converter. The DSS can also generate triangular waves, squarewaves, sawtooths, and reverse sawtooths. The frequency can vary from 2^{-16} to 2^{+16} Hz. It is specified in two parts, a 16-bit integer and a 16-bit fraction. The initial phase angle of the signal can also be specified with 16-bit accuracy. Two or more systems can be interconnected to produce frequency modulated signals, amplitude modulated signals, or to repetitively sweep a range of frequencies.

Another component of the DSS is due to the necessity to reduce the amount of energy frequencies other than the one being generated during the period when the signal is turned on and off. This is accomplished by multiplying the signal by a trapezoidal waveform that has a programmable rise/fall time. A 16 x 16 bit digital multiplier is used to perform the multiplicaton. One advantage of this approach over the use of an analog multiplier is that it does not introduce any distortion when the signal is fully on since the signal waveform is merely multiplied by a constant value. The rise/fall time of the DSS can be varied from 0 to 125 msec. There are 14 settings that change by a factor of 2 except for the zero rise/

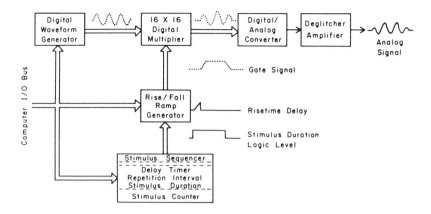

FIG. 9.6.   The relationship between the enabling logic level and the trapezoidal gate. The duration of the gate signal is identical to the stimulus duration. The waveforms are shown with dotted lines to emphasize that they are digital until they pass through the digital-to-analog converter. The stimulus duration logic level is generated by the stimulus sequencer, which consists of three timers and a repetition counter as shown in Fig. 9.2.

fall time. The trapezoidal gate signal is generated by a pair of 16-bit counters. The first counter generates the rise-time delay, and the second counter generates the gate signal, the trapezoidal waveform, after the expiration of the rise-time delay as shown in Fig. 9.6. Therefore, the generated signal is always displaced in time from the stimulus duration timer by an amount equal to the rise-time.

The final step in the synthesis is the D/A conversion. This is the step that limits the accuracy of waveform production. Theoretically, a 16-bit system should result in a system that has harmonic distortion in the neighborhood of 2^{-16} or -96 dB. The present system achieves about -74 dB (0.02%) distortion that is quite acceptable for most auditory experiments and is comparable to the best transducers for sound production. The limiting system component is the digital-to-analog converter or DAC. Any DAC can produce "glitches" or large undesirable pulses in output when undergoing transitions in input addressing that involve a change in the state of a large number of bits (e.g., 001111111 to 010000000). A deglitcher amplifier is used to suppress these transients; this is a fast sample-and-hold circuit that maintains the output of the DAC at its previous value until the input address has had time to change and the output of the DAC has stabilized.

A philosophy incorporated into the design is to make most of the functions of the system capable to both manual and computer control. This allows initial exploration of neural unit responsibility without the need for computer inter-action. It is also useful for maintenance of the system.

Waveform Generator.   In certain auditory experiments, it is desirable to combine 3, 4, or more harmonics of a given frequency with specifiable amplitude and phase. The cost of building a separate sinewave synthesizer for each harmonic becomes prohibitive and has resulted in alternate methods of synthesizing harmonic complexes (Wolf & Bilger, 1972). One method of accomplishing this is to have a "variable" length circulating buffer that stores one cycle of the desired waveform. For example, if the 9th, 10th, 11th, and 13th harmonics of 100 Hz were to be combined, the basic or fundamental period of the complex wave would be 1/100 sec or 10 msec. Therefore, a 10-msec sample of this waveform must be stored and the desired stimulus duration achieved by repeating the 10-msec waveform. If the maximum size of the buffer is to be 16,000 words, at a sample rate of 64 kHz, the maximum period obtainable is 250 msec. This period can be increased by lengthening the buffer or by decreasing the sample rate. This device can also be used as a simple buffer for delivering stimuli of arbitrary duration and shape by merely transferring data from a computer disc file to the buffer (e.g., speech, phonemes, or animal sounds). There is no restriction on the contents of the buffer, and waveforms of arbitrary complexity can be generated.

An alternate approach to the fabrication of a special device to generate waveforms is to use a computer to compute and present the waveform. If the sample rate is not beyond the capacity of the machine, this may not only be the least expensive approach but also the quickest, easiest, and most flexible. Many of the applications in visual and the somatosensory system could be handled along with many in auditory systems. As mentioned previously, the economics of computers are still undergoing rapid change. Each experimental requirement needs to be evaluated under the current technological conditions.

Other Stimulus Generation Devices.   The previously mentioned devices are, in a sense, generic. They find application in investigating every sensory system at any level of the nervous system. The types of stimuli depend on the sense being explored, but the "electronic" devices are often nearly the same. The range of frequencies necessary to investigate the auditory system is from 10 to 100,000 Hz, while the tactile system does not require much more than 200 Hz. The types of waveforms are often the same. The delivery of the stimulus varies mostly between sensory systems. To give a few examples, audition requires speakers or earphones; vision, a tangential screen or TV display; touch, a mechanical stimulator; and taste, a delivery system for liquids. It should be restated that many of the digital devices for stimulus generation and control will be similar regardless of the sense system and the specifics of the experiment. An example of this is that individual DACs find application in many areas in controlling magnitudes of stimulus parameters. Also, pseudorandom noise generators (Anderson, Finnie, & Roberts, 1967) are used in a variety of applications where the properties of the noise stimulus can be utilized to aid in characterizing the system under investigation.

Data-Collection Facilities

The principal data collected in our laboratory consist of trains of all-or-none neural spikes or discharges. Frequently encountered data types include averaged evoked responses and continuous physiological signals, such as EEG recordings, respiratory variables, body temperatures, expired CO_2. Several devices have been designed that are used to collect these separate date types, including a multiple-event timer, event histogram binners, a programmable A/D system, and a digital spectrum analyzer.

Event Timer.   The conversion of the all-or-none unit activity to a discrete sequence of "times of occurrence" is by far the most important activity in the lab. Each time the voltage recorded from a microelectrode exceeds a specified threshold value, the time is recorded as indicated in Fig. 9.7. The event timer designed to perform this task resolves events by using a time base that can be varied from 1 μsec to 1000 μsec under program control. The use of a 24-bit register permits an 8.3-sec period to be timed with 1 μsec resolution without overflow in the counter. The event timer can time up to 16 events and includes a 32 work buffer (a FIFO, or First-In-First-Out buffer) to store event times. This relaxes the need for rapid response to timer events by the computer system. An alternative to a FIFO is to use a direct memory access (DMA) channel to read in the event times into the computer's memory.

The event timer can be turned on and off by computer command or by a selectable synchronization pulse that can arise in any of the three DSSs or an external source. The sync pulse occurs whenever the signal is first turned on. The event timer is stopped by a terminate pulse that occurs whenever all the stimuli have been presented, and the repetition interval time has elapsed. The elapsed time for any events such as the neural discharge time or a bar pressing time are all recorded and stored. The event timer has another mode that only records the Nth event time. This is useful for determining the period, hence, frequency of an oscillator. The desired accuracy of the measurement determines the number of timer counts, hence the N to be used.

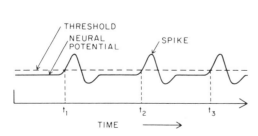

FIG. 9.7.   The sequence of times $(t_1, t_2, t_3, \ldots)$ corresponding to the time at which the electrical potential measured with a microelectrode from a neural unit becomes greater than a predetermined value called the detection threshold, which is used to differentiate the desired neural discharges from noise and other (smaller) spikes.

Analog-to-Digital-Conversion-System. The design objectives of the A/D converter system are simplicity of use and flexibility. It is a 16-channel system having sample rates as high as 100 kHz with 12-bit accuracy. The A/D inputs are single-ended, differential, or pseudodifferential. The channels to be sampled are program selectable, as is the sample rate and number of samples to be taken. The device is connected to the computer on a DMA channel so that the high sample rates can be accommodated by the system. No handling of the data is necessary, except to move it out of its buffer in the computer's memory.

Three sampling techniques are available in the A/D system: (1) rapid-scan mode in which conversion of each channel occurs as soon as the previous channel is converted until all selected channels have been sampled; the A/D then waits for the next clock or scan pulse, (2) uniform-interval mode in which the next channel is converted after a clock pulse occurs, and (3) fast-sample mode in which only one channel is sampled, permitting samples to be taken at a 160 kHz rate.

The rapid-scan technique allows one to sample effectively all channels at the same instant in time. This is especially advantageous for low sample rates, although it is desirable in general. An alternative to the quick-scan mode is to use a separate sample and hold amplifier for every channel. Due to the recent advances in this technology, this is probably the method of choice today. The uniform-interval mode is the sampling technique most commonly employed due to ease of implementation. In this mode, the rate is the channel sample rate multiplied by the number of channels to be sampled.

Advances in A/D technology make it feasible to use inexpensive A/Ds in dedicated applications. An example might be the continuous recording of body temperature where a simple IC timer would provide sampling times, and the A/D would be enabled when sampling is to occur. A dedicated program could collect and store all the data with no interaction with any other program currently being executed.

Digital Spectrum Analyzer. There are a number of data-collection problems that can overload the I/O capabilities of a computer. Fast sampling A/D, multiple event timing or event timing at a high rate can all cause problems especially if some simultaneous processing is required. An example would be obtaining an averaged evoked response in 8 to 16 channels with a high-sampling rate. A solution for this problem is a special purpose device that takes the individual samples from the A/D and adds the value to a location in its memory, then increments its address register and waits for the next sample without intervention from the computer.

This device is named a digital spectrum analyzer because in one of its modes a periodic signal can be sampled, and averaged and subsequently operated on to obtain its Fourier spectrum after the average has been read into a computer. It can handle inputs at a 200 kHz rate and average up to one-half million 12-bit

samples without overflowing its 32-bit word. It can function as a histogram computer whereby a count is added to the current address when an event occurs.

While it has been constructed with 4-bit bipolar logic, it is entirely possible
that in the near future, 16-bit bipolar processors on a single IC may be fast
enough to perform these tasks. The lab of the future will undoubtedly use
microcomputers quite liberally.

Event Histogram Binner.   A supplement to the event timer is a histogram
binner that is an extra benefit of the design of the DSS. One of the very common operations in auditory neurophysiology is the computing of a cycle histogram. This involves recording the instantaneous phase of the simulating wave-
from. In experiments where two or three sinusoids are simultaneously presented,
multiple-cycle histograms are often desired. A fringe benefit of the digital implementation of the stimulus system is the availability of the instantaneous phase in
digital form. When an event occurs, the current phase is stored in a FIFO buffer.
A single event can cause all three DSSs to record their phases, thereby saving the
repetition of the stimulus conditions that would be necessary if only one cycle
histogram could be computed at any one time.

DATA ANALYSIS

Histograms

One of the most common techniques for analyzing spike distributions that are
empirically derived is the histogram. The histogram displays the number of
events in a range of the metric being used. For example, one could display the
number of students with heights, weights, or ages as the abscissa of the display.
For convenience, one "groups" this discrete data as a function of the independent variable. The independent variable, which could be weight, height, or age, is
discretized by letting a range of the variable be defined as a bin. For example,
one year, pound, or inch could be the bin width. The number of events that
occur within a specified range determine the height of the bin.

The computing of a histogram is basically a counting process. The domain
(independent variable, x) is divided into a contiguous set of uniform intervals of
length, Δx. Each of these intervals is called a bin. We define N_j to be the contents of the jth bin of x. We also define an integer function, INT, such that INT
(y) = the integer portion of the argument y. Then, computing a histogram is defined as counting the number of events within each interval of the range of the
histogram where the range is $N\Delta x$. That is,

$$N_j = N_j + 1 \quad \text{when } j - 1 \leqslant \text{INT} \left(\frac{x_i}{\Delta x} \right) < j;$$

$$x_j = \text{the measure of the } i\text{th event} \tag{1}$$

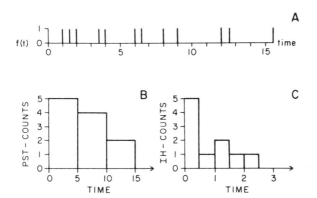

FIG. 9.8.   (A) The occurrence of events in the random process, $f(t)$, are indicated by a line of height equal to one. These could correspond to the time of occurrence of neural discharges as shown in Fig. 9.7. (B) The time axis is divided into equal increments of 5 sec. All the events of $f(t)$ within each increment are counted with the individual sums indicated by the height of each bin. This is called a *poststimulus time histogram*, or PSTH. (C) The intervals between successive events are determined. The time axis is divided into 0.5 time increments, and the number of intervals in each bin are indicated. This is called an *interval histogram*.

Note that the 1st bin covers the range $0 \leqslant x < \Delta x$, and the 2nd bin covers the range $x \leqslant x < 2\Delta x$, etc. A random process is illustrated in Fig. 9.8 with two types of histograms computed from it. The form of a histogram can vary from the bar graph presentation, to an outline of the histogram, to the use of cross-hatchings to indicate two or more superimposed histograms.

There are several types of histograms used in various applications, including poststimulus time histograms, latency histograms, cycle histograms, that will be discussed in conjunction with the analysis of the discharge of neurons.

Neuronal Spike Trains in the Absence of Stimuli

Interspike Interval Histograms.   It is a working hypothesis (1) that there is a wealth of information about the structure and function of the nervous system that can be derived from a study of the timing of spike events; (2) that analysis of these signals can shed light on the mechanism of spike production within the observed cell, on the presynaptic input to the cell, and on the mechanisms by which the latter is transformed into a postsynaptic output; and (3) that observations of multiple units can reveal details of interconnections and functional interactions (Glaser & Ruchkin, 1976; Perkel, Gerstein, & Moore, 1967a, b).

We are primarily concerned with information processing by the nervous system. The use of some simple statistical measures allow a relatively concise characterization of the output of the neuron, which may be useful in the description, comparison, and classification of nerve cells. The underlying neuronal processes have a degree of randomness that gives rise to its characterization at a stochastic point process and the subsequent use of statistical methods of analysis. The methods of analysis will vary depending on the experimental circumstances and whether we are concerned with intra- or interneuronal phenomena.

In a neuronal-spike train, the interspike-interval histogram serves as an estimate of the actual pdf (probability density function) of the stochastic point process. In order to construct the interval histogram, the time axis is divided into m uniform intervals of length δ. Each event (as shown in Fig. 9.6) is analyzed to determine which bin of the interval histogram it should be placed in by using the following relation.

$$N_j = N_j + 1 \quad \text{if } (j - 1)\delta \leqslant T_i < j\delta \tag{2}$$

where N_j is the number of events in the jth bin, δ is the bin width, and T_i is the ith interspike interval. There are N intervals when the number of spikes is $N + 1$. This is due to the fact that the first interval $(0, T_i)$ is not included in the analysis, only the interspike intervals. The ratio N_j/N is a smoothed estimate of the pdf, $f(t)$. Equation (3) is the probability that the duration of a randomly chosen interval lies between $(j - 1)\delta$ and $j\delta$ time.

$$\frac{N_j}{N} = \int_{(j-1)\delta}^{j\delta} f(t)\, dt \tag{3}$$

A peak in the interval histogram shows a preferred periodicity in the spike train. Certain neuronal systems will show phase locking to a stimulus that is manifest by a multimodal appearance in the interval histogram. The auditory periphery demonstrates this at low frequencies as shown in Fig. 9.9. The importance of the proper bin width to reveal the detail in the histogram is clear from the appearance of a large number of modes when the time axis was expanded.

Order-Dependent Statistical Measures.   It is of interest to determine whether successive interspike intervals are independent in the statistical sense and, therefore, whether the spike train can be described as a realization of a renewal process. The joint-interval histogram, JIH, that was introduced to neurophysiology by Rodieck, Kiang, and Gerstein (1962) is displayed in the form of a scatter diagram as shown in Fig. 9.10. Each pair of adjacent intervals in the spike train is plotted as a point. The $(i-1)$st interval is the distance along the abscissa; the ith interval is the distance along the ordinate. If successive intervals are independent, then the joint-interval histogram will be symmetric about a $45°$ line through the origin.

Proof of statistical independence requires that the joint probability be equal to the product of the individual probabilities. That is, Eq. (4) must be satisfied.

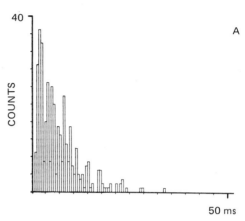

A

50 ms

FIG. 9.9.   An interspike-interval histogram. Frequency = 1300 Hz, and sound pressure level = 90 dB. A display window of 0 to 50 msec is used in A. There appears to be some large variability in the number of spikes/bin that is explored by increasing the temporal resolution of the histogram in Fig. 9.10B where the display window is set to 0 to 10 msec. The multimode histogram is an expression of phase locking that occurs at low frequencies in the peripheral auditory system.

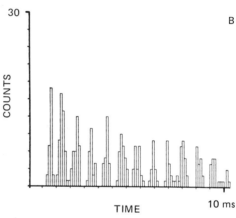

B

TIME   10 ms

FIG. 9.10.   A joint-interval histogram of the nerve activity in an auditory nerve fiber with a stimulus applied. If the points are not scattered evenly on each side of the 45° line, then the intervals would not be independent.

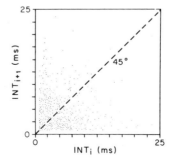

$$\text{prob } (T_i, T_{i+1}1) = \text{prob } (T_i) \text{ prob } (T_{i+1}) \tag{4}$$

In practice, a substitute is used for this test that involves computing the mean of each row and each column in the JIH. The column means are plotted vs. row, and the row means are plotted vs. column. If the intervals are independent then the means will be parallel to the axes. This is considered necessary but not sufficient for independence.

Spike Trains in the Presence of Stimuli

Poststimulus Time Histograms. Much of the previous discussion involved characterizing a stochastic point process on the basis of a spike train observed in the absence of any stimuli; that is, only the spontaneous activity is observed. In experimenting, different types of stimuli with various patterning are used. The stimuli are appropriate to the sensory modality or nervous system function being investigated. The stimuli could be patterned repetitions of sounds, a spatially modulated video display, a sequence of stepped increases in temperature, a random variation in angular acceleration for vestibular stimulation, the application of a specified concentration of a chemical, or various tactile stimuli. The Poststimulus Time Histogram, or PSTH, is an average of the spike trains due to a repeated stimulus. For example, acoustic clicks, tone pips, or light flashes may be repeated hundreds of times to obtain a PSTH that is relatively smooth.

An example of the use of an acoustic click to determine a transient response (Robles, Rhode, & Geisler, 1976) involves the mechanical events that precede the generation of neural spikes in the inner ear. Hair cells in the organ of Corti are responsible for transducing acoustic or mechanical energy to an electrochemical form that eventually results in pulses or spikes in auditory nerve fibers. The excitation of the hair cells is largely determined by the motion of the basilar membrane that is one boundary of the organ of Corti. These structures rest in a fluid environment and vibrate 10 to 100 Å at normal sound levels. A small radioactive foil (Mössbauer source) can be placed on the basilar membrane. The gamma rays emitted by the foil pass through another foil (Mössbauer absorber) and are detected with a proportional counter. The number passing through the absorber is modulated by the velocity of the membrane. A PSTH of the resulting gamma-ray activity is shown in Fig. 9.11. The acoustic click was repeated as many as 800,000 times. A computer was essential for controlling stimulus presentation and performing the data collection and analysis.

In general, the bumps and wiggles or the PSTH reflect the underlying excitatory process, and one must decide if they are significant or merely random fluctuations. The distribution of mean square deviations from mean bin level can be computed or a control case can be constructed using fictitious times of stimulus

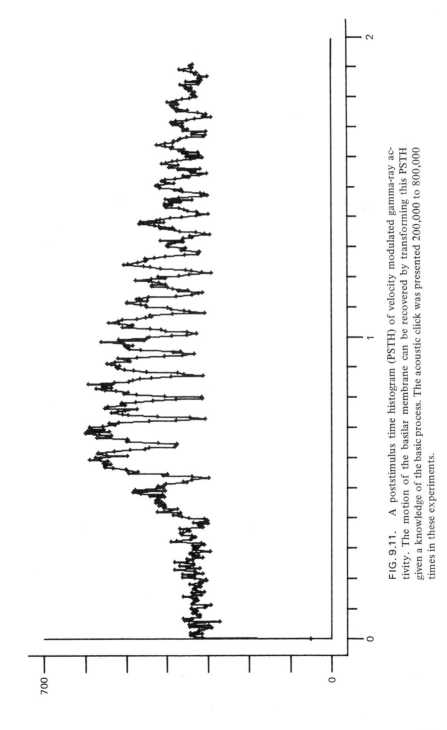

FIG. 9.11. A poststimulus time histogram (PSTH) of velocity modulated gamma-ray activity. The motion of the basilar membrane can be recovered by transforming this PSTH given a knowledge of the basic process. The acoustic click was presented 200,000 to 800,000 times in these experiments.

presentation and portions of a record where no actual stimulations were presented. In general, any features that are to be interpreted as meaningful should have a width of several bins. Note that one can always recompute the PSTH with a smaller bin width to search for greater detail. Usually, the response is obvious at all but threshold and subthreshold levels of stimulation.

Latency Histogram. The general technique using PSTHs can be used in other ways; one of which is the nth spike-latency histogram, LH. When the first spike latency is calculated, it is used to determine the average time at which a neuron will discharge after the stimulus onset. The mean and variance of the LH distribution are usually calculated. The LH is useful for studying the travel time of spikes through the nervous system. It helps to determine whether there are any synapses interposed between two recording sites, as spikes require a significant amount of time to traverse each synapse. Neuroanatomical studies of fiber size and length are a help in estimating the expected travel time between the two sites.

Cycle Histogram. Another very common analysis technique is the use of cycle histograms, CH, which have also been called *period* or *phase histograms*. They are a type of PSTH where the synchronizing event is the zero crossing or initiation of a cycle of the stimulus. It is used to reveal phase-locking behavior in the system under investigation. Cycles could be based on diurnal patterns (1 day), traffic flow (hour, day, weeks, months, year), hamburgers eaten (day), etc. The resulting histogram allows calculation of the degree of response to some underlying variable that is the stimulus.

The CH can be developed from the distribution of events around the unit circle. The sequence of events $x_1, x_2, x_3, \ldots$ are transformed to a sequence of events θ_i, with values on the unit circle $(0, 2\pi)$. The mean direction, $\bar\theta$, of $\theta_1, \theta_2, \theta_3, \ldots$ is defined to be the direction of the resultant of the unit vectors $\overline{OP}_1, \overline{OP}_2, \ldots$, as shown in Fig. 9.12. The cartesian coordinates of P_i are $(\cos \theta_i, \sin \theta_i)$ so that the center of gravity of the points is $(\bar{X}, \bar{Y})$ where

$$\bar{X} = \frac{1}{N} \sum_{i=1}^{N} \cos \theta_i, \qquad \bar{Y} = \frac{1}{N} \sum_{i=1}^{N} \cos \theta_i \qquad [\text{Let } \bar{R} = (\bar{X}^2 + \bar{Y}^2)^{1/2} \tag{5}$$

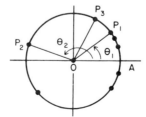

FIG. 9.12. Events are represented as points on the unit circle. OA is the zero (reference) direction. θ_i are the angles corresponding to x_i modulo 2π.

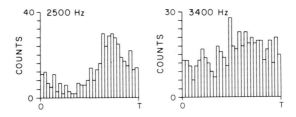

FIG. 9.13.   Cycle histograms (CHs) taken at an intensity of 90 dB sound pressure level. The discharges are well locked at 2500 Hz but much less locked at 3400 Hz since the CH is much flatter.

Then $R = N\bar{R}$ is the length of the resultant, and $\bar{\theta}$ is the solution of Eq. (6).

$$\frac{Y}{X} = \frac{R \sin \bar{\theta}}{R \cos \bar{\theta}} = \tan \bar{\theta} \text{ results in Eq. (7)} \qquad (6)$$

$$\bar{\theta} = \tan^{-1} \frac{Y}{X} \qquad (7)$$

A problem of interpretation of θ arises in trying to assign a degree of confidence to the experimentally determined value. If N is small, we clearly cannot conclude anything about $\bar{\theta}$ because of having too small a sample. This is overcome through the use of the Rayleigh test (Mardia, 1972). It is used to test the hypothesis that the distribution around the unit circle is uniform versus the hypothesis that it follows a von Mises distribution.

The CH has been used extensively in the study of the auditory nerve fibers whose discharges "lock" to the stimulus (Hind, 1970); that is, they show a preference for a certain phase of the stimulus in their discharges as shown in Fig. 9.13 for a stimulus frequency of 2500 Hz. This locking becomes less prominent as the stimulus frequency increases (Fig. 9.13, 3400 Hz) or as the intensity decreases. CHs have also been used to analyze the generation and distribution of distortion products in the inner ear. A system is said to be nonlinear if it does not obey the principle of superposition. When the input to a nonlinear system consists of two components at frequencies, f_L and f_H, then new components will be generated at frequencies that are combinations of these frequencies. In the auditory system, the most prominent distortion component is at a frequency, $2f_L - f_H$. It can be measured psychoacoustically in the response of eight nerve fibers (Goldstein & Kiang, 1960). The CH has been used to determine the amplitude and phase of the primary and any distortion components in the neural response. The search for the origin of these distortion products in the auditory system continues even today.

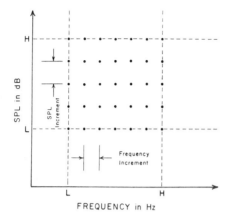

FIG. 9.14.   The portion of the frequency–intensity stimulus space to be explored is specified by low to high paramaters along with the step size for each parameter. Each stimulus in a response area corresponds to the coordinates of a point in the stimulus space.

Additional Analysis

Various stimulus paradigms will require the systematic explorations of one or more independent variables, such as frequency, sound pressure level, the phase relation between two signals, and the contrast and spatial frequency of a visual display). An example of a 2-dimensional stimulus space for an auditory experiment is shown in Fig. 9.14. The coordinates of the points correspond to individual frequency and intensity combinations to be presented. They can be presented systematically or in random order. Usually, intensities are presented in a low to high sequence to avoid biasing the response to less intense stimuli by recovery effects. If the data collected at each "point" consists of the spike timings, any of the analyses previously described could be performed. An example of PSTHs for a part of the response area is shown in Fig. 9.15, where it can be seen that the nerve responded best at 4600 Hz.

Some summary statistics are often used to analyze the behavior of a neuron. A very common one is the spike rate during some interval of the stimulus sequence. The number of spikes recorded for each frequency and intensity of sound in the response area is shown in Fig. 9.16. The resulting series of curves tell us what region of the stimulus space the neural unit responds to. An alternative way of looking at this data is the isorate curve. It is formed by plotting the intensity necessary to produce a fixed rate of discharge at each frequency. It defines the filter characteristic for the auditory nerve fiber by showing what part of the stimulus space causes the unit to respond at the specified rate.

This is very important in trying to understand the process by which sound is converted from acoustic energy to neural energy in the ear. The response area and isorate curves have been compared with the results of investigation of the mechanics of the inner ear and seem to indicate the need for an additional stage of filtering to sharpen the mechanical response (Geisler, Rhode, & Kennedy, 1974). The origin of the exquisite frequency selectivity seen in auditory nerve fibers is still a puzzle to researchers.

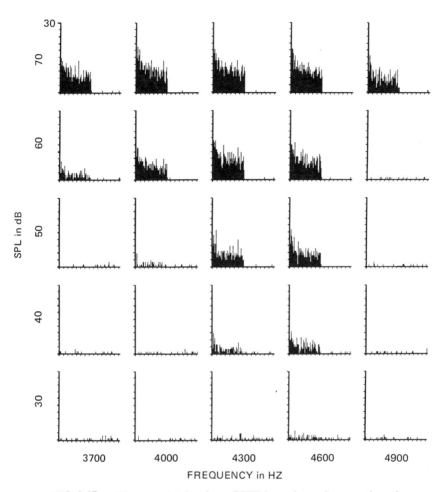

FIG. 9.15.   The poststimulus times (PSTHs) are shown for a portion of the stimulus space specified. A similar display can be generated for an interval, cycle, latency, or joint-interval histogram.

FIG. 9.16.   The spike counts/stimulus point in a 100 to 6400 Hz, 20 to 90 dB sound pressure level (SPL) stimulus space. A different symbol was used in plotting the curve corresponding to each intensity. Similar displays can be made for the mean and variance of latency, mean and variance of the period histogram, isorate curves, and cumulative phase curves.

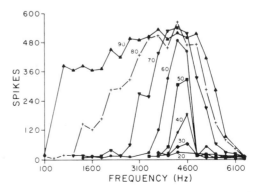

In addition to the techniques applied to the study of single units, a number of techniques have been evolved to deal with multiple units. As the tip size of the electrode is increased, spikes from multiple neurons are received. If the tip is too large, a "hash" is seen that is useful for mapping regions of the brain but may not be useful in understanding the action of individual neurons. There is a middle ground where techniques can be applied to separate individual neural waveforms (Glaser, 1970). Additionally, multiple electrodes can be used to record from several units. The resulting multiple spike trains are then analyzed in an attempt to determine the neuronal circuitry and interactions; that is, what dependencies exist between the members of the neuronal population and what is the simplest hypothesis regarding the physiology that the data will support. There are several methods of investigating these relationships (Gerstein & Perkel, 1972; Moore, Segundo, Perkel, & Levitan, 1970; Perkel, Gerstein, & Moore, 1967b). They usually rely on some cross-correlation calculation or some graphical display of mutual interaction. Often a display is interpreted by comparing it to the results of what happens in a simulation of simple neuronal networks. Although this network simulation does not permit definitive statements to be made, it does often give the simplest available explanation.

Before leaving the subject of neural unit analysis, it is perhaps appropriate for me to apologize for the lack of coverage of other sensory systems and approaches. There are many other approaches that the reader could benefit from. The extensive work of Mountcastle (1976) in the somatosensory system and recent development of behavioral techniques is especially worthwhile. In vision an example of a particularly innovative technique is a computer-controlled TV display to search for the optimum visual stimulus for each neural unit studied (Harth & Tzanakou, 1974). The display is divided into a 32×32 grid. The intensity of each section is varied according to how the unit responded to the last change along with a random variation in each intensity. The final visual pattern should be the one the unit is most sensitive to. Stimulus motion could be incorporated in the technique. Another example of quantitative studies in the visual system is the work of Schiller, Finley, and Volman (1976). They used a computer-controlled apparatus and applied various statistical analyses culminating in neural models to explain the response patterns that they observed.

Other techniques of neural-signal analysis are still evolving. One in particular has its genesis in the area called *systems identification*. An attempt is made to describe the properties of a system in a mathematical fashion that represents the response characteristic as a series of "kernels" (McCann & Marmarelis, 1975). This is being applied in the investigation of nonlinear systems. One of the drawbacks of the technique is that the resulting model does not relate well to the physiology, therefore leaving the biologist with an uncomfortable feeling. There are many approaches to systems identification dealing with both linear and nonlinear systems. The use of white noise as the stimulus is often dictated, as in the use of the reverse correlation techniques (DeBoer & Kuyper, 1968).

AER — Averaged Evoked Responses

Although the first recording of evoked potentials in mammals occurred in 1875, it was not until the introduction of the electronic amplifier that the recording of brain potentials through the unopened skull was demonstrated by Hans Berger.

There were problems in analyzing evoked responses that are obscured by the larger EEG activity. It was decided to enhance the low signal-to-noise (S/N) level of the evoked activity by averaging responses, evoked by a repetitive stimulus.

The basic idea is very simple. Activity or electrical signals that are time locked to an event will sum according to a linear relation whereas incoherent signals, e.g. noise, will sum in a root mean square (RMS) manner. This is the basis for S/N enhancement as M repetitions of the response are added. If M signals, $x(t)$, are added, $S = Mx(t)$ while M segments of noise $n(t)$ will grow as $\sqrt{M}$. Therefore, the S/N improvement is equal to $\sqrt{M}$. That is, adding 4 repetitions together will improve the S/N ratio by a factor of 2. If 100 repetitions are necessary to obtain a noticeable evoked response, then 400 responses would be necessary to improve S/N by an additional factor of 2, whereas 1600 responses would have to be averaged for a second factor of 2 improvement. The point is that the fastest improvement occurs for small Ms. If S/N is not sufficient for some reasonable M, then further improvements will come only at great expense. The additional problem that must be faced is whether the system under investigation will be constant (stable) over the averaging period.

The details of recording have been discussed in sufficient detail elsewhere (Goff, 1974). Whether nonpolarizable electrodes are necessary is dependent on the necessity of D.C. recording, the measurement of interference effects, and on the required ease of placement. Needle electrodes reduce skin surface potentials but exhibit an impedance that is inversely proportional to frequency.

In order to facilitate the comparison of EEGs, a standard electrode placement was proposed in 1947 and named the International 10-20 electrode placement. Some AER investigators realized the need for standard placement and have suggested the use of the 10-20 system as a reference. In general, the purpose of the experiment and the type of subject should determine electrode placement. The primary considerations are: (1) the sense modality being studied, (2) the study of the early or late response, and (3) the minimization of contamination by "extracranial potentials." Topological studies of VER (visual evoked response), AER (auditory evoked response) and SER (somatosensory evoked response) are available as guides.

SER stimuli often consist of electrical shocks to the median nerve at the wrist or legs. VER stimuli are often flashes of white light, and AER stimuli are usually clicks presented via earphones.

If short-latency AER components represent neural activity in the primary auditory receiving area, one might expect their focus to be in the temporal areas of the cortex. Several researchers (Goff, 1974) have found them to be at maximum in the vertex region. This leads to two questions: Are they of neural origin? Are they generated in the primary auditory cortex? The use of scalp and subdural electrodes at points near the vertex demonstrate that the AERs have the same waveform and latency at both sites. A similar waveform in the temporal region supports the conclusion that the early AER components are cochleoneurogenic. The latency, duration, and configuration of scalp potentials are not comparable to those recorded directly from the human primary auditory cortex. Barbiturate anesthesia suppresses early AER components at the vertex, supporting the idea that they are not primary auditory components.

Another issue in AER recording is whether monopolar or bipolar electrodes should be used. Bipolar recording looks at the algebraic difference between two electrodes. The basic problem is the interpretation of the bipolar records. By recording both bipolar and monopolar signals and varying stimulus intensity, it can be seen that monopolar recordings are important in the interpretation of the bipolar recordings because of differences in the topographic distribution of various AER components and intersubject variability. Assuming that the "indifference" of the reference electrode is good, then the interpretation of records is simpler in the monopolar case. The polarity of the signal recorded with bipolar electrodes is usually meaningless without independent assessment from monopolar recordings. In addition, if the monopolar recordings are stored, simple subtraction will produce the equivalent bipolar records whereas the opposite is not true.

The AERs are used to correlate brain activity with sensory and motor behavior. We seek information on the timing, magnitude, and location of neural events that take place in the brain during some sensory of behavioral sequence. Since scalp-recorded brain potentials provide a substantially degraded indication of intracranial processes, evidence of these events may be ambiguous. Timing information is the most unequivocal form of data. The magnitude of neural activity is must less secure and the interpretation of it is ambiguous.

The recorded brain potential, $V(t)$, can be represented as the sum of an evoked response, $E(t)$, and the background EEG plus noise, or $G(t)$ as in Eq. 7.

$$V(t) = E(t) + G(t) \tag{7}$$

We want to characterize $E(t)$ and its variability and describe the statistical features of the EEG.

In sampling these signals, we are subject to the same constraints as are applicable to any signal-analysis problem; that is, the sampling rate must be at least twice the highest frequency present in the signal. The sample interval will be Δt, and $V(t)$ will be sampled at $t_i = i\Delta t, i = 1, \ldots, m$.

The mean and variance of $V(t)$ are given in Eqs. 8 and 9.

$$\bar{V}(t) = \frac{1}{M} \sum_{k=1}^{M} V_N(t) \tag{8}$$

$$\sigma^2\left[V(t)\right] = \frac{1}{M}\sum_{k=1}^{M} (V_k - \bar{V})^2 \tag{9}$$

The autocovariance of $V(t)$ can be evaluated in Eq. 10.

$$R_{VV}(t_1, t_2) = \frac{1}{M}\sum_{1}^{M} \left[V_k(t_1) - \bar{V}_k(t_1)\right]\left[V_k(t_2) - \bar{V}_k(t_2)\right] \tag{10}$$

This gives a measure of correlation between points on the same record. A useful method of displaying averaged evoked responses is to plot the standard deviation, $\sqrt{\sigma^2}$, which is the root-mean-square deviation from the signal mean and is expressed in the same units as the data. As σ decreases, we can begin to trust the bumps and wiggles present in $\bar{V}$. Remember, the reduction in the standard error, S, is proportional to $\sqrt{M}$. A general guideline for choosing M is to reduce the fluctuation in S to 10% of $\bar{S}$, the average.

There are several problems that are being addressed using AERs, due to the availability of computers for data analysis. They include: (1) the detection of evoked potentials at psychophysical thresholds that requires the application of statistical detection methods to the evaluation of the AER. A nonzero $\bar{V}(t)$ and an increase in the RMS voltage or a change in the autocovariance could all signal a significant change in the AER. (2) The second problem is the evaluation of differences in AER waveform in those instances where the reliability of differences in the AER is important. The two main approaches to evaluating differences are using the t test for the significance of differences between means and assessing differences in correlation of averages obtained under different conditions. The latter technique employs a product-moment correlation that yields a single number. Unfortunately, the nature of waveform differences is completely obscure. (3) The resolution of AERs into simple component waveforms is important since a major objective of brain-potential investigation is to define the physiologic origin and functional significance of the AER components. The problem of component identification (Donchin & Herning, 1975) is essentially a physiologic problem. (4) Waveshape sorting (Bartlett, John, Shimokochi, & Kleinman, 1975) has been used to sort single ensembles according to their likelihood of containing one or another of two predefined mean components.

Signal Analysis and the EEG

In EEG as in art, one person's signal is another person's noise. Whereas in AER the EEG was a confounding signal that interfered with the evoked response and had to be averaged out, it has been utilized to provide corroborative information for suspected clinical conditions. It is a record of more or less rhythmic fluctuations in electrical potentials that arise in the brain. These potentials are greatly attenuated by virtue of the fact that they are recorded from the scalp. The attenuation is undoubtedly greater for cortical potentials that are very localized in origin. Although there are many concerns about the recording process itself (the need to use nonpolarizable electrodes, placement of electrodes, monopolar vs. bipolar recording, patient state, movement, and a variety of artifacts that must be screened for by the EEG technician), the focus here is the analysis of the EEG. Reading EEGs is still somewhat of an art form. Certain signs are regarded as abnormal, such as the absence or reduction of rhythms, the presence of abnormal waveforms, slow waves, sharp waves, and spikes. The description of these abnormal waveforms usually includes the period, amplitude, incidence, location, sites of probable origin, reactivity to eye opening, effect of hyperventilating, and photic stimulation. The EEG has been used to classify the stage of sleep and is an indicator of the level of anesthesia in surgery. The lengthy evaluation time and lack of a quantified evaluation of the EEG has led to attempts to develop alternate, objective methods that could result in compressing the typical one-half-inch-thick stack of 14-channel recordings to a summary description. The techniques of signal analysis that have been applied are of interest in themselves and have application in other areas (Rabiner & Gold, 1975). The literature dealing with EEG analysis (Brazier & Walter, 1973; Gevins, Yeager, Diamond, Spire, Zeitlin, & Gevins, 1975) is every extensive, and the interested reader is encouraged to review it.

The analysis of EEG signals employs many fundamental techniques of signal analysis. The most fundamental is Fourier analysis, which is the determination of the frequency content of a signal and is predicated on being able to represent a signal as a sum of sine waves and cosine waves. The procedures used to analyze a lot of data was often tedious and expensive until the relatively recent introduction of the Fast Fourier Transform or FFT (Brigham, 1974). This clever algorithm has revolutionized signal processing by permitting once infeasible computations to now be performed.

A randomly varying signal can be represented in the form of Eq. (11).

$$X(t) = a_0 + \sum_{r=1}^{\infty} (a_r \cos \frac{2\pi}{T} rt + b_r \sin \frac{2\pi}{T} rt) \tag{11}$$

Normally, the quantity we are interested in is the magnitude, C_r, of each component.

$$C_r = \left| a_r^2 + b_r^2 \right|^{\frac{1}{2}} \tag{12}$$

where the fundamental frequency is $1/T$, and T is the length of the segment we are analyzing. All the components of $x(t)$ are multiples of the fundamental frequency. In Fig. 9.17 a signal, $x(t)$, and its spectrum are shown. It is clear that there is a prominent frequency component near 3 Hz. There are problems that arise with the analysis of signals such as the EEG that vary in their basic characteristics as a function of time. Signals of this type are called nonstationary; that is, their statistical properties are different depending on the interval of time analyzed. To overcome this problem, small time segments, 1 to 8 sec, are often ana-

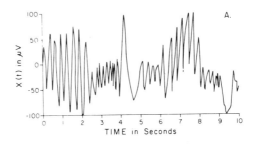

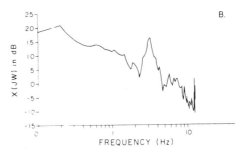

FIG. 9.17.   A time signal that could correspond to an EEG signal and the resulting Fourier spectra. The signal was entered into the computer using a graphic tablet.

lyzed, and the individual spectra are graphed in a 3-dimensional display called a *compressed spectral array* (Bickford, Fleming, & Billinger, 1971). This has the advantage of showing changes in the frequency content of a signal as a function of time. These spectra are sometimes averaged across time or are smoothed across frequency in order to reduce the variability of the estimate of the amplitudes of the frequency components. These are basic operations that may be useful in a variety of problems. One can divide the frequency axis in several bands in which the energy is summed and then plotted as a function of time. This makes it obvious when any major shift in frequency content of the signal occurs. Various statistics (Matoušek & Peterson, 1973) can be developed using the sum, difference, and ratio of these energies in an attempt to discriminate between patient populations. There are many other manipulations that individuals have applied in analyzing EEGs where two channels are analyzed simultaneously. For example, a cospectra is a correlation of the individual spectra and shows what frequency components are common to both signals along with their mutual phase relations.

An important measure of signal correlation is the coherence. If the power spectrum of a signal is defined as

$$S(\omega) = E[Z(\omega)Z^*(\omega)] \tag{13}$$

where Z is the Fourier transform of the time series and * denotes the complex conjugate. The cross-spectrum is defined in Eq. (14).

$$S_{xy}(\omega) = E[Z_x(\omega)Z_y^*(\omega)] \tag{14}$$

and

$$C_{xy}(\omega) = \frac{|S_{xy}(\omega)|^2}{S_x(\omega)S_y(\omega)} \tag{15}$$

The coherence in Eq. (15) gives a measure of the squares of the correlation between two time series for each frequency component.

These are but a few of the techniques that have been applied to EEG analysis. Autocorrelation, period analysis, toposcophy, amplitude analysis, and several others have all been used. The understanding of the EEG and its origin is yet to come. Perhaps the use of models (Wennberg & Zetterberg, 1971) will facilitate experiments that may lead to a further advance of our understanding of the source and nature of the EEG.

NEUROANATOMICAL ANALYSIS

In recent years, computers have been used to assist in the analysis of neuro-anatomical material in a number of ways (Lindsay, 1977). One of the simplest is the use of a graphics tablet to enter either cell counts or contours of the cell body and nucleus. An example is shown in Fig. 9.18. From this rather simple process, the cell-size distribution can be computed along with several other measures such as cell circularity and orientation. The advantage of using this rather simple device is that it is easy to use and facilitates quantitative studies. One can easily test hypotheses regarding cell size, number, and distribution in brain developmental studies.

One can readily guess that it would also be very important to be able to study the entire 3-dimensional structure of neurons. One of the problems of working with anatomical material is the lack of contrast between very densely packed structures. In order to circumvent this, a variety of histological staining techniques have been evolved. One of these, the Golgi staining technique has the characteristic that only a very small percentage of the neurons in a section of brain tissue accept the stain. Another of its characteristics is that usually the entire dendritic tree is stained. Techniques for injecting dyes into cells also permit the entire cell to be visualized. The anatomical material is sliced into thin sections, with structures of interest often being distributed in several sections. Even when a cell is contained in one section, its entire 3-dimensional structure cannot be seen at any one time under the microscope. To overcome these deficiencies, techniques that allow the entry of 3-dimensional structures have been evolving over the past few years. The data can be derived from photographs and light microscope and electron microscope images (Macagno, Levinthal, Tountas, Born-holdt, & Abba, 1976; Shantz, 1976), with different techniques required to handle each one. The techniques are becoming quite sophisticated, and many use a graphic display to show the resulting neural structure. Stereo pairs and rotating stick figures have been used to impart the impression of 3-dimension.

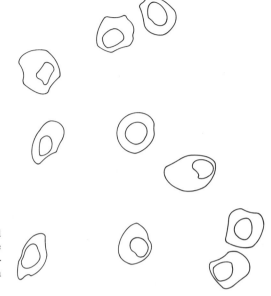

FIG. 9.18.   A group of neural
cell body contours along with the
nucleus contours that were entered into the computer through a
graphic tablet.

Another use of the computer in anatomical processing is to count silver grains
in a photographic emulsion. The technique of autoradiography is used to study
neural connectivity in the brain. It involves injecting a radioactive material that
is absorbed by certain neurons and then transported by their axons. When the
photographic emulsion is developed, the density and location of the silver grains
is studied. The automation of this technique (Wann, Price, Cowan, & Agulnek,
1974) has helped in digesting vast amounts of data normally gathered in a very
tedious way.

It is worthwhile pointing out that the data explosion that occurs in processing neuroanatomical data suggests an obvious need for computer-assisted analysis. In using an electron microscope to study tissue ultrastructure, researchers
section the material into slices that are often on the order of 500 Å. For example, a 1-mm block of tissue could be cut into 20,000 sections. If a 1 mm^2 is
magnified 10,000 times, it becomes 10 m^2. Multiply this by 20,000, and it is obvious that to digitize and store this amount of material is impossible. The material needs to be selectively analyzed and the data compressed for storage.
These are problems that will continue to challenge us for some time.

DATA-BASE MANAGEMENT SYSTEMS

Out of the brief considerations of neural-unit analysis and neuroanatomical
structural analysis, a feeling of inadequacy in dealing with the data sometimes
arises. The program development of large analysis systems is expensive and often

a long process. It is important to use the very best of tools, both hardware and software, to facilitate these developments. Computer science has advanced operating systems, compilers, real-time computing along with the area called Database Management Systems or DBMS. It is worth devoting much attention to this latter area (Date, 1975), due to the importance and expense of collecting, maintaining, and analyzing data. Unfortunately, one often collects vast amounts of data without giving consideration to analysis. The data often become virtually inaccessible, rendering them incomplete and useless. It is worthwhile to be aware of DBMS technology, because it may enhance one's programming system design.

In each area, Soni and I have developed an integrated system that usually includes a nonresident command processor that is responsible for interpreting commands and initiating the required programs. An example of this is the response area program (Rhode & Soni, 1976) that performs the statistical analyses described previously. We applied some DBMS concepts by using a Data Description Language to specify the type of data and its organization within the data files. A separate description of the parameters that are required by each analysis program is also provided. A processor then "reads" both of these descriptions and passes data from file to program, performing any necessary formatting during the process. This results in a system that is easily modified and extended when the needs arise.

A well-documented approach also facilitates the ease of transferring the maintenance of the analysis systems to new programmers. The primary objective, however, is easier program development and interfacing to analysis packages for various statistical analysis. A consideration is the development of data files that contain summary information about the neural units investigated. That is, we often select certain features of the data, such as characteristic frequency, threshold, spontaneous discharge rate, and dynamic range, to provide a characterization of the neural unit. We may apply statistical analyses to this data to determine whether any distinguishable populations exist, such as cluster analysis or discriminant analysis.

In a comprehensive data-base system, methods of passing data to analysis programs are provided. Data manipulation programs and, occasionally, query programs with a few simple statistical routines are provided. The ideas are worth study, but their actual implementation is difficult and often expensive.

SUMMARY

Many of the hardware and software techniques used in neurophysiology have been briefly described. They are all important to an understanding of current computer use in this area. The literature references will provide a substantial entree to other uses and techniques. Unfortunately, one chapter could not cover all the important analysis and instrumentation techniques.

REFERENCES

Anderson. G. C., Finnie, B. W., & Roberts, G. T. Pseudo-random and random test signals. *Hewlett-Packard Journal*, September 1967, 1–12.

Bartlett, F., John, E. R., Shimokochi, M.., & Kleinman, D. Electrophysiological signs of readout from memory, II. Computer classification of single evoked potential waveshapes. *Journal of Behavioral Biology*, 1975, *14*, 409–449.

Bickford, R. G., Fleming, N. I., & Billinger, T. W. Compression of EEG data by isometric power spectral plots. *Electroencephalography and Clinical Neurophysiology*, 1971, *31*, 631–636.

Brazier, M. A. V., & Walter, D. O. (Eds.). Evaluation of bioelectrical data from brain, nerve and muscle, 11. *Handbook of electroencephalography and clinical neurophysiology*. Amsterdam: Elsevier, 1973.

Brigham, E. O. *The Fast Fourier Transform*. Englewood Cliffs, N.J.: Prentice-Hall, 1974.

Brown, P. B. *Computer technology in neuroscience*. New York: Halsted Press, 1976.

Clark, W. A., & Molnar, C. E. A description of the LINC. R. W. Stacy & B. D. Waxman (Eds.), In *Computers in biomedical research*. New York: Academic Press, 1965.

Date, C. J. *An introduction to database systems*. Reading, Mass.: Addison-Wesley, 1975.

DeBoer, E., & Kuyper, P. Triggered correlations. *Institute of Electrical and Electronics Engineers Transactions on Biomedical Engineering*, 1968, *15*, 169–179.

Donchin, E., & Herning, R. I. A simulation study of the efficacy of stepwise discriminant analysis in the detection and comparison of event related potentials. *Electroencephalography and Clinical Neurophysiology*, 1975, *38*, 51–58.

Geisler, C. D., Rhode, W. S., & Kennedy, D. T. Responses to tonal stimuli of single auditory nerve fibers and their relationship to basiliar membrane motion in the Squirrel monkey. *Journal of Neurophysiology*, 1974, *37*, 1156–1182.

Gerstein, G. L., & Perkel, D. H. Mutual temporal relationships among neuronal spike trains: Statistical techniques for display and analysis. *Biophysical Journal*, 1972, *12*, 453–473.

Gevins, A. S., Yeager, C. L., Diamond, S. L., Spire, J. P., Zeitlin, H. M., & Gevins, A. H. Automated analysis of the electrical activity of the human brain (EEG): A Progress Report. *Proceedings of the Institute of Electrical and Electronics Engineers*, 1975, *63*, 1382–1399.

Glaser, E. M. Separation of neuronal activity by waveform analysis. In S. Fine & R. M. Kenedi (Eds.), *Advances in biological and medical engineering* (Vol. I). New York: Academic Press, 1970.

Glaser, E. M., & Ruchkin, D. S. *Principles of neurobiological signal analysis*. New York: Academic Press, 1976.

Goff, W. R. Human averaged evoked potentials: Procedures for stimulating and recording. In R. F. Thompson & M. M. Patterson (Eds.), *Bioelectric recording techniques*, New York: Academic Press, 1974.

Goldstein, J. L., & Kiang, N. Y. S. Neural correlates of the aural combination tone $2f_1\text{-}f_2$. *Proceedings of the Institute of Electrical and Electronics Engineers*, 1968, *56*, 981–992.

Harth, E., & Tzanakou, E. Allopex: A stochastic method for determining visual receptive fields. *Vision Research*, 1974, *14*, 1475–1482.

Hind, J. E. Two-tone masking effects in squirrel monkey auditory nerve fibers In, R. P. Plomp & G. F. Smoorenburg (Eds.), *Frequency analysis and periodicity-detection in hearing*. The Netherlands: Sijthoff, Leiden, 1970.

Lindsay, R. D. *Computer analysis of neuronal structures*. New York: Plenum, 1977.

Macagno, E. R., Levinthal, C., Tountas, C., Bornholdt, R., & Abba, R. Recording and analysis of 3-D information from serial sections micrographs, The Cartos System. In P. B. Brown (Ed.), *Computer technology in neuroscience*. New York: Wiley, 1976.

Mardia, K. V. *Statistics of directional data.* New York: Academic Press, 1972.

Matoušek, M., & Petersen, J. Automatic evaluation of EEG background activity by means of age-dependent EEG quotients. *Electroencephalography and Clinical Neurophysiology*, 1973, *35*, 603–612.

McCann, G. D., & Marmarelis, P. Z. *Proceedings of the first symposium on testing and identification of nonlinear systems.* Pasadena: California Institute of Technology, 1975.

Moore, G. P., Segundo, J. P., Perkel, D. H, & Levitan, H. Statistical signs of synaptic interaction in neurons. *Biophysical Journal*, 1970, *10*, 376–900.

Mountcastle, V. B. The world around us: Neural command functions for selective attention. *Neurosciences Research Program Bulletin*, 1976, *14*. (Supplement)

Perkel, D. H., Gerstein, G. L., & Moore, G. P. Neuronal spike trains and stochastic point processes I. The single spike train. *Biophysical Journal*, 1967, *7*, 391–418. (a)

Perkel, D. H., Gerstein, G. L., & Moore, G. P. Neuronal spike trains and stochastic point processes II. Simultaneous spike trains. *Biophysical Journal*, 1967, *7*, 419–440. (b)

Rabiner, L. R., & Gold, B. *Theory and application of digital signal processing.* Englewood Cliffs, N.J.: Prentice-Hall, 1975.

Rhode, W. S., & Olson, R. E. *A digital stimulus system* (Monograph No. 2). Madison, Wisconsin, Laboratory Computer Facility, 1975.

Rhode, W. S., & Soni, V. Neural unit data analysis system. In P. B. Brown (Ed.), *Current Computer Technology in Neurobiology.* Hemisphere, 1976.

Robles, L., Rhode, W. S., & Geisler, C. D. Transient response of the basilar membrane measured in Squirrel monkeys using the Mössbauer effect. *Journal of the Acoustical Society of America*, 1976, *59*, 926–939.

Rodieck, R. W., Kiang, N. Y. S., & Gerstein, G. L. Some quantitative methods for the study of spontaneous activity of single neurons. *Biophysical Journal*, 1962, *2*, 351–367.

Schiller, P. H., Finley, B. L., & Volman, S. F. Quantitative studies of single-cell properties in monkey striate cortex. *Journal of Neurophysiology*, 1976, *39*, 1288–1374.

Shantz, M. J. A minicomputer-based image analysis system. In P. B. Brown (Ed.), *Computer technology in neuroscience.* New York: Wiley, 1976.

Szenthágothai, J., & Arbib, M. A. *Conceptual models of neural organization.* Cambridge, Mass.: The MIT Press, 1975.

Wann, D. F., Price, J. L., Cowan, W. M., & Agulnek, M. A. An automated system for counting silver grains in autoradiographs. *Brain Research*, 1974, *81*, 31–58.

Wennberg, A., & Zetterberg, L. H. Application of a computer-based model for EEG analysis. *Electroencephalography and Clinical Neurophysiology*, 1971, *31*, 457–468.

Wolf, V. R., & Bilger, R. C. Generating complex waveforms. *Behavior Research Methods & Instruction*, 1972, *4*, 250–256.

10 Future Trends

T. R. Dolan[1]
Parmly Hearing Institute,
Loyola University of Chicago

I. Pollack
Mental Health Research Institute,
The University of Michigan

INTRODUCTION

The previous chapters in this book have been concerned primarily with the technical details by which mini- and microprocessing systems may be utilized in various areas of research. These chapters have been written in a manner that, hopefully, will assist practicing scientists in the development and utilization of hardware and software applications to their research interests. This final chapter is concerned with two additional but related facets in the use of computers in research. The first is a brief discussion of information exchange: how can the scientists' use of a processing system be enhanced by their peers' parallel efforts in other laboratories, and vice versa? Are there any systematic and relatively simple strategies to exchange information that will hasten the development of a system and enhance its capabilities?

The second aspect has to do with the long-term prospects for fiscal support to purchase processing systems. At the present time, it is commonplace for scientists to include appropriation of a computer system in the budget when submitting a research proposal to one of the National Institutes of Health (NIH) or to the National Science Foundation (NSF). Is the long-term funding situation such that each new scientist will be able to purchase his/her own computer system? If not, what are the alternatives, and how may they be facilitated?

---

[1] On leave to NSF, Washington, D.C. 20550.

INFORMATION EXCHANGE

There are a number of journals that attempt to facilitate exchange about processors and their programs. In the minicomputer field, *Behavior Research Methods & Instrumentation* has been servicing the psychological research community with articles on instrumentation, techniques, and program abstracts. In the large computer field, *Behavioral Science* has provided program abstracts for the entire social sciences community. In addition, computer manufacturers, through their users groups, have provided a program interchange.

With all of these resources available, why does it appear that each investigator must "reinvent the wheel," in that new programs are laboriously written from scratch for each new application? Among the answers to the question are: The small processors are being used for many new and highly original applications; until recently, the high cost of memory precluded the use of operating systems with higher level languages; and programming is a highly creative activity such that, even when programs are written in higher level languages, it is difficult to determine what a program does simply by reading someone else's program (Weinberg, 1971).

Information exchange may be most helpful to the researcher for *convergent* applications, such as in the area of general statistical techniques or experimental design that manipulate abstract entities, irrespective of their origin. The availability of such programs also greatly simplifies the task of describing the statistical techniques employed. By this means, complex new techniques (e.g., multidimensional scaling) have diffused through the research community far faster than would have been possible had each investigator been forced to master the technique before application. Information exchange has also been aided by the fact that statistical programs have been written in machine-independent languages available to most computing centers.

Information exchange has been frustratingly poor in the area of *divergent* applications, such as experimental control, despite the availability of standardized experimental procedures. Here, each investigator is producing a unique experiment and is usually working with a unique and, often, a minimal equipment configuration.

We see no easy way out of this dilemma until experimental controllers are equipped with operating systems with higher level languages. But, even with such operating systems, specific features of experimental control may not be possible, although procedural techniques should be good candidates for standardization. Much more thought and standardization is necessary before programs for experimental control can be readily interchanged among investigators.

Among the methods for improving information exchange are: development of classification systems for describing programs in detail; standardization of interfaces, devices, and languages within restricted research areas; and establishment of National Centers within restricted research areas.

Classification systems can be best established through learned and professional societies working in conjunction with user groups. We must also face up to the possibility that the field of experimental control through the use of processors may not yet be ready for rigid classification. But a serious effort in this direction will, at least, highlight the important areas of ignorance.

The standardization of interfaces, devices, and programs within restricted research areas short-circuits many problems in information exchange. An NIH-sponsored effort in neuropsychology and neurophysiology resulted in the development of the LINC system with a turn-key package of processors, interfaces, and programs. The sponsor also wisely provided funds for purchasing the entire package by a number of qualified groups. The immediate availability of the most sophisticated techniques to the research community made a profound impact on the rapid development of neurosciences.

The development of National Centers has been slow in psychology. A noteworthy exception, and an excellent example of a successful centralized operation, is the Haskins Laboratory. The Haskins Laboratory was awarded an NIH grant to provide synthetic speech stimuli for research purposes. An overwhelming number of the researchers in synthetic speech have utilized this facility. The advantages are obvious: standardization of stimuli, abbreviated descriptions of materials, and a central clearing-house for related activities. The disadvantages are also obvious: extended travel time and arrangements, necessity for nonadaptive experimental procedures, and inflexibility for quick modification. The usefulness of the Haskins Laboratories effort would be further enhanced if there were a parallel development on the LINC model, where their unique experience could be translated into programs for a minimal systems configuration available to a number of regional centers or to the development of programs for general-purpose computers, to serve any investigator with access to a computing center equipped with a digital-to-analog converter.

Finally, we may be able to finesse the problem of exchanging programs for experimental control by circumventing the dedicated computer, at least in the initial exploratory stages of investigation. A large time-shared computer provides the neophyte experimenter with easily learned, machine-independent high-level languages, excellent file structures, and data analysis capability. We seek to use the time-shared computer without being limited by its inability to be totally dedicated to the demands of on-line experimentation.

In one clever solution, a Dartmouth group (Potts, 1976), employed a large time-shared computer with the BASIC programming language, a terminal with a video display, and an auxiliary "black box." The time-shared computer loaded the terminal with characters. The actual display of the visual material was controlled locally, either by scrolling the material into view or by activating the brightness of the display. The black box captured the response, the time of response, and yielded up its information to the time-shared computer. In this way, experiments can be constructed in a few minutes from any terminal of the time-shared system; the student can have immediate experience with almost any experiment in the entire psychological literature that employs an alphanumeric display; and, if preliminary results are promising, the experiment may be further automated or moved to a dedicated processor.

This example, obviously, does not cover the entire range of possible cases of experimental control. Even within the area of visual presentation of information, it does not permit experiments with detailed temporal-spatial interactions or provide instantaneous feedback. But these objections seem minor compared with the possibility of "instant" experimental design and experimental execution. The added black box (Polytronics, Lebanon, N.H.) is within the price range available to many laboratories ($650) and can operate with any terminal with a standard interface.

The Dartmouth approach, we believe, merits the attention of any investigator with access to at least a time-shared system for the "mock-up" of standard experiments for demonstrational purposes. It effectively employs the full capability of the large computer with the full-time dedication of a dedicated controller. And, more importantly here, it exemplifies an alternative approach to the difficult problem of information exchange for the purposes of experimental control.

LONG-RANGE SUPPORT

The availability of Federal support for the purchase of computer systems is very much related to the more general question of availability of Federal funds for all "permanent equipment." This in turn, is one part of the overall availability of fiscal support of basic research in general. Let us begin this discussion then, by examining overall support for basic research.

According to statistics gathered by the NSF, the federal government spent $630 million towards support of basic research in the Social and Life Sciences in fiscal year 1967. In 1976, it is estimated that the total federal dollars for basic research in these disciplines was $964 million. In 10 years, then, the increment for basic research in these areas was only 53%. There are a variety of methods to compute the rate of inflation over those 10 years. Unhappily, almost all of them would suggest that a 53% increment between 1967 and 1976 is less than the increment necessary to maintain equivalent support in terms of constant dollars.

An examination of federal support for basic research in psychology is even more disheartening. In 1967, the Federal government spent $60 million on research in psychology. In 1976, estimates suggest that the total dropped to $51 million. That is a decrement of approximately 15% in terms of current dollars. Needless to say, the decrement would be substantially more if measured in terms of constant dollars.

As the total support picture worsens, the outlook for fiscal support of permanent equipment can hardly improve. Nevertheless, the NSF has emphasized in support materials accompanying the proposed 1978 budget that advancement in the sciences is inextricably related to technological development, and one cannot occur without the accompaniment of the other. Consequently, the NSF has made a special appeal in its Congressional request for funds to purchase, and to refurbish, research equipment (including processing systems of all types).

At the time of this writing, it is difficult to assess either the immediate response of the Congress or the short-term prognosis of support for permanent equipment. Although the NSF has committed a substantial portion of any increment it receives in the 1978 budget to the purchase of permanent equipment, the size of this increment is not yet known. A peek at the more long-term picture is provided in a recent report issued by the U.S. Senate, and it is less positive than the short-term view. The report is the Appropriation Subcommittee's Report accompanying the 1978 Senate Appropriation Act for the Department of Housing and Urban Development, and for sundry independent executive agencies, boards, bureaus, commissions, corporations, and offices (including the NSF). Although the report is less than comprehensive, it does encapsulate some of the recent thinking in the Congress regarding permanent equipment. To quote from the report:

> The Committee recognized the central importance of modern equipment in research, for it would hardly seem possible to make reasonable scientific progress, particularly with reasonable investments of time and effort, when equipment capability and availability come to limit the work that must be done. On the other hand, research equipment is expensive, and it would seem that, no matter how much equipment can be supplied through the NSF budget, equipment shortages will never be fully satisfied. Given the nature of this problem, the Committee would recommend that the Foundation make a serious attempt to encourage greater sharing of equipment by scientists in universities. The universities themselves would apparently have to shoulder a major responsibility in this effort by keeping adequate inventories of research equipment that the Government has provided for the use of scientific faculty and by establishing appropriate procedures to review questions of how equipment might be shared to provide greater utilization. This will not be a simple problem to solve, nor will it ever be solved completely. However, for the sake of scientific progress, it would seem that there will have to be greater recognition of the fact that the equipment provided on NSF research grants is vested in the host university and that, although it may have been acquired for primary use on a specific project, it is to be available for other projects whenever possible.
>
> Since a greater sharing of research equipment can only be achieved through a conscious effort within universities themselves, the Foundation ought to give careful consideration to various incentives to focus university attention on this matter. One approach might be to require that universities cost share in the purchase of equipment, just as is now done in the NSF Chemical Instrumentation Program. Though the full 50 percent cost

sharing guideline used in that program might not be appropriate in NSF's other programs, some meaningful degree of cost sharing might be found that would heighten interest in equipment sharing without impairing the effort to maintain modern research facilities in universities.

The Committee therefore directed the NSF to determine what steps it was taking to ensure that it was not supporting the purchase of new equipment where existing equipment of adequate capability existed on a university campus.

Although the report does not specify any immediate changes in funding procedures, the tone of the discussion is indicative of the present funding situation. Fiscal support for the acquisition of permanent equipment (including computer systems) is currently tight and apparently will remain so. If the scientific community's utilization of processing systems is to continue to grow, various alternatives to the present situation must be considered.

There are at least three general strategies presently available to the scientific community that would be beneficial and lead to increased availability of central processors.

First, it is necessary to make use of *all* the mini- and microprocessing systems that have already been purchased by universities and industry. A recent Congressional study estimated that many million dollars worth of minicomputers had been purchased for use on basic research projects and later discarded. The study further suggested that an even greater number of minicomputers were not being used a substantial portion of the day. That is, miniprocessors often sat unused and available during routine working hours. Although the data in the report are difficult to assess, it does seem likely that greater use of presently available processors is possible.

Second, there are funding programs currently available and underutilized that provide funds for faculty members of small colleges (and, presumably, with more limited laboratory facilities) to spend part of their time (e.g., summer, one semester) at already existing laboratories at other universities. The NSF, for example, has a "Small College Faculty Program" in which funds are provided for this purpose. The only limitation on this particular program is that the funds must be awarded as a supplement to an already existing grant that was previously awarded to the operating laboratory. Programs of this type allow a scientist without a laboratory (and computer system) to utilize one already in existence and functioning.

Third, in Chapter 3, Yost described the structure and some possible uses of microprocessors. Although the hardware and software support from the manufacturers for these processors has not yet reached sufficient levels, it is clear that they will be a partial solution to the lack of larger processing systems. They are not only economical but are impressively flexible. Many of the laboratory uses of mini-computers could be performed just as effectively with one of these devices.

In summary, there are several strategies available to the scientific community supportive of the uses of processing systems. Although they are less satisfactory than the acquisition of a computer system for every laboratory that desires one, they are particularly helpful to the young scientist and the scientist that has not been able to procure extramural research support.

REFERENCES

Appropriation Subcommittee Report, Senate Appropriation Act of 1978 for Department of Housing and Urban Development.

Potts, G. R. Use of a campus-wide time-sharing computer to run reaction time experiments. *Behavior Research Methods & Instrumentation*, 1976, *8*, 179–181.

Weinburg, G. M. *The psychology of computer programming*. New York: Van Nostrand Reinhold, 1971.

Author Index

Subject Index